love, castro street

love, castro street

---

reflections of san francisco

edited by
Katherine V. Forrest
and Jim Van Buskirk

alyson books
New York

Manufactured in the United States of America.

Published by Alyson Books, 245 W. 17th St., Suite 1200, New York, New York, 10115-1251.
Distribution in the United Kingdom by Turnaround Publisher Services Ltd.,
Unit 3, Olympia Trading Estate, Coburg Road, Wood Green, London N22 6TZ England.

First Edition: May 2007

07 08 09 10 a 10 9 8 7 6 5 4 3 2 1

ISBN 1-55583-997-5
ISBN-13 978-1-55583-997-0
The Library of Congress Cataloging-in-Publication data are available.

table of contents

introduction

SAN FRANCISCO HAS BEEN EULOGIZED by the best. Oscar Wilde, in his oft-quoted epigraph from *The Picture of Dorian Gray*, penned in 1891, wrote: "It's an odd thing, but everyone who disappears is said to be seen at San Francisco. It must be a delightful city, and possess all the attractions of the next world." Exactly a century later, Tony Kushner, in *Angels in America*, concurred: "Heaven is a city much like San Francisco."

San Francisco has a long history of being on the forefront of social and cultural change—the beats in North Beach, hippies in the Haight-Ashbury, and gays in the Castro. More than most cities, it is a vibrant, organic, changing place. It has survived earthquakes, political assassinations, redevelopment, parades and parties, political protests, and the dot-com boom and bust.

Castro Street is more than a physical place. It is mythological. A beacon of hope for those made to feel separate and dispossessed. Geographically, the intersection of Castro and Market Streets marks the center of San Francisco's seven-mile-by-seven-mile peninsula. It also marks the heart of the Castro, the neighborhood festooned with the rainbow flag created by San Franciscan Gilbert Baker. The neighborhood, once largely inhabited by working-class Irish families, has been transformed into an internationally known mecca by gay, lesbian, bisexual, transgender, and intersex people, and, as the essays in this collection demonstrate, has become an iconic place that reflects our history and our deepest yearnings. It is not by accident that two essays in this collection refer to San Francisco as New Jerusalem.

Many people from all over the world have stories, memories, and dreams about the Castro. Stories about how the neighborhood has marked a milestone in their development, made them who they are, altered their lives. Perhaps they came from a small town and spread their wings sexually, politically, creatively. Perhaps they came to town single and partnered here. Perhaps they came of age here, in one way or another, as they bore witness to the history created here. The stories in this collection are powerful, poignant, and important. And representative of many.

Love, Castro Street doesn't delve into academic history. What it offers are deeply personal stories by some of San Francisco's finest queer writers. Stories that take place in the streets and on the sidewalks, in the bars, baths, and buses, behind the facades of those much-photographed Victorian houses. Like the Bay Area's queer communities, *Love, Castro Street* doesn't stay confined to the "gay ghetto." It travels around the region, and through time.

The Castro neighborhood is often visually evoked by the blade marquee of the Castro movie theater. Jim Tushinski and F. Allen Sawyer offer uniquely different personal valentines to this scene of so much drama—cinematic and otherwise. Other famous landmarks of the City appear, as in Jim Duggins's remarkable reminiscence of his year of working among prisoners on Alcatraz Island. Michael Nava, known for his Henry Rios mystery novels, writes from the heart about an epiphany at Candlestick Park during a baseball game. Mark Thompson vividly remembers his first visit to the City as a boy and the indelible impact made on him by two men he saw in Golden Gate Park. And coeditor Jim Van Buskirk tracks the evolution of the campy revue Beach Blanket Babylon as it parallels his coming-of-age as a gay man.

The emotional landscape of Castro Street is described in several stories such as Kirk Read's "Notes on the Castro" set during the week after Hurricane Katrina, gay pulp fiction pioneer Victor Banis's entertaining depiction of managing an apartment building in the Castro, K. M. Soehnlein's reminiscence of his "First Days," and in the evocative essays of Lucy Jane Bledsoe, Elana Dykewomun, Karin Kallmaker, and Carla Trujillo, who offer personal testimony to being in the Castro and experiencing an inner shift that became life-changing. Jess Wells, in a few short pages, offers her shifting perspective on the Castro through the years.

Several stories are elegiac. Charles Q. Forester reminisces about a night in "The Hothouse" and the joyful time of sexual freedom. Paul Reidinger offers his quietly moving story about evenings in a neighborhood park with a boy and his dog. Stephen Beachy paints a portrait of his partner's Aunt Vera, Carol Seajay vividly brings to life the lesbian heyday of Valencia Street's bookstores and its lesbian energy, and Fenton Johnson signifies the City's transformations he has experienced through the years.

The bars, ever-present in many of these essays, are an especially potent presence in "In the Bars of Heaven and Hell" by Aaron Shurin, whose journey from Berkeley to visit, night after night, the Rendezvous, was far more than a bus trip.

Many of the voices speak to our ever-changing history. Michelle Tea, Thea Hillman, and Carol Queen remember their early years in the City, and the how as well as the why of their living here. Jamison Green writes movingly about claiming his transgender identity.

As editors, we sought out writers to represent San Francisco's rich racial and ethnic diversity, and while we were not as successful as we had hoped, we have powerful essays from writers such as Michael Nava, who grew up in the barrio of Sacramento; Andrew

Ramer, who writes about San Francisco's allure to a Jewish New York; and Helen Zia, who describes the Asian community's (and her own) essential role in the history-making marriages that took place at City Hall in 2004 when our City became once more a cultural watershed.

You may well find some part of your own story here, as a resident or a visitor, as a participant or a voyeur. Whatever, we welcome you to this collection, and to the place we refer to simply as "the City." We hope you enjoy these postcards from the edge of a changed, and changing, world. As Elana Dykewomon eloquently puts it in the opening essay: "San Francisco is an archetype—sedimentary layers of immigration creating a vast striation of cultures. Subject to earthquake: The very real possibility of sudden, violent upheaval makes us, the residents of this fragile place, either fools who have no appreciation of the larger histories we take part in or adventurers, willing to risk all for beauty, freedom, community."

KATHERINE V. FORREST
JIM VAN BUSKIRK
San Francisco
2007

seeking welcome

elana dykewomon

SAN FRANCISCO IS AN ARCHETYPE—sedimentary layers of immigration creating a vast striation of cultures. Subject to earthquake: The very real possibility of sudden, violent upheaval makes us, the residents of this fragile place, either fools who have no appreciation of the larger histories we take part in or adventurers, willing to risk all for beauty, freedom, community. We like to style ourselves as adventurers, don't we? And an open, adventuresome city is a natural for queers of all kinds.

An adventuresome kid, I first saw San Francisco in 1967, the year of "flowers in your hair," as well as the year I graduated high school. I was on my way to Oregon to attend college with my first lover. We thought our loverness was a secret. Quite likely no one recognized us for who we were when we hitched from my aunt's place in Berkeley to Haight-Ashbury, where I managed to score street acid. The high came over me on the lower deck of the Bay

Bridge. Forty years later, whenever I find myself on the bridge's underside, I still fear I'm driving through the digestive tract of an elongated spider. I breathe a sigh of relief when I get to the other shore—the East Bay.

Eventually I settled in Oakland—one of the best places to cruise for views of the bay, San Francisco gleaming like the lost city of Cibola in the morning sun. Oakland is a terrific town— integrated, friendly, host to a thriving art scene, marginally cheaper to live in—and your friends can always find parking on your street when they come to visit. But when we talk about "the City," we always mean S.F., and those of us who live in the East Bay cross the bridge for culture and community much more often than those who live in San Francisco make the journey to us.

When I moved here in 1983, I came for the women—individually and in community—but it's easy to talk about loving women, much harder to explain love of place.

For me, San Francisco was an acquired taste. It's a city of many postures, of who's in and who's out, what's the coolest, tastiest, smartest, most-up-to-the-minute hipness. Sheryl Swoopes and k.d. lang notwithstanding, dykes are, let's be honest, not most folks' idea of cool. But San Francisco is the coolest, most comfortable place to be a lesbian.

While I have heard horror stories of dyke-bashing from the City that rival those of any small town in the Midwest, I have also seen how decades of organizing leaks across the Bay and stains the map of California (the world?) an appealing shade of lavender, and changes lives and minds in the places many Bay Area queers moved here to escape. As an instructor at San Francisco State, I had entrée to teach a course in a community college in Pittsburgh, California, a good forty-five minutes away in the Sacramento Delta lands that are as close to "fly-over zones" as the Bay Area has. While I didn't desire to keep that job (or commute), it was instructive to see how the name Dykewomon played in the outlying areas: nothing more than a few raised eyebrows—thanks to everything done in San Francisco.

Everything done in San Francisco includes the world's biggest dyke march! For the last six years I've been working on senior and disabled access for the S.F. Dyke March (which now boasts some of the most comprehensive access west of Michigan). I was talking to my mother about it this year, and she said, "But I'm confused. I saw in the papers about the pride marches on Sunday, but you said yours was Saturday."

"Dyke Marches happen in most big cities on Saturday, Mom, before the pride parades, but you don't hear much about them because they're run for and by women."

"Don't get me started on that!" my mother huffed, already indignant about how often what women do is disrespected.

Dyke marches started with San Francisco dykes in 1993. Many dykes find it an excuse to party, and certainly we need more parties. But the heart of the Dyke March beats political—multiracial, multiclass, intergenerational volunteers create an event that represents a raw, uncommercial vision of a better world.

Because San Francisco is a better world. Everyone knows it. Even when I was kid, my dyke organizing vision was opened up in San Francisco, to which I hitchhiked often from colleges in Portland and L.A. San Francisco: the magnetic pulse of the West Coast, where somewhere the grail of poets and perverts is secreted—we can't help it, we are overtaken by the quest to see for ourselves.

When I found myself in my first gay women's liberation meeting, I wasn't quite twenty-one; now I have the fantasy that it took place in Sally Gearhart's home. It is as likely a possibility as any (I don't think it was Del and Phyllis's place, but I could be wrong). Thirty-five years later, the memory is a fragment of a big, beautiful apartment somewhere in San Francisco. But I clearly remember thinking: This is a hell of a nice place and amazing that she would trust all these strangers in it—all these dykes!—any dyke who happened to see what must have been the flier, or the notice in a local underground paper.

I was twenty and I hadn't finished getting over my image that being a dyke banished you to, at best, the seamiest apartments in some gray gay netherworld. It was probably 1970; I had hitched from Los Angeles, where I'd cofounded the first Gay Liberation group at California Institute of the Arts. There I'd found myself an unlikely den mother, making coffee for gay men who were cruising each other; the lesbians wouldn't come near it. I went to one college women's liberation consciousness-raising group, which only confirmed my consciousness that I had little in common with straight women.

It was in that long-ago living room in San Francisco that I found myself among the lesbians for the first time. Not on the outskirts; not the only obvious one in my high school; not me and my first lover alone on the Greyhound to Portland after that bad acid trip, trying not to draw attention to ourselves; not the only dyke hanging out with a gay men's group; not lonely in a lesbian bar in Greenwich Village, underage and trying to make small talk over the din. The lesbians of San Francisco came together to talk political realities.

Somehow I found them and was welcomed in.

all the way home

mark thompson

MY FIRST TRIP TO THE CITY began with hushed whispers and in the ebbing darkness of dawn. The oldest of three siblings, I was gently nudged awake before the others. Time to trade pajamas for neatly pressed corduroys, to "knock the sleep" out of my eyes, as my father brusquely put it, and then help my brother and sister. For soon we were to set off on our big adventure.

My mother had organized the day with a general's unwavering command: sandwiches lined up in crisp waxed paper, thermos bottles filled just so, the itinerary based on a clipping from the *Monterey Peninsula Herald* about a special doing in that great city to the north, San Francisco. There was not one precious minute to waste.

The clan was ready and on our way by eight. We kids were not quite awake, but had been comfortably piled with the baskets and blankets in the back of the family's big-finned station wagon.

While Dad silently pulled the enormous car away from our little house in Pacific Grove, Mom made one last adjustment to her lipstick in a shiny compact mirror.

He drove down Pine Avenue toward Monterey and then beyond to Route 101, the famous El Camino Real, "The King's Highway." It was about two hours to the City, but the passing scenery and colorful stories about it were as enthralling to us as any movie.

Our last glimpse of home was the smokestacks of Cannery Row, where my father had worked as a teenager. Those massive canneries never closed until one day, not long after the Second World War ended, the last sardine was scooped out of Monterey Bay. My Dad said he'd hung around a bit after that, helping Ed Ricketts, the legendary marine biologist, collect tidepool specimens for classrooms around the world.

"Doc," as the locals affectionately knew him, had been immortalized in the writings of his good friend John Steinbeck. He was killed in 1948 when his car stalled on the railroad tracks going through town and was hit by a train. Doc Ricketts was a hero in my father's eyes, and my father never tired of telling stories about him. One day, some years after the accident, my father borrowed the keys to Doc's weathered old lab, incongruously wedged between the rotting hulks of two empty canneries. He was very proud of that place and wanted me to see it, too.

The plain rooms had been left just as they were the day Doc died: Yellowish specimen jars filled with odd-looking creatures lined the walls, a fine layer of dust covered a sheaf of notes left on the worn wooden table. It was a calming sight, in an eerie kind of way, as if Doc were due back home any second. The only other time I had seen my Dad so reverently bowed was in church.

The lessons in local lore never stopped as we continued northward. Did we know that a famous bandit once lived in the mountain caves not far from San Juan Bautista? I could see the old colonial mission lands in the distance as we sped our way past on the highway. And then vast, endless rows of produce growing under the California sun: Ripe artichokes and sunflowers, pungent fields of garlic, and iceberg lettuce the size of soccer balls.

Miles of orchard trees heavy with cherries, peaches, walnuts, and juicy nectarines were just around the bend. We stopped for a rest, sampling this magnificent bounty from a quaint roadside stand, little knowing that in just another decade or two all we beheld would be replaced with housing tracts bearing the names of the very things ripped up and paved over.

But such ideas were unthinkable when the beckoning City was so near. San Jose flashed by, barely noticed, as the tidal estuaries of southern San Francisco Bay came into view. Flocks of egrets and other birds made elegant patterns in the sky over lush waves of marsh reeds. Lofty cumulus clouds drifted above, like stately Spanish galleons. Those one hundred twenty miles between Monterey and San Francisco, which might otherwise seem an eternity, were but the shortest steps in time that unforgettable day.

We arrived in mid-morning, the sun glistening brightly off the copper dome of City Hall. Dad maneuvered the car off the freeway onto Fell Street, which would take us right to Golden Gate Park, our main destination. Somehow a wrong turn got us sidetracked into Hayes Valley, a black ghetto filled with run-down Victorians. There were few blacks living on the Monterey Peninsula then, and I remember thinking how different their lives were from mine as I pressed my face against the window. My mother had announced this as a "cultural outing," but the most enduring lessons in culture for me were the fleeting glimpses of kids my age playing in the street—just as we did back home but under very different circumstances.

A quick consultation with a map hastily pulled from the glove box corrected our course, and soon we were in the park with a picnic basket unpacked and lunch all spread out under a magnificent canopy of trees. We were close by the old carousel, which we pleaded to ride again so many times that nausea almost set in. I wandered while my parents dealt with my insistent siblings, exploring a path that meandered away with tempting twists and turns. I was not at all prepared to find what was waiting at the end of it.

There on a bench, in a secluded grove, sat two men embraced, kissing. They were intimate in their laughter, too, enjoying a Sunday in the park as much as I was. A few minutes passed before they noticed my curious gaze and quickly pulled apart, as if something bad had been discovered. I was thinking no such thoughts, but was merely dumbstruck by a picture that seemed utterly foreign yet somehow familiar. A part of me wanted to be on that bench, too. Calls of my name through the trees broke my silent watch, and I quickly retreated to the staid reassurance of a plaid blanket.

The rest of the day seemed quite unremarkable after that. The fish in the aquarium and pictures on the museum walls seemed colorless figments compared to the much more vivid and indelible scene known only to me. Of course, I could tell no one what I had seen. It was the first of many secrets I would from then on habitually carry inside. The day was finished when the sun began its slide down into the Pacific horizon. My last impression as we left the City was the lights of the Bay Bridge starting to go on, like gleaming jewels on the back of a giant sleeping dragon half submerged in the murky waters of the bay.

•

MANY YEARS WOULD PASS before I returned to San Francisco for a permanent stay. On the day of my twenty-first birthday, my sister and her redheaded boyfriend helped carry my possessions in the back of his truck to a small student apartment near San Francisco State University. I was enrolled to finish my college education there, taking courses in the journalism department. It was 1973, and while the campus seemed tame enough, stories of student strikes and other tumult still echoed from the previous decade. I felt keenly disappointed that somehow I had been left out of the actions of the late1960s. Little did I know that another revolution was just waiting for me.

Within a few short months my burgeoning talents as a young reporter had found a voice in the student paper, *The Phoenix*. I wrote about whatever I was assigned until one day I approached my editor with a piece of my own choosing. Timidly, I handed over the leaflet announcing the formation of a gay students' group on campus. Now, I asked, in a tone as casual as I could muster, shouldn't the paper cover this item, too? With a look verging on a wink, she agreed and sent me on my way.

I remember arriving at the meeting a few minutes late and sitting nervously in the back row. To hell with journalistic objectivity, I knew why I was really there. And apparently so did everyone else in the room. We all quickly became fast friends. My report was somewhat tepid, as I recall, but my personal commitment to this newfound cause was not. I quickly became one of the leaders of the group. Nothing else seemed as important as this.

Our little group soon became larger as other gay and lesbian students from neighboring campuses joined us in solidarity. We sponsored rap groups and potlucks. The announcements for our first on-campus social were pulled down as quickly as we tacked them up. But that night in a shabby room in the student center was undeniably memorable. With dabs of mascara and streaks of glitter in our hair (boys and girls both, for that was the fashion of the day), we danced the night through. I drank too much champagne, and woke up the next morning with my first adult-sized headache. Still, I would not have traded one moment of the evening for anything.

We had our earnest fun but were serious as well. Gay power was just beginning to become a viable political force in the City. There were marches and demonstrations. The bravest thing I ever did was stand in the middle of the street to halt an advancing bus. Our goal was to stop traffic that night in front of a theater showing yet another movie with twisted homophobic characters. Then one morning, not long after that, something else happened that would change my life in ways that are still incalculable to this day: I walked into Harvey Milk's camera store on Castro Street for the very first time.

Harvey was just becoming a perceptible force through the political campaigns he dutifully—but not successfully—waged. It was not until his fourth try for public office in 1977 that he would win, and win big: a coveted district seat on the board of supervisors. On this crisp April morning in 1974, however, he was still relatively unknown. I wanted him to explain his mission in an article for the readers of the gay student newspaper I had started, *The Voice*.

While it may sound dishy to say so here, I have always been convinced I got fleas from the beat-up red Victorian coach that filled much of the store's modest front room. But never have I known prouder fleas than these. Whether it be furniture or people, one could just sense that Harvey relished in saving things—preserving them for a better future.

"Anyone who wants to work for the freedom of not only themselves but for the next gay generation so they can have a better chance than we did, start now," wrote Harvey. He concluded his article by stating: "I am committed. Are you?"

Even though many in the past had reacted indifferently to that question, my generation of gay activists was a fairly fearless lot. We didn't have anything to lose but our self-respect. And if there is anything baby boomers possess in excess it's high self regard. So we all got to work.

It amazes me to this day how quickly the pieces of our new-found lives came together; art galleries and theater troupes, marching bands and singing choruses, neighborhood cafés and bookstores, even the first-ever Gay Games. By the mid-1970s, the

City had emerged as the de facto capital of gay cultural life. While gay arts and activism were rising in many other parts of the world, a lot of the cultural infrastructure that gay people take for granted today was coined and exported from this fervent, permissive urban arena.

I was lucky to have been tapped by the new owner of *The Advocate*, the national gay newsmagazine, just as I was graduating from State. David Goodstein wanted me to freelance for the paper, and despite the objections of my professors, who felt that such a choice would ruin my professional career, I decided this was exactly what I wanted to do. So I set to work, writing articles on just about every topic imaginable.

I flew down to Los Angeles and interviewed Dorr Legg and other venerable activists for one of the first articles to deal with being "Gay and Gray." Another trip south to Stanford University and its newly created Sexual Dysphoria Program put my readers in touch with the still-forming social world of transgender individuals. I interviewed drag queens and leathermen, politicians and plumbers. (Coming out as a working-class person was a big story back then.) José Sarria told me "if I was going to be labeled a queen, then I would be the biggest, best queen there was....Our humor is our key." And I'll never forget the afternoon movement founder Harry Hay said, "Being gay is a gift!" Those words rang a prophetic bell.

The most newsworthy angle for me was the integration of our sexuality with our spirituality, which was being redefined apart from mainstream religion and expressed in fascinating ways. Performance groups like the Angels of Light and Gay Men's Theater Collective placed a lot of emphasis on spiritual ritual and storytelling in widely acclaimed productions such as *Paris Sights Under the Bourgeois Sea* and *Crimes Against Nature*. Audiences were spellbound, for never had there been as magical a mirror in which to view our authentic selves. These tribal conversations would later

lead to the formation of groups like the Sisters of Perpetual Indulgence and the Radical Fairies and the rapidly growing gay and
lesbian spirituality movement of today.

While covering my beat I also enjoyed countless talks with
artists of every imaginable stripe. My favorite was cabaret singer
Bobby Short, whose annual concerts at the Geary Theater I slav-
ishly attended. No, he didn't quite come out when I asked him if
he was in love with anyone special. But he did admit, "I'm in love
all the time. Being in love is the difficult part. It's such a fleeting,
ephemeral thing in so many of our lives."

There was no way I could disagree with that. I was having as
many "gentleman callers" as everyone else in the City, each one
with his own special lesson to teach me. I'll never forget the afternoon Carl Whitman and I had just finished giving each other
rug burns on my new carpet when he looked up after the requisite minute of satisfied silence only to say that my "class consciousness" needed work. Carl was the famous Socialist author of
the era's most influential polemic, *Refugees from Amerika: A Gay
Manifesto*, and despite our apparent differences, we sparked like
crazy. Few people knew about this seemingly improbable affair—
radical leftist leaving love bites on a towheaded boy from
Carmel—but it worked for us. It's funny how and when one's real
education begins.

Carl correctly viewed us as refugees from an ugly and insensi-
tive America. But most of those arriving by the hour at this gracious city by the bay saw it only in the most opportunistic way: as
a gay mecca in which past worry and hurt could easily be dreamed
away. I could see almost from the beginning of my time there that
this was not so easy, or even desirable. Rather than alleviating sins
from the past, we just as often passed them along unseeingly to
the next person. There was a lot of bad behavior going down in
the name of righteous love. People didn't always see the contradictions inherent in their self-absorbed choices.

Internalized homophobia was only one dimension of a mounting problem. The growing forces of repression and backlash were just as obvious. But sometimes it was hard to see clearly enough through all the popper fumes. It would take tragedies of monumental proportions to wake everyone up to the consequences of their actions. Soon, all too soon, an awful season of death and disintegration was to descend on us.

It was 1978, and citizens of the City were stunned one morning in early November to learn the fate of nine hundred followers of the Reverend Jim Jones, a charismatic San Francisco social and religious leader. They had compliantly lined up in the jungles of Guyana and poisoned themselves with cups of cyanide-laced Kool-Aid. Accounts of the mass suicide deeply shook the local establishment, from the mayor on down. They had supported Jones's messianic plans to relocate his People's Temple, which served the poor, in this remote region. And now all that was left of the congregation were corpses piled up in the South American heat.

Eight days later, on Monday, November 28, a general sense of dismay was compounded into horror when former city supervisor Dan White coldly assassinated Mayor George Moscone and Supervisor Harvey Milk in their chambers. Yes, Harvey had finally won his race. He was the first openly gay man to be elected to high public office in the land.

White, a self-appointed standard-bearer for the blue-collar voters feeling displaced by the City's sudden influx of gays, among other rapid changes, had recently resigned his post. He'd pleaded stress but then just as impulsively asked for the job back. When Moscone declined, the enraged former cop sneaked his .38-caliber revolver past City Hall metal detectors and, high on Irish pride, blew away the mayor and the man he had long considered his political nemesis.

The trial was a mishmash of homophobic justification, with the defense pushing a plea of diminished capacity due, in no small part, to White's diet of junk food. The conservative, winnowed jury bought the reasoning—as feeble as it was—and found White guilty of voluntary manslaughter rather than premeditated murder. The lesser charge meant no more than eight years in jail with time off for good behavior. White would probably walk free within five years.

By the evening of the jury's judgment on Monday, May 21, a furious crowd of five thousand protestors assembled in front of City Hall. It didn't take long for the action to turn ugly, and the mob almost succeeded in burning the building down. Flaming torches and chunks of asphalt rained through the night air. A row of police cars was set ablaze, sirens wailing like dying banshees. Dozens of people were badly hurt and dozens arrested. The fiery melee only served to thicken the atmosphere of dread and fury clutching the city like an implacable fog.

It had been half a year of bad Mondays. Most gay and lesbian San Franciscans, already disillusioned by recent happenings, were pushed to the edge of paranoia. Despite the gains of the last decade or so, it seemed maybe there really wasn't a place for them at the City's table. What was going on?

Little could anyone at the time comprehend the finality this sequence of events was signaling. A decade—the gayest ever—was over. But so was an era. Unfettered liberation, the sexual revolution itself, was rapidly coming to a close. In the following year, the first signs of a deadly pandemic would appear. It would slaughter tens of thousands of young men in this cultured metropolis and points far beyond.

I was twenty-seven years old the night I stood and watched City Hall burning. My objectivity as a reporter was too much in place for me to join in and throw a stone, even though a part of me wanted to very much. Violence is never an answer, I knew that. But sometimes the fires of rage and indignation that burn bright inside have to be boldly expressed. So too do the dreams of peace and personal joy that still shine as clearly within today—an equal number of twenty-seven years after that riotous night.

Our endless struggle to become—to find ourselves and our right place in the world—has always been signified to me by that simplest of human acts: a kiss. From the very first moment when my gay consciousness was born by witnessing two men kiss on a park bench. To the very last instance when that sweet kind of innocence was never to be the same. It's all been defined by a kiss. For as I stood there in the midst of the flaming debris of torched cars and incinerated trees, I saw again two men kiss. Backlit against the raging crowd, they kissed passionately and hard and with all the proper defiance that two men in love could ever declare.

wonder

for Robin

lucy jane bledsoe

1: 2006

LAST WEEK, AFTER THE DYKE MARCH, I danced in the street at the intersection of Market and Castro. I arrived amid a throng of dyke marchers just as the music truck was swinging around for optimum speaker position. I admired the driver, a flock of tattoos flying up her arm, muscles flexing as she wrestled the truck's steering wheel to perform her bidding. I don't expect to recognize dance music anymore, but I loved that the entire truck throbbed with it, sending out waves of vibration that charged the cells of the women and men celebrating dykedom. So

I was surprised but also primed when Aretha started demanding her brothels and respect. I pulled Pat up close to the speakers and let loose.

•

THROUGHOUT THE NIGHT we stayed close to a group of very young women who were dancing as if they owned the world. I loved their hubris, their innocence of doubt. This, their dancing bodies seemed to say, this, dancing in the street with lesbians of all colors and ages and genders and abilities, this was the answer. I also loved the part of me that still believed they were right.

One girl in particular caught my eye. She might have been eighteen years old, or even younger, Chinese-American, fully decked in can't-help-myself butch attire, including very short hair that stood on end all over her head. She hung out on the edge of the group with her hands shoved deeply into the pockets of her big, baggy plaid shorts. Sometimes she shuffled her sneakers in an effort to look like she was dancing.

I couldn't stop watching her. It wasn't lust. Nothing maternal, either. Nor do I glorify youth for youth's sake. What broke my heart was her sense of wonder. It was the outline of fists in her pockets, the angle of her elbows, the feet-apart stance with one knee slightly bent. It was the slow way she turned her head to take everything in, careful not to gawk, not to make a single body movement that might be construed as uncool.

Thirty years her senior, I was unafraid of uncool dance steps, of what my body said to anyone who cared to look, of inappropriate flirting. I played with her shyness, made a conscious choice to let her know I was watching. I looked, smiled, admired, looked away for as long as I could, then turned back. She noticed. I thought she might slide into the crowd, away from my gaze. But she didn't. She stayed within my vicinity as carefully as I stayed within hers. If our groups drifted apart, I'd see her searching me out, and when her eyes found me, suppress a smile, look away quickly, paw the ground with her sneaker, look again to see if I'd turned away. I hadn't. She liked me. Though I was easily old enough to be her mother, something about my attention moved her. I considered walking right up to her ear and saying something quick and sweet, and then disappearing. But it was more fun to see how far I could go with eye contact.

2: 1976

THE GREYHOUND BUS lumbered into Rincon Annex well after dark. Robin was fast asleep on my shoulder, her drool soaking my hooded sweatshirt. I was loathe to wake her. I loved the weight of her head, her dead-to-the-world oblivion to what anyone thought of the affection between us. Awake, Robin was terrified of anyone knowing we were lesbians. She'd go to church on Sunday mornings to ask forgiveness for what we'd done the night before. These eighteen hours on the bus from Portland to San Francisco were filled with back-of-the-bus bathroom stench and the snores of old men. But the dark enclosure, the rumbling engine, the anonymous miles of freeway were a kind of freedom in themselves, lulling us into believing in the possibility that we could be free together.

Robin had come home with me for Christmas, and the visit hadn't gone very well. Already our year-long relationship was strained by differences of race, class, and temperament that we managed to bridge but not without much effort. I still have a picture of her on Christmas morning when I'd managed to coax her out of her bedroom hideaway for gift-opening. She's wearing a turtleneck sweater of multicolored stripes and sits huddled in an armchair, as if she wished she could slide down into the neck of that sweater like a real turtle. She'd given my little sister the *Family of Man* book of photography, which my sister still cherishes. I fear that Robin has no memories from that holiday to cherish.

We'd gone to her home in Richmond, Virginia, for Thanksgiving, a visit that was no less challenging. She'd had a fight with
her mother before the holiday about bringing me there at all, and
then requested that I duck down in my seat as we approached her
African-American neighborhood so that the neighbors didn't see
her with a white girl. It wasn't my whiteness itself so much as my
color being a cue to the nature of our relationship. Once in her
home, her mother ran me through a series of tests, all of which I
failed. At dinner, it was, "Lucy, you'll say the blessing." I didn't
know any. In the morning, it was, "Lucy, you make the biscuits." I
didn't have a clue how to make biscuits. As she fried the chicken,
she called out the biscuit-making steps, which I managed to follow, but I was so nervous that I didn't commit the instructions to
memory. The next morning, when she said, "Lucy, the biscuits," I
had to ask for help all over again.

Robin and I had spent the year of our coming out filling our
heads with Mary Daly, Pat Parker, Robin Morgan, Audre Lorde,
Adrienne Rich, Monique Wittig, every lesbian-feminist text we
could get our hands on. We were in school in Massachusetts at
the time and even found a couple of witches in North Adams
whom we visited. A straight woman brought Elaine Noble to our
campus, and in one evening the congresswoman organized a gay
student union. Later, I brought Rita Mae Brown to speak and got
to be the one to pick her up at the airport. The year had been full
of heady, awestruck revelations and joys.

Now we'd come to mecca. I gently lifted Robin's head off my
shoulder, refrained from kissing her, and told her we'd arrived. I
meant Arrived. We tumbled off the bus and found our suitcases in
its hold. Robin has never been very good at waking up, so I linked
an arm through hers to pull her into the bus station, dimly lit by
glowing vending machines. I studied my San Francisco map to
find a good route to the room I'd booked at the YMCA. Then I
steered Robin out to the dark street.

Robin woke up enough to realize that we were two girls holding on to each other in front of a seedy Greyhound bus station. She shook me loose. We marched bravely on, side by side, in search of our digs.

Years before the Loma Prieta earthquake took down the Embarcadero Freeway, there was a dirty little YMCA tucked under its dark reach. At nineteen, I was still under the impression the word "Christian," as in Young Men's Christian Association, referred to brotherly love that might extend to sisterly love, too. I assumed a YMCA would be safe and welcoming. Also, at nineteen, my assumptions often overrode my perceptions, and so we walked on undaunted to our lodging, despite the cues that we were far from the tourist district. After getting our key at the front desk, I did notice, as we passed the open doors of the other lodgers at the Y, that they seemed to be living in the dorm-sized rooms. I remember one young man especially. He wore a too-small white T-shirt and sat in his sock feet on the edge of the stained, thin mattress on the metal-framed, coil-spring bed. I made a conscious choice to ignore his listlessness, the obvious end-of-the-road state he was in, sitting there in his Y room, the door open as if to invite a glimmer of hope. I looked away. For me, this was the beginning of the road. I was brimming with anticipation.

3

I CALLED ROBIN LAST WEEK, the day after dancing in the street at the intersection of Market and Castro. A continent and an ocean separate us now, and thirty years have passed since we arrived for the first time in San Francisco, but we talk whenever we can, visit occasionally. I asked her what she remembered about our pilgrimage to San Francisco. Just the mention of the trip triggered a long, deep laugh.

I prompted, "That was when you were seeing Blanche."

"I was not."

"You were. You'd sneak off to find pay phones to call her."

"You thought I was calling her. I wasn't doing that."

"You were, too."

"I wasn't."

Oh. Thirty years later, still arguing about other lovers. Who can't appreciate the continuity? I'd threatened to call the whole trip off—Christmas in Portland, the jaunt to San Francisco—if she intended to continue her affair with Blanche. Robin swore it was over, the girl was crazy, and that she wanted nothing more to do with her.

"But why didn't we just go to New York?" I asked Robin on the phone. A friend had asked me the question earlier in the week.

"San Francisco was easier to drop in on. Slower and friendlier. Remember the bus rides from the YMCA to the Castro? As we drew closer and closer, the bus got gayer and gayer. It was like pigs to the trough. We were so happy. We were okay and we were gonna survive."

"Yeah." I found myself whispering into the phone. "Yeah."

4

WE CROWDED ONTO the small mattress to sleep that night. Then, intrepid, we set out the next day. We knew no one. We had no names of specific women's bars or centers. In fact, we had no addresses whatsoever. We knew two words: Castro Street.

It took us the morning to get there by bus. We breakfasted at the donut shop and then started looking for the women. In 1976, there were a lot of hunky men but no women on Castro Street. We were happy to be there, but the scene felt a bit tight, humorless, less freewheeling than the preview of lesbian culture we'd glimpsed elsewhere.

I know there's a persistent belief that lesbianism in the seventies was a dull and stern affair, and I constantly wonder how that story became the dominant history that is told, because it differs so from my experience. For me the late seventies and early eighties were a time when nonmonogamy was the rule, when covens of witches brewed and spelled and dressed in deep purple, when lesbians engaged in hours-long, paradigm-bashing theoretical discussions about everything, and then had sex. It was a time when poets thrived, when bars thrived, a time when we could dance and talk and create.

Robin and I were thrilled to be on Castro Street, among gay people, but something important, something more vital, felt just out of our reach. It may have been simply the future. I could feel a humming in the pavement under my feet, a sense of all that was to come. The fiercely guarded gender code would break down. Everyone would develop better senses of humor. We would move backward, yes, but also forward. This was a couple of years before the emergence of the Sisters of Perpetual Indulgence, but I felt them there, about to burst out of the cracks in the streets.

But right then? We wanted lesbians. We stopped a couple of guys and asked where we might find some. They directed us to a bar called Scott's, which took us another couple of hours to reach by foot. When we finally found the small neighborhood watering hole, we stopped on the sidewalk to check our fake IDs, which Robin had meticulously created using an X-Acto Knife and a fine-tipped black marker. Then we stepped inside.

A row of four flannel shirts sat at the bar. Did any of them turn to look at the two teenage girls blinking in the dark at the door? I don't remember. But I do know that if any of those older women were moved by our youthful wonder, they didn't show it. Maybe they were just racist and didn't appreciate our integrating the bar. Maybe we were just ageist and didn't show enough respect for their hideout. We didn't stay long. But before we left, we did manage to get the names of a few other establishments.

Soon we were handing our fake IDs to the gloriously big bouncer at the foot of the stairs at A Little More. My adrenal glands rejoiced at the idea that a mob of lesbians accompanied that pounding disco music coming from the loft upstairs. However, the bouncer shook her head at our IDs and sent us away. Again, no chuckles at our sweet innocence, just get the fuck away from the bar before you close us down. Luckily, we weren't easily daunted. We got a bite to eat, then circled back, hanging outside the door, waiting for a crowded moment. It was the same bouncer, but this time she waved us upstairs. We thought we'd fooled her, but it's more likely that she just figured we'd climb the building's brick exterior and come in through the window if she didn't let us in. She was probably right. Up the stairs we went into a roomful of dancing women.

I danced for the next ten years.

The choice of venues in San Francisco was breathtaking. The bouncers at the foot of the stairs at A Little More continued to be heart-stoppingly tough. I never grew tired of marveling at Peg's beehive as she sat at the end of her bar in Peg's Place. Maud's was great for a game of pool. Across the bay, you couldn't beat the Jubilee for getting away from the too-cool atmosphere of the San Francisco bars. At the Jubilee everyone danced. You couldn't stand alone for more than ten seconds without being asked. To dance, and more. One night my girlfriend and I were invited home with another couple. The Bacchanal (we called it "the Bok") in Albany was where you went for conversation. One night I listened to Jill Johnston mock Martin Heidegger from one of its bar stools.

5

ROBIN AND I FLEW back to Massachusetts after New Year's. We arrived late at night and took a cab from the airport to our college campus, arriving around midnight. As the cab pulled past the chapel, Robin directed the driver to Blanche's dorm. There she opened the door, grabbed her suitcase, and got out.

I sat alone in the dark backseat of the cab as it wended through the campus to my own dorm, where I climbed the stairs to my room, threw my suitcase on the floor, and climbed into bed. I tried to summon the four tough women in flannel shirts at Scott's. The hours of abandoned dancing at A Little More. All the lesbian-feminist poetry and theory I'd read. None of that addressed my nineteen-year-old broken heart.

Then, just a few minutes later—not long enough, I quickly judged, for sex to have occurred—my dorm-room door opened. Robin slipped in without saying a word. She undressed and got into bed.

6

ROBIN AND I DECIDED to move to San Francisco in the fall. She'd be graduating and I'd transfer to Berkeley. At the last minute, though, she took a job in New York instead. I'd already transferred, so I went on to Berkeley.

We never did break up. After all, we'd been practically children. We just drifted into other relationships, and our friendship remained intact. Robin now has a medical practice, a partner, and two growing sons.

When I talked to Robin yesterday, trying to mine her memory for more stories about our San Francisco adventure, she kept turning the conversation back to Christmas in Portland. "Your mom was a fierce Ping-Pong player. Your brother was so sweet to me. Your little sister was just the most wonderful thing. Mount Hood took my breath away. I still think of it." Maybe she has a few cherished memories from that holiday after all.

Robin's mother and I still stay in touch via e-mail. She sends me cards signed with love. I send her some of my books and pictures from my travels.

A few years after the San Francisco trip, Blanche and I happened to visit Robin in New York at the same time. We took acid together. Blanche and I sat cross-legged on the floor of the living room and stared at each other's faces, which we found hilarious. We laughed and laughed and laughed. Robin, who hadn't indulged, puttered about the house, annoyed with us.

Lately, I hardly ever think about my sexual orientation. I even forget I'm a lesbian sometimes and get surprised when I notice someone else noticing. It's just that there are so many other more pressing, and frankly interesting, things about my life these days.

But every now and then I catch a glimpse of that wonder, how it felt to have just popped out of the dominant paradigm, the breathtaking view from that new summit. To witness someone else seeing that view for the first time is a little like falling in love. I wanted to tell my friend at the Dyke March party, the girl with the plaid shorts and stand-up hair, "If I were eighteen, you'd be all I want."

I'm not eighteen. But I am dancing in the street. That night last week, the Castro teemed with dykes of all genders. The Sisters of Perpetual Indulgence were on the scene to keep it peaceful, sane, loving, and doing all that with humor. I closed my eyes for a moment and felt the rumble of that Greyhound bus, smelled the stench, heard the old men's snores, felt Robin's head on my shoulder. We still had a long journey ahead, but we'd been right to believe in the possibility of being free.

in the bars of heaven and hell

aaron shurin

O, damn these things that try to maim me
This armor
Fooled
Alive in its
Self
　—Jack Spicer

In time Cupid himself, healed of his wound, escapes and joins Psyche
and Love may thus be said to have rescued the mind.
　—W. Jackson Bate

A SERIES OF FALSE STARTS, holes, memory in junk mode, flashing signs that won't hold, missing letters: wet pain for wet paint, urn for turn, trance for entrance.

A sequence of overtures, preludes, entryways leading to the same core, a hub of alleys in the heart of the underground city, San Francisco of bright men in dreamtime and lost boys all me, 1965–69, who will become a civic stalwart and one of the seen-it-alls, furious partisan within ten short years, for forty years and more. Imaginary metropolis, *fleur de ciel*, balm for a wound and the wound's own inflamer, city of promise or pleasure or pain, city of the heathenly heavenly gate, city of all gratification given or lost in place, still there, still here, still there.

A net into which I am pushing myself, falling, talking to origin, walking home, walking away, counting backwards: 58, 47, 36, 29, 18! December 1965, when the siren began to wail, the house shake from its foundation, the wildflower open that wouldn't close, perfuming the small rooms, the glittering streets, the lowering classrooms and lecture halls, infusing the bus in motion, the ever-streaming sky, night-driven, electric, westward into the city...*e lucevan le stelle.*

•

AT THE AGE OF EIGHTEEN, toward the end of my freshman semester at UC Berkeley, having been plucked by a young man in Boston and kept vibrating on the telephone for five months, sharpening my skills at melodramatic exhortation and blame—cornered as I was in a shared dormitory cubicle casting a stark modernist light on my nineteenth-century poses (fainting in a ripped negligee on the forlorn floor of an imaginary boudoir)—I burned up the phone line unassuaged and unexamined, pleading, ignited, exquisitely selfless and thus self-absorbed, tenderized by long distance, and thoroughly invaded. Fingering the black rotary phone's empty alphabet holes—His name? My name?—I heaved and sank, palpitating like an anemone and laid bare like a shucked mollusk. My bottomless susceptibility encouraged Al to listen while talking little, but his Boston realism brought closure to conversations I hoped to extend. Frustrated to surfeit at last, I leaned into a decision for action: I would go to a gay bar across the bay in San Francisco and test my errrr testicles.

And so began a journey of a thousand nights and more in these bars, oscillating between exaltation and despair, as I tried to get laid in the name of love and got laid in some other name and walked back into the night to try again, the bars' names—vibrating rhythm—a vatic invocation: Pearl's, The Rendezvous, The Capri, The 524, The Rainbow Cattle Company, The Mind Shaft, The Stud, continuing for decades, sacrificial rite in which my body was meat to placate the hungry/angry god but also the god's own feral pleasure brought to fruition. It's hard to register, now, the charge the mere phrase "gay bar" had then, with its overtones of forbidden treasure and perilous, secret shame, its aura of biblical topos recalling both burning sin and angelic rising, its contradictory tenor fusing the phrase into a single Janus word—"gaybar" —where one side was leaping in joyous release and the other was locked for eternity in a penitent cell. There was no other community site, no other avenue, no public visibility, no other home away from home.

At my venture out, in December of 1965, the nights were dark and the sex was still (thrillingly?) secret. The gay movement's—not yet a movement—epiphanic libido and horizontal fraternity had not yet come to purpose, though a telepathic reaching toward light was imminent, subject to history's own propulsive network of radical connectivity. You couldn't yet see the combustive, allegorical power in naming your urges out loud to follow them into flame. The circuit through erection and deflation began again each morning or night with impossible innocence and welcome erasure, without yet stringing the stations together—shared bed/empty bed—into a linked strategy of social recognition, petition, and redress. At eighteen I merely gathered myself sobbing or gathered myself thrilled and combed my hair—I will tell you how I combed my hair—and mapped out the even now antipodal

trajectory from Berkeley to San Francisco, coded in the form of
the F bus, laconic bullet into the heart of pulsating distance,
whose course of freeway to bridge was almost ludicrously symbolic. I paid my fare—the price was admitting I wanted to go—
and cast myself into the classic fog in search of reciprocation.

•

MY POINT OF VIEW at every point is ineluctably recursive:
Later I would come to see or in time I would think that or after a
few years I started to. So many days and nights collapse into each
other, so many hours went in circles, so many men traded faces,
so many dicks went up and down. My superannuated lenses double, triple, quadruple events. Down a side street, through an alley,
across a corridor, behind an unmarked door: these were repeated
coordinates, and the first of many sets of indices attaching eros to
underground, splitting it off, Dante-esque, from *la diritta via* to
find or lose its only other way, in the night and of the night, and
cast off into the castaway arms of the Tenderloin, the emptied financial district, of neon-wicked North Beach. But winding wide-
eyed into these alleys I didn't even know to say hello and good-
bye—a little boy with a hobo sack made of a polka-dot scarf and a
wand—because I couldn't then see the contraindications of audience, old family and new family crossing in opposite directions.
(Five months later, already long removed from the machinery of
home and former friends, spiraling into new networks of bar-go-
ers and bed partners, I walked the dormitory grounds one spring
evening with Lela, oldest and dearest pal, who turned suddenly to
me and pleaded, "What do you do all those nights you say you're
doing nothing?") Now in the dark, bus-weary but alive with singular focus, I tucked in my striped shirt and settled my stomach,
which had lurched the first of a thousand or more lurchings; I
took off my black glasses to cast my lot with being seen over seeing. This Tenderloin bar was Pearl's, an after-hours club open to

underage explorers. A couple of weeks ago I'd been initiated with my good friend Mark after we'd mutually removed our masks—girlfriends! —and formed a scandalous compact of adventure. This time I was on my own. I smiled at the doorman like a practiced pro—a thin, wavering smile, for sure, but bravely set—and swam into the bowl of a room with naïve guppy enthusiasm, all goggle eyes and forward momentum.

I emerged into the peopled circumference of a dance space, whose center was occupied by bouncing boys, semicollegiate or flightier than that, wiggling to the Supremes while the circumference slid around them at a slow, ogling pace. Far in the back, on a stagelike dais, was a civilized set of tables, gents talking to gents, vestigial normalcy. Colored lights fractured and energized both circulating loop and throbbing core, and everything else throbbed, and I throbbed, too. I stood at once airy and leaden, predatory and perfectly succulent, putting on my thick, black-rimmed glasses to scan the crowd, then taking them off in case anyone had noticed. I put them on and took them off, put them on and took them off, wading slowly through the periphery, pennyloafers leading the way. I was as neat as a cutout silhouette and about as loose; my oxford shirt was tucked in all the way to my shoes, and my hair—well, I will tell you about my hair—but I managed to get some depth of perspective by grooving to the music from the outside circle without committing shamelessly to the inner dance.

As I casually pocketed my glasses one more time, a baritone voice from behind me whispered into my ear, "Why not just keep your glasses on?" I turned around; he smiled slyly, swept away in the moving current, leaving me achingly self-conscious but deliciously exposed, caught between sweet blindness and sweet sight. He had a dollop of thick, blond hair—the kind you merely push back with your hand and call it a day—and a stevedore's torso stuffed in a white, cable-knit sweater; he was tall with a fair, freckled complexion, and an air of confident athleticism. I started to twitter under the nourishment of his parting eyes.

Time distended as the circling masses looped back. I pre-
tended to be on top of my eyeglass problem (I kept them deter-
minedly off), and did my best to shimmer in the dim light. I
hoped that I was being watched, maintaining a passively alert
stance, urged toward clairvoyance by my near-blind state, trying
to descry a blond fin carving the surface of the crowd. Martha and
the Vandellas matched the beat of my knocking knees; I moved
my arms like I was dancing in place to mask their tremor, though
in truth I was now almost drowsy from stimulation. Then a voice
flavored with molasses warmed my ear from behind, enunciating
with great, slow, care: "I'd . like . to . fuck . you."

Reader, can you picture me in my starched pinafore, punctured
by this impregnating voice? Can you catch my prim shock at the
sudden vernacular, my unskilled, flustered propriety; can you feel
the pointedness of the remark in that age at my age, before noto-
rious bathhouses, before leather and chains, before public orgies,
before AIDS? Beyond that, my entire sexual repertoire was cir-
cumscribed by Boston Al's generous rubdown, and he'd even
asked me with fine politesse if I wanted to try something new before he scooted down to blow me, secretary licking a letter. If I
was alarmed and maybe even affronted (What kind of girl did he
think I was? etc.) I was also titillated out of my pants. But I didn't
even know his name!

Such decorousness I communicated without much trouble,
given the full extent of my dropped jaw and nervous giggle. The
silver shark who'd cruised the room with bloodlit, discriminating
intent now bowed low, transformed into a courtier dusting my
feet with the florid plume of his hat. Certainly he was sorry,
hadn't realized what kind of guy he was dealing with; would I like
to take a seat? We removed to the theatrical dais where I tucked
up my knees in self-congratulation and began the essential conversation.

Bill, it turned out, was educated, literate, preparing to get an
advanced degree at SF State, with enthusiasms that matched my

own: a belief in the lasting value of *Who's Afraid of Virginia Woolf?* (my favorite current literary argument!), and a devotion to the Theater of the Absurd in general. From there I was all unstoppable run on:

"I go to Berkeley I'm a poli-sci major but I'll probably study English want to be a writer I'm living in the dorms love Ionesco came here once before a couple of happened in Boston for the first but now I'm really ready about love not sex I plan to meet then I'll forever."

Bill nodded ceremoniously, eyebrows raised in approval, laughing as he patted my leg, genially committed to letting me verbalize my entire past and even my future with him. He greeted a couple of passing boys as I fondled my Coke, then we talked for an hour about literature and more. Late in the night as Pearl's grew thin, after I was convinced of his genuine interest and had convinced him of my serious purpose, he took me home to his apartment high on a hill above North Beach, precipitous climb to a small but modern studio, plate glass and bleached wood, with a wide, rumpled bed almost thrust through the picture window like a gangplank, overlooking the far, glistening, lubricious Bay. And there, gentle reader, without further ado, he turned off the lights and fucked me till the stars were wet with dew.

•

GOING TO PEARL'S was inconvenient at best, given its after-hours schedule (starting at two?) and my dependence on the F bus, whose last ride back to the dorms left the East Bay Terminal in downtown San Francisco a few unaccommodating minutes later at two-thirteen, not to resume its returning crawl till early rush hour. The real goal would have to be the Rendezvous, cleanest and cruelest of all the collegiate bars, up a long stairway behind a prohibition-style unmarked door on a quiet denuded street at the edge of the financial district. For a couple of months I dared an "I'm with them/I'm invisible" slide (being three years under the age limit), and sometimes the bouncers went blind as I nervously held my breath, but soon enough I scored a fake ID in dependable radical Berkeley, and my fate was sealed by a hasty wave up to the landing.

The Rendezvous of my near-virginity; the Rendezvous of my counting how many men so far on my fingers; the Rendezvous of sighing across the room while Fontella Bass sang "Rescue Me" and I thought she meant someone else; the Rendezvous of cold, bitter shoulders and men as remote as they were before I said I wanted men; the Rendezvous of window dressers imperious in precision slacks; the Rendezvous of the last stand, of being a cute kid, of saying less than I knew so I could be thought worth doing; the Rendezvous of complete impersonation and lusting after a look of alluring indifference, of purveying a masque of decorum in profile; the Rendezvous: a sweater bar; the Rendezvous of the hunt, and shriven nights, and pointless mornings of long walks to the bus, and somewhere, somewhere buried now because it won't release, moments of wild pleasure and affection in the company of gentle men—but the Rendezvous won't let loose those nights from its faceless unnamed speakeasy doors I would rip from their hinges, impatient for payback. Nowhere did the prosaic malevolence of the social closet pervade more thoroughly, a mutating force that narrowed men into their slimmest moral territories to fit the imprint of second hand normalcy—a charade of entropy with a mixed drink—not the multifarious community we would come to be but the constrained, devalued projections into one or two or three tight molds, provisional, good for a quick glance and one moment's respite of being alike instead of different. Cleaned up and smoothed down, brushed off, polished, impeccable, unassailable exteriors.

Today—forty years later!—confirming my history of gay bars in the San Francisco Public Library archives, I happened upon an exhibit of men rounded up and exterminated in Nazi Germany

under the aegis of the infamous Paragraph 175—banks of photos
of their faces, the sweet fairies of Germany I hardly needed to examine to recognize, the schoolteacher and artist and writer and
yes, the window dresser—so I'm having to remind myself that my
own foolishness, my frailty, my comrades' unlovingness, the unmarked doors of their hearts, our unmet Rendezvous, were surrounded by real not imaginary terrors, of police roundups, and
lost jobs, and public shame and family disgrace. Last call at the
Rendezvous—we stood around drinking, eyeing, and we went
home and sometimes talked and sometimes didn't and spread our
legs or got spread, we licked and bathed each other in sweat and
sometimes traded tender kisses that seemed to matter and sometimes didn't, a repertoire of intimate address played out in a microcosm of distance: the one-night stand, the trick; the Rendezvous which had no warning printed above its legendary
unmarked door into which I entered shivering a hundred nights,
all in my youth, eighteen, nineteen, not yet part of an army of
natural lovers—but I will get there, it will come—not quite yet
one of the soldiers of ecstasy.

•

EVERY NIGHT A NEW NIGHT, every wardrobe not yet
tested, every shower a purification, each afternoon a systematic
prelude. With all the other students gone on movie dates at normal dating hours, the dorms reached a point of (merciful) hushed
emptiness as I began my preparations for a ten departure to the
City. I was slim; I had nice bones and a twinkle above them when
I managed to relax, but my hair—oh, my wiry, independent, shtetl
hair, my Ukrainian ribbons from my mother's side, folkloric bon-
net of curls, was out of the question, way too heavily accented,
ruefully unacceptable, untidy, un-Californian, un-Rendezvous. So
I stepped out of the shower and looked right and left to make sure
I was alone—I was always alone or I wouldn't have begun the

process!—and blotted my hair, careful not to rough it up into frizz. I crept back to my room, sat down, took a towel and folded it lengthwise with studious application—my weekly midterm—into an absorbent strip like a civil war bandage, to heal my wound. Dreamily I thought of clean-cut, uninflected men, exhibiting no scars, no wayward intentions, no minds of their own. I combed my hair down over my brows, wet straight bangs, and wrapped the folded towel across it, knotted behind my head, hair plastered to dry flat on the griddle of my forehead. In half an hour, dressed for recovery, bandage removed, the vicissitudes of organic growth had been countered by a smooth semi-industrial layer of perfectly straight strands, my fall of grace. Like a surgeon I pried, parted, and patted. With a comb I lightly pressed and shaped the units—no one would ever know—(later no comb could make it through my afro of sausage curls) into a pompadour-like contraption of near-solid organization, neat, discrete, unshakably—or so I hoped—under control. I unwrapped the telltale, offending towel and put it on the rack. The mirror confirmed my magic from all angles. I flashed a pleased, bitter, triumphant smile, tucked in a loose strand, and hit the door with trembling anticipation, hairdo firmly in place, a swagger enclosing my swish.

•

I GOT ON THE F BUS TO THE CITY. I kept my head down and my hopes high. There weren't many people on the bus that late. A tired woman stepped up with a couple of stuffed shopping bags, looking at me with disgust for the shame inscribed across my face that everyone could see in spite of my near-perfect hair. I kept my head down and my hopes high, as the bus wove on through the ghettos and warehouses of Berkeley, and I traced in my mind the long dark stairway up to the Rendezvous, boys at the top. A drunk sat down across from me, sneering contemptuously at my leaking corruption, my stinking catalog of projected caresses. I kept my head down with my hopes high, scanning under lowered brow for the towers of the bridge, and beyond them the spangled towers of the city, *fleur de ciel*, the bridge itself a stairway and the city rising. The bus stopped at every lonely outpost of the East Bay, lost workers working too late, ascending and descending as the murky waters of the bay drew nearer. A skinny man with levitating hands I recognized from one of the bars took a seat in the back, sweeping his eyes across mine then lowering them in secret humiliation. I too kept my eyes down but my hopes high, catching the first string of lights on the Bay Bridge, diamond necklace around my trembling throat, as the bus hit the incline, the sour smell of Bay mud drifted up, the bridge unfolded its stairway, the boys of the Rendezvous waiting up there, down there, my skin beginning to itch, my pulse quicken. And there at the crest between the big suspension towers from the top deck heading west the City began to sparkle into view over the salted gray steel, one tall building lit up, another glittering group, a huge gesturing neon sign, the tall silhouettes arced with scintillations, a sense of streaming purpose, one glinting community of buildings with night-vision eyes alive in the dark, glimpsed always through the bars of the sloping cables, an actual other side I drank the elixir of, keeping my head up, now, for clear sight and my abiding hopes rising. A complicity of electricity burned high as I neared the shining metropolis all vicissitudes of school or traffic or psychiatry or family couldn't deny, a shimmer of the western wave exactly at its crest, this fluorescent tournament of arrivals, radiating city at the water's edge unbound.

Even in 1966 I could map its locales as if they were part of my body, and my body recognized the incoming city as a form that fit, though I was too young, I was too small, the city was too big, it had too much to give and I had too much to be taken. If it wasn't yet mine it would become mine. And it is always and still this apparitional San Francisco, glistening with the immediate future, starlit, as seen through the scratchy windows of the accelerating

F bus from the upper deck of the Bay Bridge as I set out late in the evening to get lost or found—flickering spires between spires—my nose pressed right to the glass in the middle of a night at once pitch black and luminous I hoped would never end.

●

THE EAST BAY TERMINAL spilled its contents into the un-peopled nether streets of the financial district, below Market Street, it was said, with an emphasis on the low. The proverbial canyons were indifferent to my forward-leaning walk except in one respect: together they polished an unrelenting wind arriving somehow off the Bay, batted it from their right angles to sharpen the chill, and hurled it down Mission Street like a bowl-ing ball of air. The target, of course, was my precious hairdo. I ducked and danced like a prizefighter, keeping my head down and my hands up, a gesture somewhere between vigilance and pained helplessness, fanning my fingers in a frantic attempt at maintenance.

The route to the Rendezvous required navigating only these glaciated throughways. I scampered from entryway to entryway, wedging my body close to the walls, darting out of the aim of sniping gusts, re-plying loose strands as soon as they were grabbed by the teeth of the wind. At a few sacred posts along the way old-fashioned mirrored columns offered their charity. With quick, alarmed focus I assessed the damage, and dexterous as Ari-adne trilled my knowing fingers around my head. At the foot of Sutter I held my breath and dashed up the street to the Ren-dezvous, one hand raised like a bronze shield, turning my face right and left against marauding squalls that tried to lift whole sections from my head in a last-ditch attack. I arrived at the door-way shaken by the volatility of this fifteen-minute walk from transportation to transport, winded almost to tears by frustration and exertion but richly enlivened by the chase.

•

I WASN'T SPECIAL THERE; it wasn't special that I was there; it's what I knew and where I went. I was younger than most, and some looked up to me for that and some looked down; some looked through me, as they often did, and some looked me over— almost, but not quite, as often: inviolable algorithm of gay bars. Sometimes, in fact, I went with Mark or Roosevelt; sometimes I arranged to meet up with Jim and John; but at all times I was there alone, filled with incomprehensible yearning, chattering in the foreground while my eyes fed on strangers in the back. I shuffled my impatient feet, ready to follow them in the trance of a suggested direction like an ouija board: B=L=O=N=D. Sometimes they pointed me out the door with Del or Danny, then trotted me back the next week for Danny or Del.

One blustery night in October I pushed my beginner's luck dangerously through to last call. After a long set of gin and tonics, I heard the bartender's ominous shout, then dared to have one more; I blinked my brown poppy eyes and no one blinked back. Desperate, I tried to prevail on a casual friend for shelter to no effect—sorry, kid—and so, grabbing my coat, with the last scuttling men blending into the shadows like shadows, dashed out the door—two!—racingly retracing my fraught steps with the now-welcome wind pawing my back, eastbound without a moment to think of lost opportunities and no further second to spare. I arrived at the terminal at two-fifteen, to breathe in the treacherous fumes of the just-departed last bus to Berkeley, leaving the station empty, chilled, and silent till six the next morning—and where was I now in my hairdo and high hopes?

•

ACROSS FROM THE TERMINAL, at First and Mission, was the sad castle of my keep: Foster's Cafeteria, open all night for my unending night, the nonnegotiable duration of despair. One out-post in a depression-era chain across the City, it had steam-table food, tank-brewed coffee, and translucent lime Jell-O; nobody there wanted to be there because nobody there had anyplace else to go. I ordered a coffee and sat in a corner with my busted wings in my lap, as far away as I could from the homeless men and mut-tering drunks and street crazies, to differentiate my predicament from theirs—but only as far as the plate-glass walls would allow, because I was part of their company now, inside the zone of dis-possession, undone by the faulty mechanics of my lust, of even my tender, untested, zealous love. The gulping loss took my throat so that I couldn't swallow: no one to be there for me, no there for me to be, vanished in plain sight under a neon spray of disinfectant accommodation, some last-chance saloon of a world-weary cafe-teria —but this was my first chance!

•

I MAY HAVE ENDURED one or two such nights again in the coming months, and each tore down another part of me, broke me more deeply against the rocks of what my privilege was de-signed to protect me from, a middle-class kid in search of affec-tion within the frame of a polite dream of possibilities and posses-sion, kicked below the line, thrown away, so that each time I cried in my coffee a little bit harder, cursing the predilection, unchosen, that alone was enough to cancel out my parents' fine stucco house; my good, lucky genes; my college training-in-progress; my dreamy sense of purpose; my benevolent vision. I sat stupefied for hours by the suddenness and thoroughness with which I'd come undone, in a bottomless heartache as hard and sharp as my body could translate into sentient pain, a loss equal to the future of my promised homoerotic heaven for which the dorms had disgorged me in the false triumph of my own determination. I staggered home in the morning drained and somnolent from so much sadness, blinking back frayed visions that were self-accusations that made my condemnation complete: an attenuated spiral of shame.

•

BUT BY THE SECOND or third descent something settled at the bottom of my cup, a small reflective dreg that started to mirror things differently. Perhaps by then I'd already let my sideburns snake half an inch toward my jaw or, just a few months removed from the dorms, swallowed a tab of acid and permitted the trees to carefully show me why. Within the year, I know, I'd met a couple of curiously cast men at the bar: impish Jeremy who played me an LP of Edith Sitwell reciting *Fáade* in the pruniest British trill, a high flute of melodious rhyme that still hasn't quieted, and Rasputin-like Jim, who explained wild-eyed in self-transfixing tones how he'd lit up a lightbulb in his gripping fist, a mysterious narrative I found perfectly useful to believe. At the outer edge of the student district in my newly rented room I spasmed in psychedelic collapse, then came out the other side with a reading list starting with Plato, a wall-print from the cave at Altamira, and a boxed set of buoyant Bach concerti.

Around campus, on an almost weekly basis, demonstrations and student strikes had begun to fracture the university's fictitious calm. It's hard to keep the timeline in focus, its sequence of rapid initiations, inundations, transformations. Some or all of these incidents collected in my cup in the form of a suspended inchoate question or brooding lapse in the sequence of pain, and began to leak into my marooned isolation, as the ache wore down my nerves and I built up a tolerance for the bitter sacrament of cold coffee. If I was tossed out with the partisans of Foster's Cafeteria, perhaps the view from within—from without—had its own compensatory perceptual angle.

I might not have put it together in the glare of that brutal aquarium of night, but in my forced truancy of desperate, unsleeping wonder I began to catch a wavelength arriving from another part of the Bay, where, unanticipated and unlooked for by either side, my proximity to the discarded habitués of Foster's Cafeteria began to resemble something more like solidarity.

•

A CATHEXIS OF TIME IN SPACE: The foreshortened crush of events in San Francisco 1967–68—the Haight-Ashbury, the Summer of Love, the antiwar movement, Janis Joplin and Jimi Hendrix—accelerated maturation, limbs growing from other limbs, personal and civic body politics rumbling, a protean up-heaval underneath the streets as ferocious as the fabled earth-quakes. I lose the thread by which I can declare intentions my own, subject to a multi-directional and constant stream of cultural invention. In the narrower terms of my vexed romantic explo-ration, the tide shifted me away from the circumspect, self-loathing Rendezvous, and toward the randier bohemian shores of North Beach, with its post-Beatnik libertine glow, its practiced, seamy boulevards, and free-floating literary sheen. On upper Grant Street, just two blocks from the illustrious City Lights Books, the tiny, cramped, smoke-thick Capri became, for a while, the righteous center of my exploration.

I drove over with friends, or for a short while in my own VW bug, or even stood on the freeway ramp at University Avenue and hitched my way across the Bay with careless, confident ease, with the same incandescent fantasy appearing like a promise at the apex of the bridge, and the same leap into my throat of wide-open anticipation. Inside the Capri, at the very back, which is to say the other end of a dark lozenge not big enough to have a back, we danced in a modest frenzy, shook our hair, which was just about long enough to shake, nuzzled a neck with a mustache or baby beard, rattled a couple of beads, and semi-furtively passed a joint—the old-fashioned kind that took two stogy missiles to give you a buzz. My own hair was now a wavy nest looped behind my ears, proudly accented by a bandito mustache that conspired to make me look even younger by showing how hard I was trying to look old. But I was an adult now—no more fake I.D. for me—and poetry and high lit were steadily invading my conversation, ably handled by the quirky intellectuals frequenting the bar, many of whom made North Beach their home, down Grant Street inside minuscule rooms in a seedy residence hotel that clearly had never seen better days, with the inspired lyrical name of The Bachelor's Quarters, just one short step removed from Tennessee Williams's infamous Tarantula Arms.

But I'm wrong to put a spider web around The Bachelor's Quarters, because it became my sanctified home-away-from-home, in the skinny but well-formed arms of Stephen, in the cramped thick of his tiny room and single bed, under the fall of his long, straight hair, his lean hawkish gaze and critical wit, in a happy grace incomprehensible to him who both lusted after me with relish and wearily tolerated my youth in equal measure. He was twenty-eight to my twenty-one, and treated me like the pleasant pup I couldn't understand I still was. But in that maddening close chamber stuffed with books and sheet music and bigger books again, under the spell of his independence and in conversation with his friends—a writer, a harpsichordist, a gardener, a historian—I began to see a place for myself in a totally queer collective zone I would later come to know as "community."

By the fall of 1968 the air around the Capri was salted with historical imperative, as if a solution had reached its maximum saturation and was ready to be transmuted into another property entirely, atmosphere becoming ground. In and out of the arms of Stephen, and with other men in and out of mine, I (we) turned passionate encounter into play, and body friction into recreation (many years later, someone at the café suggested, "Don't say 'slut,' say 'sexually generous,'") In a gathering political synthesis still liminal but impinging, I sensed a common ground with radicalizing elements at large, and though I couldn't yet precisely see the purpose we shared, the flower had already cracked the bud in me and was unfolding.

It was no big deal to test last call at the Capri: In a jam, I just held out my thumb on Broadway and a VW van picked me up and took me back across the bridge. Let's say one night in November I stayed too late carousing, and hadn't yet arrived at an acceptable conclusion. Let's say a number of other men were similarly disposed, if not quite sure of their direction. Let's say some of us knew each other and some of us wanted to, and one or another of us meant to, and somebody had to, and when the bar expelled us into the dimly lit street a reluctance that was an excess of libidinal energy and fleshy goodwill restrained our feet, and we didn't blend into the shadows. Let's say one person put his back to a blue parked car and leaned, scuffing his boots, and then another stopped and talked, and soon a small set of tired but still-alert men milled around in the smoldering dark out in the open as the safe house of the bar shut down, in the nightglow but not of the night.

With a smile I put my comradely arm around Michael, who was always flirting, though I had eyes just then for his friend from Modesto. And the still air was sharp and clear and, yes, *e lucevan le stelle*, as we shuffled in place under the dim streetlights chatting toward any destination at all, and our small, friendly gathering was perfectly visible and absolutely audible to anybody wanting to listen or look—for a good twenty minutes right there on a short stretch of Grant street in 1968 in front of the Capri bar in the middle of the vivid dark of the city we came for together—and then the circle relaxed its hold.

I uncurled my toes on a deepening breath, bid a sweet good night to Michael and "Modesto" without regret, ambled a few blocks down Broadway to where the freeway ramp floated off to the Bay, buttoned up my peacoat, and stuck out my thumb.

the rock
and a hard place

jim duggins

1

AT THE FOOT OF VAN NESS AVENUE, I waited for the
Warden Johnston, the launch ferrying back and forth to Alcatraz.

My employment counselor had reported only a single listing, a
job at Alcatraz Island for a commissary clerk with merchandising
experience. I needed that job. Following the breakup of my first
committed relationship, I had fled to San Francisco to lick my
wounds and to start a new life. I was twenty-two.

Drenched in morning sun, the Rock and its attendant lighthouse glowed from its perch atop the island. I could imagine the
massive white building as a palace in the Aegean Sea, its companion

lighthouse a way station for mythic sirens seducing sailors. But I knew its foghorns mourned the misery warehoused amid the splendor of one of the world's most beautiful harbors.

I trembled a little from more than the bay-chilled wind at the entrance to the prison. Up close, it had none of the romantic illusions seen from the bay. The white structure, so blinding in full sun, was actually a fog-whipped gray of patched and stuccoed-over cement. Nearly windowless at eye level, the long stretch of unadorned concrete most resembled a chalky cliff or the fortress wall about a medieval town.

•

THE ADMINISTRATIVE OFFICES of the island couldn't have been more government-issue, dull and tasteless, devoted to the idea that economy trumps imagination. Gray doors opened onto gray halls from gray offices furnished with gray steel military surplus desks.

At the end of the hall, a man in a dark blue suit sat before a typewriter. He rushed around, arm outstretched, to shake my hand. "Mr. Duggins. I'm glad you can join us. I've got some papers for you to fill out, then I'll take you in to see the warden. After that, I'll help you get started."

Constantine Belieuski was well over six feet tall and gave the impression that he hovered as he bent down for face-to-face conversation. His Roman nose called attention to his face, but his placid brown eyes revealed no emotion. His thin lips scarcely moved when he spoke, and his voice seemed to emanate from the back of his throat. I quickly concluded from his guarded comments and evasions that we would never be friends away from the office.

Half an hour later, Warden Paul Madigan took my elbow to direct me to a chair opposite his desk. For his office, he had traded the gray colors for a bilious green and had abandoned the gray metal furniture in favor of dark thrift-shop wood.

Madigan was a friendly, long-faced, blue-eyed fellow with big ears that my mother called "the Irish curse." Softspoken and well-mannered, he was the sort of man one feels comfortable with on first meeting. An unusual attribute for the head of America's harshest prison. "My door is always open," he said so repeatedly and forcefully that I couldn't resist peeking back at the closed door.

After a few inconsequential questions, he led me back to Mr. Belieuski's typing-stand desk and, after a reassuring pat on my shoulder, disappeared into his office, shutting the door behind him.

My own office turned out to be a tiny space at the end of the hall. It barely had room for a metal desk and file cabinet, a typewriter on a stand, and two chairs, one for me and one for my typist.

I had been hired to operate a store for inmates. I would also keep their "bank," an accounting of what they'd earned in prison industries, a carpentry shop, the kitchen, and bakery. Other jails had small prison exchanges where inmates could buy luxuries—cigarettes, candy, toiletries, and the like—but Alcatraz had no store. Inmates were permitted to buy only selected reading materials—never anything of violent or criminal content—and hobbies, art supplies, and musical instruments.

Inmates placed their purchase requests on a simple Federal Form 1a, called a "cop-out," the same form used by snitches and stoolies to notify the warden that they were ready to rat out other convicts. The cop-out forms came to me to decide whether to accept or deny each request. When orders arrived and items like palette knives in art-supply kits and guitar strings that might serve as garrotes were removed, I distributed them to the inmates during daily sick call.

"Why did the previous commissary clerk leave?" I asked Constantine.

He studied my face before answering. "Well, it all began at the movies. The inmates get a free movie every Sunday afternoon if they're on good behavior. You order the movie."

"I do?" I rolled my eyes, mocking my ability to remember yet another duty.

"Anyway—when officers have nothing to do on their shifts, they fill in the time by searching inmate cells. It's called a shakedown. It's all legitimate, and cells shaken down are recorded in a log so searches are randomly distributed throughout the population."

I wrinkled my forehead.

"The cons hate it. Most all of 'em have some contraband seized in a shakedown, but it's like one more assault on their dignity."

"And, so?"

"So, Jonesy, that's 753 Jones, returned from the movie one Sunday and found his cell had been shaken down. The next day, Anderson, the old commissary clerk, passed the stairs when Jonesy walked by. He asked, 'How did you like the movie?'" Constantine paused, his face pale. "Jonesy thought Anderson was belittling him for having his cell shaken down during the movie. Well, Jonesy went ape that morning. He went up to his cell and got his trombone and brained Anderson with it. Beat his brains out. Killed him."

A long silence followed before I managed to ask, "What happened to Jonesy?"

"The courts in town added another twenty years to his time." He looked at me and grinned. "And we went looking for a new commissary clerk. That's you, Jimbo."

"But Anderson didn't do anything. It was cold blooded-murder!"

"That's not the point, Jim. Get that out of your head or you won't survive here. Your typist's name is Granger, 987 Granger. The way he tells it, he's in for auto theft. Naturally, he doesn't tell you that he needed the car because he'd held up a navy exchange. Also, there were passengers in the car, people he'd held as hostages as part of his escape. To listen to him, it's all a bum rap. You know when he's due to get out?"

"No, when?"

"It's 2074."

In spite of myself, I caught my breath. "2074? Oh, God, imagine what it must be like to have that over your head."

"The point is you've got to be careful, Jim. A man who ain't gettin' out till 2074, he ain't got a lot to lose no matter what he does. He'll die here. Cons think like that. It don't matter if they kill somebody. Now, do you see?"

I quit arguing.

"So watch your ass. Grow eyes in the back of your head. Always know what the man is doing behind you. Don't trust anyone here—that includes a lot of the screws. The inmates got nothing to lose, and they've been conning people for more years than you've been alive. Keep your eyes and ears open and your mouth shut."

I sat a moment, sullen, my lips clamped together. "Okay, I'll remember that."

He tapped the face of his watch. "How 'bout I come by at twelve-fifteen and show you about lunch? In the meantime, you can start working on those papers—put aside the ones you have questions about." He stood and turned to go.

"Thanks, Constantine."

"Nothin' to it," he said over his shoulder. "Just be careful."

·

I RUSHED HEADLONG into my work. The office area felt sterile and hollow. High ceilings, tile floors and cement walls, footsteps, delivery men, clerks in the hallways, noises unrelieved by carpeting or draperies. I consciously blanked them out to focus on the scatter of papers on my new desk. Attacking the bank statements

first, I was astounded to see that several of the lifers had balances of
more than a thousand dollars—not bad at twenty-five cents an hour
for work in the kitchen.

After two hours with the accounting entries, I couldn't resist
peeking at the inmate requests. The four-inch by four-inch cop-out
form had a line for the inmate's number, name, and the date submitted, and "Dear Warden, Sir:" followed by a dozen blank lines.
The hair on the back of my neck rose. These were the written
records of some of America's most violent men. Childish scrawls, a
quick jab of downstrokes, a mixture of cursive and block printing,
and uneven squiggles shouted out "illiteracy." Who were these men
fueled by a rage so hot it had incinerated human conscience?

One form near the bottom of the pile snagged my attention.

1057 Smith. April 9, 1958.
Dear Warden, Sir: Mr. Duggins:
    Welcome, sir, to Alcatraz Prison. I'm sorry what hap-
pened to Mr. Anderson. He was a good man and everybody
knows Jonesy is crazy.

Yours Truly
Smith (1057)

Its grammar-school neatness suggested it had been painstak-
ingly copied, probably many times. Furthermore, he had carefully
drawn little circles to dot the letter *i* on his note. I laid it alongside
the pack as I pondered what on earth it meant. Who was this
man? What did he really want?

Constantine reappeared to take me to lunch. Rolling Granger's
chair alongside, he dispatched my questions about purchase
orders—rejecting books with crime themes and metal pens that
could be used as weapons. By the time we'd finished working together, I felt proud of my progress. I forgot to ask about 1057
Smith.

When we stood to leave, my heart quickened: This was my first view of the cell house where inmates lived.

Officer Tompkins—"We call him Bubba," Constantine told me—was a lanky good ole boy from Georgia. He stood duty at the gate—a heavy steel door with a bulletproof glass window. At our approach, he unclipped a ring of keys from his belt and opened the massive door. The main entrance was secured by a sally port, a waiting area between two gates. When we had stepped inside the port, about the size of a freight elevator, built to hold a chain of a dozen manacled prisoners for transfer, Bubba banged his door shut, a deafening sound that reminded me why prisons are referred to as the slammer.

I stood there feeling foolish as an officer on the other side peered through his window to identify us, opened up, then slammed it closed as we passed through.

"We're in the main cell house now," Constantine muttered. "The ground floor is called the flatlands and the aisle between the two main cell blocks is called Broadway."

He paused and glanced at me in a way I thought protective. "Look straight ahead. The inmates will be checking you out because you're new. Don't do anything to attract attention. They can make your first day miserable, and once they find a soft spot, they'll rub it in for the rest of your time. I've seen them make wolf calls and whistle at new staff. If you think it's bad for us, you should see what they do to a new fish, especially one they think they can punk out."

Two hundred pairs of eyes focused on me. A thousand pins prickled at the base of my skull. Men sat on their bunks, some reading, some staring at the wall. One sat unself-consciously on the toilet as we passed. I'd seen bigger cages at the dog pound.

My teeth began to chatter. The cell house was dimly lit from a single source three stories above. It was also chilly with the damp bay air outside. I asked, "Is it always so cold in here?"

"Mostly so," he answered. "We don't have heat. If it was warm well, frankly, this many men together—two showers a week, three-day socks—they'd smell."

"I don't think I could stand it twenty-four hours a day."

"You'd be surprised what you'd get used to if you had to. They used to have inmates in D Block facing the bay—had a view and afternoon sun when there is any—but the inmates didn't like it. Couldn't see one another the way they can over here. Now D Block's used for TU, treatment unit—inmates call it the hole. That's where they put prisoners for punishment. A cell with a beautiful view of the bay but no privileges, two hours a week for exercise, no talking allowed."

As we neared the end of Broadway, about the length of a football field, Constantine muttered again, "Ahead of us is the gate to the mess hall. Without moving your head, look up. See the man in the wire cage? Above the gate? That's the East Gun Gallery. You didn't see it but we passed under the West Gun Gallery when we came in." He nodded solemnly. "The officers up there have rifles and forty-fives and cannisters of tear gas. They're the only officers inside the joint who carry weapons. Even if inmates kill an officer, the officers don't get a weapon. All the others are unarmed."

A wave of admiration washed over me as I considered these men who worked, unarmed, in daily contact with convicted murderers. Then, I realized, so do I. And my thoughts turned to Anderson, my predecessor.

Constantine took my arm to stand alongside the officer at the entrance to the chow hall. "I've brought you here a little early because I wanted you to see this."

Toward the sally port lay a clear view of Broadway. The two gigantic cell blocks, B and C, faced each other, three tiers high and surrounded with steel banistered walkways past the minuscule birdcages in which two hundred sixty men lived out their lives.

Constantine then told me in great detail about the count. The heart of Alcatraz Prison beat with the constant counting of its population. Inmates were counted no fewer than twelve times a day. One hundred eight times a week. Three hundred sixty times a month. Four thousand three hundred eighty times a year. Year after year after year.

At the height of a standing man, at the ends of cell blocks B and C, a flat iron lever the length of a crowbar extended out from the wall. The nether end of the lever notched a wheel with teeth that gripped and released a series of gears and cams that opened and closed the steel-barred doors of cells on the tier. A single door could be opened for one man or a work crew could be released from various cells. In the same way, the placement of a shim could be used to "lock down" an individual or a group on the tier.

No matter how many or how few, whenever any prisoner at Alcatraz was moved, all the others were counted and reported to central command. So long as a single man was unaccounted for, the entire prison was locked down until everyone was found, counted, and reported.

To take the count of a cell block, officers on all three tiers of B and C began at the end nearest the entrance and, under the surveillance of the armed guard at the West Gun Gallery, walked the line, visually identifying each man. When the officer passed, the man must be standing behind his name and number in a steel holder welded to the bars.

Over the years of their confinement, the hundreds and thousands of counts had taught the old hands a rhythmic ballet of the precise number of steps and turns needed to reach the front bars. No matter where they'd been when the count was called, sitting or lying on their bunks, standing at the back or against a wall, their calculated steps had been choreographed on their brains and they were there at the split second it took for the officer to pass.

At mealtimes, when the Gun Gallery officers over the gate received word from central command that every man had been accounted for, they signaled to the officers on the flatlands who called to the guards on all three tiers to "Let 'em out!"—to open the cells.

It was now lunchtime. The men left their cells, turned, and fell in line in a stream—a river of blue-denim pants and shirts—toward the mess hall to descend the circular stairs at the end of the block. Their leaden-footed shuffle seemed a synchronized dance. The great hall rang with the sloosh-slap of their steps on cement. Their silhouettes momentarily darkened the bars of the cells, doubling the eeriness of their passage. When the first man from cell block B and the first from cell block C met three feet from the gate, the halted shadows in the cavernous space seemed to hold their breath in silent anticipation.

I stood there transfixed by what I'd seen and what I suspected it meant—man is ultimately as trainable as a dancing bear—and I'd just seen evidence of how the human spirit can be bent. Leaning closer to Constantine, I wanted desperately to ask him how he'd come to accept it.

The Gun Gallery officers above and behind us with their view of the entire cell house and the double line of waiting inmates croaked a few staticky words into their walkie-talkies to the officer in the flatlands where we stood. That man immediately hustled over to open and slam aside the gate, whereupon the double line of block B and C strode into the mess hall.

Ahead of us lay a long, double-sided steam table, in the center of which stood six inmates in white jackets and chef hats. The two columns from the cells separated at the steam tables, B going to the left and C to the right. When the inmates had passed the steam tables with their partitioned trays, they automatically took their places at the long tables. Ten men sat at each table, four and four across from each other and one man at each end.

As I tagged along behind Constantine, I said, "Wow! That was something. I can't get over how orderly it was—like a drill at the navy base in San Diego."

"Don't let it fool you. It's not always like this. The inmates know exactly where they're going to sit because they're assigned a table and can never change—it's in the same order as their cells. Then everybody goes through the chow line, and they can ask for as much food as they like, but if they don't eat it all, they get a reprimand. Hunger strikes are strictly forbidden. The only men who can get up from the table during a meal are the ones at the head and the foot. The man at the foot can get up for more bread for the table, the one at the head for pitchers of beverage."

"Still, you've got to hand it to them for discipline."

Constantine looked over at me; a frown creased his forehead. "What you're too new to know, Jim, is that the mess hall is the most dangerous place in any prison. Contrary to movies and dime novels that show riots beginning in the prison yard, actually most riots start in the mess hall. Here's where fights between two men break out—and spread to the rest. Imagine sitting at the same table every day with the guy you hate most in the world. And did you see block C go to the right, toward the windows overlooking the bay? Fantastic view, no? Well, did you also see the two officers outside the windows on a catwalk with machine guns? Try having a nice lunch with that staring you in the face."

Constantine led me through the mess hall, turned sharply to the left, and stopped while a uniformed officer opened a steel-wire door into the kitchen.

We entered a room behind the kitchen with three tables set for four people each. An employees' lunchroom, it had been painted in the warden's putrid green. Two middle-aged men, dressed in kitchen whites, stood at the back wall, legs apart, arms behind their backs in military parade rest. They looked up, broke their stance, and came forward.

"Good afternoon, Mr. B," said a blond man who looked to be my father's age. "How are you today?"

"Excellent, Cooper. This is Mr. Duggins. He's the new commissary clerk."

981 Cooper smiled and tipped a mock military salute. "Glad to meet you, sir. Heard a lot about you. Welcome to Hellcatraz."

"Easy there, Cooper. You never had it so good. I want you guys to take good care of Mr. Duggins. Remember, he says whether or not you get your Commissary orders."

Cooper's colleague in the officer's mess, 1005 Bukovnik, chimed in, "Welcome, Mr. Duggins. Glad to have you here, sir. Let us know if there's anything you want."

I learned from Constantine that both men had been bank robbers in the 1930s and had worked their way up the federal prison ladder to Alcatraz by repeated assaults on officers. By some mysterious chance, they had ended up together in the officer's dining room, a much-sought-after prison job. They became the closest I had to true friendship on the island.

2

DAYS PASSED, a week, then two, and I was finally able to mail my first order for inmate purchases. I was surprised to learn how many cons painted in their cells after evening lockdown; how many had decks of cards and musical instruments; most of all, I was surprised by the dozen or so who took extension courses from local universities.

In the meantime, still more cop-outs came from 1057 Smith. His requests were always for books, often titles I'd never heard of. Each book was requested on a separate cop-out, and each carried some special greeting to me. Intrigued with the titles, *Nine Coaches Waiting*, *The Once and Future King*, *The Days in the Wind*, and *The Hard Blue Sky*, I called Froggy Davis, my new supplier at Western News Agency, and asked him.

"Yeah," he said. "Those are very popular titles right now." He paused. "But they're all women's romances."

"Are you certain?"

"Got one right here—let me read you the back cover. 'But the life she lives never measures up to those she reads about.' Are you sure you want them?"

"Yes," I said. "Thanks, Froggy."

As confusing as the orders were the facts about them. How did 1057 Smith know about these books? What did the questions on his cop-outs imply? "Have you read this book? If so, please let me know what you thought about it." I'd not set the form aside before I felt a hand on my shoulder and I must have jumped six inches from my chair.

"Whoa!" Constantine laughed. "Sorry. I didn't realize you were concentrating that hard. How's it going?"

"Good. I'm all caught up with the banking, and I'm sending in my first orders today."

"I just came by to tell you there's fresh coffee in my office when you're ready for a break." A rattle of chains at the entrance almost drowned out his sentence. I stood up and strained to see the cause of the commotion. I recognized the officer, Bubba, in a civilian suit and tie, holding the end of a chainlike leash attached to the cable of an inmate manacled at hands and feet. The con was taller and appeared younger than most of our old bulls.

"That's Colby—1073," Constantine said. "Bubba's bringing him back from court in San Francisco."

In pressed tan chinos, a pale yellow dress shirt, and dark blue coat sweater, the con had an attitude halfway between arrogance and aloofness, as though he recognized his superiority and saw no need to discuss it. Obviously a man who spent his cell time body-building, his muscled arms bulged in the sweater and his big chest angled to a V at his waist. Prominent nipples puckered the dress shirt over his pecs. I was gawking but couldn't tear my eyes away.

Constantine touched my arm. "Forget you ever saw that man. He's just got an additional forty-two years—and for a San Francisco court, that's a major victory for our side. Jurors don't believe us when we take prisoners to court. They think this place is a medieval torture chamber and we're all sadists."

The first gate opened and Bubba led Colby—leash, chains, and all—into the sally port, and the guard slammed the gate, shutting out the clamor of chains.

My office felt strangely empty without the sight and sounds of the prisoner and his captor. "What did he do?"

"I'll make a long story short. He began with truancy and petty theft, came from the usual hopeless family. You know, drugs and booze, prostitution, and a new "uncle" every weekend. Too many kids, not enough money. Finally, a judge gave him the choice, join the marines or go to jail. Serving in the Corps made him even more lawless. He just never could live by rules. He went AWOL for a weekend and got a week in the brig. He hit a guard that week and got two years in Leavenworth. That's when the real trouble started."

I blinked. That good-looking man's story resembled others I'd read. Small stuff. I remembered a bumper sticker I'd seen some-place: Don't sweat the small stuff. It's all small stuff. A marine is busted for taking a long weekend and freaks out when a guard gives him a raft of shit. For that, he gets two years.

I saw the contradictions in Colby—his classic body developed to attract attention, and the distance he seemed to put between himself and his audience. There had to be more to the story. I took a hard look at Constantine. "So?"

"So plenty. At Leavenworth, Colby developed a relationship—if you get my drift—with another con. The punk was two-timing him. By then Colby was famous for saying no matter what it took, he always got revenge. One day in the yard, he stabbed the guy with a knife he made from a sharpened metal pen fitted into the handle of a toothbrush. That's why they transferred him to the Rock."

"And now? Another one?"

He nodded. "Here at Alcatraz, inmates get a shower twice a week. Same time they get clean uniforms. They strip down in a change room and throw their dirty clothes in a barrel in the shower room. Two officers stand guard outside the showers along the wall. After showering, the cons go back to the cage at the far wall, where an officer gives them clean clothes.

"Colby had to wait six entire years to get in a shower rotation following the one that his boyfriend was in. When the time came, he comes in from the change room, throws his clothes in the barrel, turns, dives into the shower, and hits his former friend so hard with a homemade knife that it cut his heart in two. He'd made the shiv from a razor blade and a metal support from the frame of his bunk. Happened like lightning before the officer on watch knew what was going down."

"Jesus, Mary, and Joseph!"

Constantine smiled wryly. "At least he proved he's a man of his word. He got revenge. The moral of the story is these cons got nothing but time. They can wait."

Constantine arranged for my delivery of orders during sick call in the cell house. The medical assistant had put a table near the entrance to the mess hall, covered it with a white sheet, and set up a medical cart containing the most common treatments for colds, headaches, and minor cuts.

We stood a few feet away near a rolling library cart holding the purchases that I'd labeled and shelved alphabetically. At least a half-dozen officers stood eyeing the inmates at the base of blocks B and C.

Constantine muttered, "Only eight men at a time will be sent down, but it's still a lot in such a large space. No one ever knows when something will set someone off and a fight will break out." My knees shook when I considered the possible consequence of a wrong order. I didn't want to be brained for a vendor's mistake.

The duty officer shouted, "Block C! Let the first eight go."

The officer on block C, third tier, set the pins and pulled the lever to open three inmate cells. Second tier released another five.

They formed a line at the base of the cell block, waiting to be called by the doctor. Many came for cures to the common cold, a popular remedy being an aspirin and a one-ounce paper cup of codeine turpenhydrate for their coughs. Based on the number of complaints, you'd have thought the cell block was a TB sanitarium.

"What's going on?" I mumbled under my breath.

"They hold the codeine in their mouths until they get back to their bunks, where they spit it in a bottle. When they have a full bottle, they can trade it on the prison black market."

My stomach churned.

After the sick call was finished and the inmates returned to their cells, the duty officer released the prisoners for commissary call. All at once, I found myself wildly curious about my customers. In the six weeks I'd been there, I'd thought about them, but only as numbers on a bank account or a cop-out form. Now I itched to place faces on the ledger page with facts, hobbies with real people. What kind of man ordered a paint-by-numbers kit? Who wanted a package of clarinet reeds? Then, there was 1057 Smith, my cop-out pen pal—the relationship could never be more than one-way, nor would I dare to call attention to him, for I felt certain he'd be punished—the man of the perfect Palmer Method penmanship.

From his position at the corner of the table, Constantine called out the inmate next in line so that I could have the purchase ready.

"1057 Smith," Constantine said, and I thought I discerned a bit of a quizzical look playing about his lips. I'd tried to hide my concerns for any prisoner. Could he have guessed my fascination with this inmate?

Smith approached from the line at the cell block with a rolling sailor's gait. More amazing still, he had a brilliant ear-to-ear smile spread across his boyish face. At first sight, he appeared to be very young, no older than a Boy Scout. Try as I might, I couldn't keep my eyes from straying away from his face to see how the rest of him was put together. A young man of medium height, he had the lean body of a runner, narrow-hipped, more gristle than muscle.

His truly incredible feature, his eyes, were the electrifying blue-violet color of Elizabeth Taylor's.

"Afternoon, Smith," I said, handing him his book.

"Thank you, sir."

As he took the book from my hand, he audaciously slid his fingertips forward to brush against mine. A caress of less than a second, but I snatched my hand back as though I'd touched a hot poker. There being nothing further he could do or say, Smith turned abruptly on his heel and fled back to cell block C and up the iron stairs to the second tier. Just before he entered his cell, he paused a moment and I thought I saw him risk a slight waggle of the fingers of his left hand in good-bye.

As we packed up our papers, the signed inmate receipts for their merchandise, and my tally of inmates and purchases, I found a neatly labeled package left over, Robert Stroud, 594. "Oh, God, Constantine, we missed somebody!"

"No, we didn't. That's Stroud. He's up on D block, hospital TU."

I remembered the order for a Latin grammar book and thought it odd at the time, but had shrugged it off as just another eccentricity in an institution of two hundred sixty eccentrics, not counting the staff. But commissary orders to TU, the hole? Inmates over there get no privileges: no visitors, no mail, only an hour a week in the yard.

Constantine stared at me, a crooked smile playing about his lips. "I thought you knew. Stroud's our last celebrity now that the thirties mobsters, Al Capone, Machine Gun Kelly, and that bunch are all gone."

I stood there, looking dumb and feeling stupid, for the life of me unable to figure out what the hell he was talking about.

"It's Birdman," he said. "You know, Birdman of Alcatraz? The book by Gaddis?"

As the light dawned I slapped my forehead. "Oh, that Birdman!"

"Yeah," Constantine said, laughing at me. "And this Alcatraz!"

•

WHEN WE REACHED HIS CELL in D block, Stroud 594, aka Birdman was lying on his bunk, listless, not making an effort to raise his head or to acknowledge our presence. Constantine had explained that the man's celebrity station with amateur ornithology had made him a darling of the press and public who made continual demands for special treatment for him. Under enormous pressure from the public, President Wilson had commuted his death sentence for killing a guard at Leavenworth to life in prison in solitary confinement.

The officer who unlocked the door to let us in remained at the door while we entered. I stared hard at the old man who had been in that cell for seventeen years. At last he stirred himself and sat up on his bunk.

Completely hairless, Stroud resembled nothing so much as a gnome wrinkled with age. Although he was sixty-eight, I'd have guessed him to be at least eighty, and a rickety octogenarian at that. His beady eyes shot us a glance of such malevolence as to cause me to fear him despite his decrepit state. He dismissed us with a wave of his arm, bony fingers pointing toward the door and waiting guard.

Faced with the legendary old man's ferocious look, my tongue fumbled in my mouth.

"We've brought your commissary order, Stroud," Constantine put in. "If you're having attitude problems, we can take it away until next week."

"Give me my fucking book," he snarled, extending his clawlike hand. "And I'll thank you to get the hell out of here."

Constantine dropped the book on the bunk next to him and the two of us left without another word. Outside and away from the cell, I said, "Damn! That old man is sure a corker. He acts as though he's in charge."

"Yeah, well, he's been like that in every prison he's been in.

You'd like to feel sorry for him—solitary's getting to him—but he's so foul, when you begin to feel a little sympathy you end up hating him."

"He's been here seventeen years?"

"Yes, and twenty years before at Leavenworth. And all of it hard time. He never gets to talk to anyone. They even take him to the yard when there are no other inmates around. As I say, it's getting to him. He's tried to commit suicide twice in the last few years. But he's so rotten he won't let you feel sorry for him. Prisoners hate him, too."

3

THERE HAVE BEEN TIMES—the shock of the sudden death of my father, my lingering recovery from an undiagnosed ailment, the day-to-day care of my bedridden partner—when my obsession with those singular events overshadowed the rest of my life. My employment at the federal prison on Alcatraz was one such experience. I remember little else of my life in 1958.

Spring slipped into summer and then crashed into autumn. Rain. It rained by the buckets. The Warden Johnston skipped across the whitecaps to and from the island. I bought a fancy new oilskin sou'wester but more often than not was drenched in the driving rain on the thirty-minute crossings. I wryly observed that the turbulence outdoors matched that growing in me.

No longer intimidated by the harsh life of prisoners or the terrible things they'd done to earn it, I had learned to accommodate activities as aberrant as murder, kidnapping, and rape as normal things that some men do. The realization of that change crept into my head and horrified me.

I'd begun to break one of the rules, as though my sympathy for the inmates had led me to join the other side. Even as I did so, I recognized the slippery slope of the thinking behind the act.

I smoked filter-tipped mentholated cigarettes. The odd menthol taste was prized coinage on the underground market at the Rock. With an inexplicable rush of goodwill toward Granger, my typist, a man who would never see the outside of a prison, I began slipping a single cigarette into the center drawer of my desk before I left for lunch. When I returned, I always found the cigarette gone. Neither of us ever acknowledged the infraction of rules by so much as a nod.

1057 Smith had continued writing his flowery and humble cop-outs with each request for a romance novel, asking for suggestions of things I might have read. After the order itself, he'd invariably write another thanking me for my attention. His penmanship became more and more exaggerated with curlicues and fillips. I realized he must have spent countless hours planning what to say in those carefully crafted notes, and his apparent infatuation intrigued me. Over the weeks that stretched into months, the color of the ink he used slowly changed from black to gray to blue, then finally violet. Could anything have been more obvious than that?

I couldn't untangle precisely what the series of cop-outs meant to me. Certainly, I was aware that it was a hopeless game, but at its core what fantasy is not? I knew, too, that time—that ocean of waves rolling across the shores of our lives—seemed as expendable to Smith as Colby's six-year wait for revenge. Still, I felt touched by the pent-up energy in Smith's Lilliputian love notes.

As the number of his communiqués increased over the weeks, I kept them from some dumb notion of sentimentality, a running diary of his emotional state. I stored them in the back of a file in my desk, adding the new arrivals—unfolded and stretched out— lest there be a blackmailer, guard or inmate, who'd been silently recording them.

I saw him only infrequently at a distance and at commissary call where I froze my face and mumbled, "Afternoon, Smith," handed him the newest book, and waited eagerly for the swift touch of his fingertips before he moved on.

Meanwhile, also roiling the drama taking place about me was my resistance to the warden's demand for me to take the civil-service exams to become a permanent employee. To add to my perplexity, I was invited to interview for a job with the American President Lines steamship company.

4

I WAS THINKING ABOUT 986 BRITTON when I looked up to see Constantine hurrying down the corridor. Britton, a massive black man with fingers as thick as bananas and long enough to circle half a basketball, frequently ordered watercolors. With those enormous hands, he painted florals, small, dainty subjects, pansies, petunias, and daylilies, and he laid the color down so lightly it seemed almost transparent. I'd not completed Britton's order when Constantine reached my desk.

"Warden wants to see you, Jim."

My question wrote itself across my face.

Constantine's demeanor held the pale, guilty look of a boy caught in the cookie jar. "It's not good," he said.

All my office reviews had been superior, the warden's comments highly complimentary. Had I been reported for fraternizing with Cooper and Bukovnik in the officers' mess? Some chickenshit guards would do that. What about the daily cigarette to Granger? Had some big-house censor reported the notes from Smith? I'd done nothing but ignore them.

The warden's door stood open.

"Come in, Jim. Close the door."

I halted about halfway between his door and his desk, and stood quietly while he finished scribbling corrections on a typed letter. He'd not asked me to sit.

When he looked up, I missed the trademark twinkle in his eyes. "Jim, we know each other too well for me to beat around the bush. I've received a telegram saying that the FBI can't clear you."

My mind flashed back to my first applications at Alcatraz, including a requirement for a thirty-two-year summary of residence and employer references. At the time I'd snickered at this requirement from a twenty-two-year-old who had never lived anywhere but at home and in the navy, but I had lightheartedly played their game and did the best I could at filling in blanks. I had an honorable discharge from the Navy. I had no criminal record, not even a parking ticket. I had no bad debts. My friends had told me the FBI had interviewed them, but essentially there was nothing to tell.

I felt my face redden. There was nothing to tell—but that. And not even that, only the appearance of that. This was what our nation was coming to fear.

"Warden, you said the FBI can't clear me. Do you mean can't, or won't?"

"The telegram says 'can't.'"

"Can you find out why?"

"No." He closed his eyes. "No."

"Can I appeal it?"

"No," he said, and I saw the first flicker of irritation in the face of a man who had always been good to me. "Because you're a temporary, there's no appeal. Now, if you'd taken the test and been admitted as a probationary civil servant, you could appeal it. But."

Standing there like a powerless child in the principal's office, I felt an anger rising in the back of my mind, a coming futile fury that I didn't want to unleash. From somewhere—God knows where—I heard myself saying, "Well, Warden, I'm sorry. I enjoyed being a part of your team. But what's happened isn't really so bad. After all, I was looking for a job when I came here."

At twenty-two, I had stood up to the most powerful person in the toughest prison in the United States.

"Can you stay till the end of the pay period?" he asked. "As a favor to me? It would give you a chance to clean up loose ends."

5

MY LAST DAY AT ALCATRAZ remains indelibly written in my memory. In less than a year, I had been changed in ways I'd have thought unimaginable. The cons had taught me how to work alongside—to genuinely like—men who had committed loath-some and atrocious acts against other human beings. What's more, those crimes had been perpetrated without conscience or regard—and totally without remorse—for their victims. Yet I'd found them likable human beings.

Of course the prison was abuzz with the news—the cons prob-ably knew it before the warden. Screws and cons alike hailed me with a clap on the back, a thumbs-up from a distance, or a hearty, "Take care, man. Don't ever say it hasn't!"

When I walked through the mess hall dining room, the guys—no longer cons or inmates—looked up at my passage and took what I interpreted to be a moment of silence, a nod, a flick of the fingers in salute, and went back to their plates. I clamped my teeth together to keep a stoic look in place.

In the officers' mess, Cooper looked up, flashed his eighty-four-toothed smile. "Hey, man, sir. What's this I've heard about you. Heard you got sprung from the joint. Where ya goin'?"

"Thought I'd try a steamship line. Maybe see the world some."

"Ain't never robbed no ships before."

"When I find out how, I'll drop you a line."

"Naw, man, sir." He nodded toward Bukovnik. "We got you figured out."

One day, I'd told them that I thought I might start robbing banks, to which the two of them responded that I should begin as a cotton foot, slang for a cat burglar. Laughing again at the old joke between us lessened the tension of saying good-bye.

Later, as I gnawed my way through the chief steward's rubbery lasagna, Cooper came by, looked about, reached over my shoulder, and put something in my shirt pocket. "It's a note from Smith, sir," he muttered close to my ear, and left.

When I'd fathomed what had occurred—I'd actually received a note from a convict—I felt my cheeks burn and my heart rate rush. As surreptitiously as I could, I palmed the note from my pocket and held it in my lap below the tablecloth. "Sir, please send me your address on the outside."

In order to make its way to me, that scrap of paper had to have been given by Smith to either the bread or the beverage man at his table, who transferred it to a server at the steam table who sneaked it on to one of the pantry men. All of this under the vigilant eyes of six officers on the floor and two armed men on the catwalk outside the dining room. Next, a pantry man must have carried the message until it could be handed to Cooper or Bukovnik. Incredibly, this tiny incriminating scrap of paper had sailed unnoticed under the noses of ten guards.

As the logistics unfolded, I envisioned two officers rushing in from central command, cuffing me and dragging me away to throw me in the hole to wait for Washington to advise Warden Madigan about what to do with an employee caught in a prisoner plot. Although seemingly an innocent crime, passing notes remained the most watched for infraction among prisoners. Notes communicated the traffic in drugs and sexual favors. Notes told of racial feuds and reprisals. And notes were invariably an integral part of planning for jail-breaks. I could only guess at the courage it must have taken for Smith to send it. For my part, I had no intention of being caught red-handed with such evidence.

Without a second's hesitation, I faked a cough, put my hand over my mouth and slipped the note inside, then calmly chewed it up and swallowed it. The steward's elastic lasagna and iced tea performed admirably in pushing the paper through. Taking a couple of deep breaths to will away the heat gathered in my ears, I thought, *Let the fucking FBI eat that.*

Twenty minutes later, Cooper leaned close again. "Smith wants an answer."

I grunted without moving my lips, "Tell him it's in the phone book."

I quickly finished my lunch, made a show of shaking hands with Cooper and Bukovnik, and waved good-bye to a table of officers who had just sat down.

I looked straight ahead toward the solid steel door under the West Gun Gallery and slowed my step to a casual, innocent-appearing saunter. Barnes, the duty officer, unlocked and held the door before I reached it. Taking one last look over my shoulder, I saw 1057 Smith smiling and slowly nodding. He'd gotten the message.

The Rock, a hard place indeed.

an old wives' tale

carol seajay

I SUPPOSE I MAY AS WELL ADMIT IT—it was thirty-five years ago—I was angry. Very, very angry. And I didn't know what to do with it. Women weren't exactly encouraged to express their anger in those days.

I'd just been outed by a straight friend who seemed to think that if the medical community and the funders for the new abortion clinic knew that the ringleader of the women's liberation activists and abortion counselors was a lesbian, she'd get the job running the new clinic instead of me.

It wasn't that I minded being out publicly—I was twenty-three, fiercely feminist, believed passionately in gay liberation, had been calling myself a lesbian since I was 15, and was very out in my circle of lesbian, gay, and feminist friends. But being outed in a work situation, in the Republican town of Kalamazoo, Michigan, in 1973 meant I was no longer hirable. No one in social services could risk their funding by hiring a known lesbian. Being gay was still grounds for dismissal, and the gay personnel officers at various companies, to whom we all turned for jobs in a pinch, wouldn't dare hire me. The Supreme Court had legalized abortion a few months earlier, and my movement-wages job coordinating abortion counseling for the crew of clergy and feminists who had been quietly helping women get to Japan and England, then California and New York, for safe and legal abortions (and closer to home for illegal abortions) was drawing to a close as safe, legal abortions became more accessible. But I needed to work.

So I did what I'd do again and again in my life when faced with impossible circumstances: I went traveling. Canoe trips were my preference, but this time a canoe wasn't going to take me far enough.

Where to go? I knew there were gay people in New York City—I'd read about them in Ann Aldrich's *We, Too, Must Love*, and, more recently, an acquaintance had moved there after having been caught in a lesbian witchhunt at the high school where she'd taught. (No more local employment for her, either.) I knew there were enough lesbians in San Francisco to publish *The Ladder*, which I'd been reading for years, and had subscribed to myself as soon as I was twenty-one. I knew lesbian feminists in Detroit through the Michigan Women's Liberation Union, and that there were lesbians in Chicago from reading *Lavender Woman*, and because I had an ex who'd lived in Old Towne in the sixties. But neither Detroit nor Chicago were far enough away for a grand gesture, and I was too much a product of the open-fields countryside I'd grown up in to make it in cement canyons of New York. So that left San Francisco.

I needed to make enough money to buy some wheels, so I took the only job I could get—a cocktail waitress in a college bar—and swished my hips for tips until I had enough to buy a two-cylinder Honda 450 and a stash for gas and food. I put a flower in my hair and set out. The fact that I'd never ridden a motorcycle before was a small detail: I had a Helen Reddy song in my mind—something about getting on your bike and riding, going places you'd never been. It wasn't until decades later that it occurred to me that she meant a bicycle. The motorcycle didn't make it to SF, but I did, and found a huge, thriving lesbian feminist community. There were all kinds of women's events and workshops and groups. I found a room in a lesbian household in the Mission, a job on a women's job board, signed up for a class called "Lesbianism, Socialism, and Feminism" at the Liberation School, and went to women's events of one kind or another almost every night. There were so many things happening that sometimes we had to split up and go to different ones. Then we'd meet up afterward at Scott's or Kelly's or A Little More to catch each other up on what had happened, to debate the issues of the moment, and to dance. We saved Peg's and Maud's for the weekends—we were Mission dykes and didn't have cars to get out to the Avenues.

Everyone was organizing something—marches and protests and demonstrations. There was a collective for everything, from the people's food stores to the Women's Yogurt Collective, and a zillion different organizations and projects. I fell in with Women in Apprenticeship to get tutoring and training to take the electrician's apprenticeship test, the idea being that if women learned to do *every*thing ourselves, we'd never again have to be dependent on getting men's permission or approval for something we wanted and needed. Meetings were constants, but they never, to me at least, seemed like a chore—they were where you met women, saw your friends, and got the news and gossip, and they provided a ready group to go out with afterward. Whenever anyone needed something, or thought of something to do, meetings were called, and something got done. Someone complained that she didn't know how to meet women at the bar, so we scheduled practice sessions at A Little More—with me as the coach! I was still trying to maintain my motorcycle-dyke image, albeit a long-haired one, and drank my whiskey neat. It seemed to work: some of the sessions were very effective, at least for me. Other women started a Women's Skills Center and a Women's Press Project so women could teach and learn trades. We thought that if we could just organize the lesbians, we could right every wrong, resolve social injustice, socialize medicine, end poverty, stop war, and overthrow the patriarchy. Everything seemed possible; everything seemed to be just around the corner. It was a wonderfully heady time.

•

DURING MY FIRST WEEKS in San Francisco I found a flier taped to the inside of a stall in the women's bathroom at the San Francisco Public Library, inviting women to help start a women's coffeehouse. In those days, starting something meant renovating the building ourselves, from stripping and painting the walls to pouring the cement floor for the kitchen. My tasks were more mundane: I remember scrubbing the entire floor and scraping off as much paint as I could (the original plan had been to replace the floor, so no one had used drop cloths when painting the ceiling and walls) the day before the grand opening.

The Full Moon was fantastic—lots of sprouts on the sandwiches, and musicians performing, from Rosalee Sorrells and Malvina Reynolds to Meg Christian, Cris Williamson, and Margie Adam, to any band or group that women put together locally, and poets read their best new work. Women hung art on the walls, and another committee filled a small room—about the size of a Murphy bed—with books and declared it a bookstore. The collective and volunteers ran the coffee machines, made the sandwiches, bought the food and books, and did everything it took to keep it open and thriving, including arguing through differences and misunderstandings. It closed in 1977 because, in the anarchy of the day, no one had thought to get a cabaret license—or maybe we were just too pig-headed and anarchistic to ask the city or anyone else for permission to do something for women, and the Full Moon lost its lease due to neighbors' complaints about late-night noise.

Meanwhile, I'd gotten mad again. My temporary job for the state had turned into a permanent job—but somehow I hadn't been allowed to apply for it and the job was hustled off to the returning-from-the-military son of the head of my division. No point in appealing, I was told, his other parent was on the State Personnel Board. I was offered jobs in Sacramento instead, but I hadn't moved all the way to California to live in Sacramento. I'd taken the electrician's apprenticeship test by then and, thanks to Women in Apprenticeship's tutoring, I'd ranked seventysomething out of two thousand applicants, a score that assured me a place in the second apprenticeship class. That class wasn't scheduled to start for a couple of months, so I fulfilled a long-held dream and headed for India. I flew out on Halloween night, missing most of my first Halloween in San Francisco. What had I been thinking? A friend borrowed a car and we drove though streets thick with merrymakers, many in drag, on our way to the airport.

•

AH, BUT THERE WAS A RECESSION ON. Electricians, along with everyone else, were out of work, so no new apprentice classes were started. When I got back I found that unemployment was so high that special legislation had been passed to allow state employees to collect unemployment and, having been laid off four months previously, I was eligible. My unemployment benefits provided a higher income than I'd ever had, except for the six months I'd worked for the state. In those days San Francisco could be a cheap place to live if you did it right. MediCal provided emergency medical services—no one had health insurance—and I actually managed to save money. There were certain rituals that all of us movement workers on unemployment learned to follow: Never be late for your biweekly appointment. Fill out the paperwork to perfection. Apply for jobs as required—but in places that weren't hiring. And alternate working and collecting unemployment in such a way that there would always be money in your unemployment account. I called my unemployment my "California Grant for the Arts" and went back to the novel I'd been working on when I left Kalamazoo.

Some of the women from my Lesbianism, Socialism, and Feminism class had continued on as a writing group working on lesbian and feminist theory. I rejoined them and one evening one of them, Gretchen Milne (a.k.a. Forest), who was one of the four women who started ICI-A Woman's Place Bookstore in Oakland, said, "You have some time. Why don't you come over to the bookstore sometime? There's lots to do there."

The bookstore was in a V-shaped building at the intersection of College and Broadway, and shared space with the Women's Press Collective. The first day someone put me to work cleaning old fliers off the bulletin board—a great way to catch up on everything that was happening. Later, someone set me to learning my way around the various sections. I'd been in the bookstore before, but not often, as it was more than an hour away via public transportation. I fell in love with the lesbian section: two whole shelves of lesbian books—more lesbian books in one place than I'd ever seen before. It turned out that one of the perks of volunteering in the bookstore was that you could borrow the books as long as you didn't get spaghetti sauce on them or otherwise render them unsalable. I was hooked.

At first I spent one day a week at the store. Then it was two days a week, and then three. I learned how to staff the counter and sell the books, how to log them in, and, eventually, how to order them from publishers and—even more fun—to go to Bookpeople and LS and other local distributors and pull books from their shelves for ours. I swept floors and learned to build bookcases to hold the ever-expanding inventory. It was all a part of making a bookstore and information center for women. The idea, or at least the idea as I understood it and practiced it for years yet to come, was that women would come and find information (ideas, poetry, fiction, facts, inspiration, support for their own thoughts, confidence, connections with like-minded women)— whatever they needed, and that they would do whatever was appropriate with the information. We didn't presume to think we knew what they should do with it. It was a time—and a practice— of exhilarating anarchy, with new ideas, new facts, new women, and new connections arriving every day. During these early, heady days, much of the information arrived in poetic form: leaps of imagination that often preceded the gathering of facts or the writing of longer works of fiction, and the store was rich with chapbooks from poets and writers, many of whom would later become national and international literary treasures.

Every morning Natalie would show us the work that the Women's Press Collective had printed the night before: pages of a book, artwork, record jackets for women's bands that changed every night as the printers laid down the next color. I came to understand that making the books—being able to print and publish what we wanted—was as essential as collecting them in one place for women to find. I heard stories over the counter of women taking their books to other local bookstores (including Cody's, the bookstore that had risked all to display and sell Allen Ginsberg's *Howl*) that refused to stock these new books. "Who'd be interested in books about women?" they'd say to the women who had written and published the books. Nor were they interested in stocking many of the mainstream published books that we stocked. I remember Gretchen saying, "It would have been worth all the work to start this store even if the only book we had was *The First Sex*." Written by Elizabeth Gould Davis, it was the first book to document that women-centered religions had flourished before the advent of contemporary patriarchal religions.

But new books and magazines and newspapers and journals—
each filled with new ideas more exciting than the last—kept on
coming. Eventually, I learned other parts of running the store—
paying bills and keeping the ledgers and filing tax returns. Making
the ledgers balance was the hardest part, and I found myself, one
leisurely afternoon at home, having an orgasm to a fantasy of having an entire ledger page balance the first time I added it up. Or
maybe I was actually thinking about that handsome butch collective member from Texas who was also learning the ledgers.

●

IN MID–1976 my unemployment was due to run out again. I
didn't have much in reserve, and I'd just lost my part-time sand-
ing job in a furniture factory. The owners were getting a partial
reimbursement on wages for hiring and training someone who
was currently unemployed. They weren't supposed to lay anyone
off in the process, it was just coincidence that there weren't any
more hours for me, and so one more woman lost her trades job to
a young white guy. He didn't have the requisite light touch with a
belt sander, and I'd watched him burn through the veneer on several expensive desks over the course of my last day and wondered
if they'd make or lose money on the deal. Or if they just wanted to
go back to being an all-guy shop. I missed the job, the clean smell
of sawdust, and the satisfaction of seeing what we'd made in a very
material way. The economy sucked, the electricians' union still
wasn't starting classes, and I was trying to figure out what do next.

●

I WAS STILL WORKING two or three days a week at the bookstore, but having moved back to the Mission district and away
from my ride, I often took the bus both ways, traveling as long as
an hour and a half each way to work, for free, to keep the book-

store open. And then it occurred to me: If I was willing to go to that much effort to get to the bookstore, there were probably a lot of women who also wanted to get to the bookstore, or to get there more often, who also didn't have cars and/or weren't willing to go to quite so much trouble as I was. The Full Moon had its tiny bookstore, but not nearly the range and depth of stock that a full bookstore could have, and the lefty store, Modern Times, stocked a lot of women's books, but, again, not a full selection of what was available, and it wasn't a woman's space, either—something that was rare and prized in those days. So I began to think about opening a women's bookstore in San Francisco.

•

BY THEN I WAS LOVERS with Paula Wallace, the handsome butch from Texas. I asked her if she'd be interested in starting a bookstore in San Francisco with me, and I talked to a couple of the most experienced women at A Woman's Place. They thought SF probably needed its own bookstore for many of the same reasons Paula and I did. There was more than enough need to support two bookstore/information centers.

•

MEANWHILE, one evening, after a reading at the bookstore, June Arnold, the founder of Daughters Press, and many of the women who had attended the reading, reconvened at the Bacchanal, the East Bay feminist bar, and dreamed up an idea about organizing a conference for all the women who ran women's presses, magazines, bookstores, distribution companies, and the printers, and typesetters, and illustrators, and graphic designers— the women who managed the means of production for the burgeoning Women-in-Print movement. And then June went home and organized it, and I was lucky enough to be able to go.

•

THE FIRST national Women In Print conference was held at a
Campfire Girls camp in Nebraska—a site that was equal driving
distance between the two coasts. At the opening session, everyone
introduced herself and her organization, named a skill or area of
expertise she could share, and was invited to ask for information
she needed. Shortly before I left for the conference, Paula and I
had applied for a loan from the Feminist Federal Credit Union to
launch the store, and Paula called me at the conference to tell me
the loan had come through, subject to finding an acceptable
cosigner. So I asked the conference, "If two women came up with
six thousand dollars to open a feminist bookstore, would that be
enough money to launch the store and generate an income that
could support them?" The idea of supporting the workers was a
radical departure from the volunteer-based economy of most of
the women's movement at that time. The next day two women
came up to me and outlined their different but similar situations
—Karyn London from Womanbooks in NYC and Gilda Bruck-
man from New Words in Boston. And to put everything on the
table at once, just before I left I'd received, finally, *the* letter from
the electricians' union saying they were starting a class the week I
got back and so many people had dropped out in the intervening
two years that I'd be in that first class.

It was decision time. Armed with the credit-union loan, the additional burst of confidence that came from two women telling
me they'd had the same idea and similar amounts of money and
made it happen, and my own clear vision, I took a deep breath,
said yes to the bookstore, made my apologies to Women in Apprenticeship and the union, and stepped forward in a new direction. I've always been grateful, though, to the idea and belief that
I was going to be an electrician, a goal that held me steady while I
wandered through the lesbian feminist movement in San Fran-

cisco, happened into the bookstores, and found what I was going to do with my life.

•

THE MOMENT I GOT BACK, we plunged into opening the bookstore. New friends from the conference suggested Old Wives' Tales for the name, and I added a subtitle: Women's Visions and Books. We scheduled our opening for Halloween, two years after I'd flown to India—somehow I kept missing Halloween on Castro Street—less than three years after I'd arrived in San Francisco. I was twenty-six at the time and setting out to open a bookstore in two and a half months seemed entirely sane and possible.

•

WE LOOKED FOR A STOREFRONT in the Mission. The boys were all moving into the Castro, but the Mission was what most dykes could afford. And it was important to us to locate the store in an area that made it easily accessible to women of color, to women traveling by public transit, and to dykes and feminists. The intersection of Valencia and 16th Street was a movement nexus: home to the George Jackson Defense Committee, the Tenants Union, Rainbow Grocery (the newest stepchild in the people's food system), the Roxie Cinema, and the Communist Party Bookstore, and it was across the street from La Cumbre, one of the best taquerias in town. And, for a bonus prize, there was a laundromat next door. Women could come on a Saturday, do their laundry, buy their groceries, browse the store, and buy their books all in one fell swoop. During the week, women grabbed burritos on their lunch hour and ate them while they browsed. The taqueria owner pointed us out to any likely-looking customers who didn't already seem to be headed our way. Our landlords were the San Francisco Club for the Deaf, and we rented their meeting hall upstairs for events that wouldn't fit in the bookstore. We signed up to be the polling place on election day. We opened a bookstore for women, and made a place for ourselves in the community.

•

THE BOOKSTORE FLOURISHED. I was right: Women in San Francisco wanted a bookstore. The store achieved break-even in a phenomenal six months. Granted, we were paying ourselves only two hundred dollars a month (and nothing before the store actually opened) but by sharing a house with four women and shopping at the food co-op—and, given that we spent virtually every waking hour at the bookstore—it was possible.

•

THE STORE CONTINUED TO GROW. New women discovered it every week. Some walked around the block several times before garnering the courage to enter. Many were stunned to see so many books by women, about women, for women. Many said they had no idea women had written so many books (and we stocked only what was currently in print). Many came for the lesbian books, and more than a few lingered in the shadow of the conveniently placed filing cabinet that sheltered them from being visible through the front window. The books multiplied like rabbits. More and more feminist and lesbian books were being published, and more and more exciting new journals and newspapers, and we did our best to stock them all.

The second fall we were open, a sales rep stopped by to apologize for the sad fact that he didn't have any new books for us that season: His publishing house had concluded that "the women's-liberation thing was over." My jaw must have dropped as I told him, "Not here—our sales doubled last year." He took the word back to the home office, and he had books for us the next year confirming what we already knew: that mainstream publishers would continue to publish books for us only as long as we proved the market. And that "proving the market" required having both our own visionary publishers and our bookstores to lead the way and open the door to books on new topics—lesbian fiction and nonfiction, books for battered women, books about incest, women's history, women's lives, and everything else that expanded the understanding of who and what women were.

The store wasn't just for book readers; many women came for the bulletin boards, to find a housemate or a home, to check out what was happening. Women came to meet and hang out with other women. Sometimes it was enough to be around women, around other lesbians, and to feel a part of the vibrant energy of the community. We made a point of stocking buttons and T-shirts and posters so that women who weren't into reading would also feel that the store was their place, too. But with our welcoming air and cheerful, careful matchmaking between readers and books, we turned many "non-readers" into book junkies, as women who had never seen much use for books—lesbians especially—found their lives reflected in the books at Old Wives' Tales. I called it "teaching the literacy of expectation." We put the books by and about women of color at the heart of the store—right next to the sales desk—so that women waiting in line perused books by women of color by default. Because both of us who founded the store were white women, we took care when we added staff that the women in the store represented the complexities of the community in which we lived. Our first hire was an Asian immigrant teenager—my lesbian foster daughter's best friend. By the time I left the store, the staff were from three continents and from the West Coast, the East Coast, and the Midwest. We spoke English with a variety of accents, covered a huge range of reading tastes, and each of us had her own priorities for changing the world. One thing we all agreed on was that the bookstore was one of our best tools for achieving any of our agendas.

But the heart of the store was the books. Women came in and found ideas in the books—and validation—that changed their lives forever. Some of those ideas have become cultural norms and the writers became cultural icons, but they got that way, one woman at a time, during some very turbulent decades.

The vitality wasn't limited to books and publishing: women's organizations, visions, and culture were exploding all around us. A women's bathhouse, Osento, opened farther down Valencia. Artemis, a new women's coffeehouse, at the corner of 23rd Street. Organizers at the Women's Centers were looking for a building to buy and wanted something in our neighborhood because so many women were already coming here for the bookstore. They bought an old fellowship hall on 18th Street and turned it into what is today the spectacular four-story Women's Building. Within a few years there were a feminist hair salon—Garbo's—and a woman-owned barbershop cutting hair for both women and men. When we outgrew our space and moved to a larger storefront on Valencia at 21st Street, the Women's Press Project moved into our old space. It was a vibrant and exciting community, with each new business breaking new ground. We even had our own street fair one year, and every December Old Wives' Tales hosted a holiday crafts bazaar, renting the hall above the store or a vacant storefront. When we ran out of spaces large enough, we donated the event to the Women's Building as a fund-raiser, one of Old Wives' Tales's legacies that continues to this day.

Old Wives' Tales and other women's bookstores had different goals than most general independent bookstores, and we invented new ways to achieve them—many of which have since become industry norms—"just-in-time ordering" (ordering and stocking only the books you need for the next few days or week, then restocking), handwriting notes with personal opinions about books, and a consistent practice of customer education and encouraging customer activism.

We also sponsored readings and other events. There was *something* going on at the bookstore every Thursday evening, and often at other times as well. We brought writers to our community and helped many famous (and many not-yet-famous) writers connect with their audiences. "Information not yet in books" was one of our themes, and we hosted many discussions, some of which led to topics for books. We took a lot of flak for hosting controversial events but stood by our agenda: to provide a place for women to discuss the new ideas in our community and to come to their own conclusions. We got in trouble with the Equal Employment Opportunity Commission and the "liberal" governor of California for refusing entry to a male journalist who wanted to cover a program about incest that was specifically for women survivors. One of the most densely packed events we hosted was a discussion with women from Samois, the new lesbian S/M group. It's hard to remember how controversial either subject was, but the newer or more important a subject was, the more grief we got for it, usually a mix of "you didn't do enough" and "you shouldn't have done anything at all." But sometimes there was gratitude as well. Seeing women's lives change was, ultimately, the best and most sustaining reward.

•

WHEN I FIRST THOUGHT ABOUT opening the store, I didn't have a vision of what would happen next: maintaining it. Early in the planning process, I had one image of a future—that the store would be in a small storefront with a Dutch door. I saw myself a couple years later, portly and wearing a three-piece suit and leaning on the half-open door. It wasn't a future that I wanted, so I decided not to worry about the future—I just did everything I could to ensure that there would be one. But as the years passed, I came to understand that what had been missing from that vision was the women. That the image I'd rejected was of a shell of a bookstore—the walls, the book cases, the storefront. That the vitality came from the women who used the store, from the women who came in to run it with me, and from the women busily building a vibrant community all around us. In just a few years, these women, working together and independently, built a world that none of us could have imagined just a few years before.

There was one night when it all came home to me. The store was still in the original location on Valencia at 16th Street, and I was living down on 21st Street, half a block up the hill from Valencia, with my roommates and foster daughter. I was walking home from an event at the Women's Building. And as I walked down Valencia toward home, I took the time to cherish each women's organization and business in the neighborhood, and to appreciate all of the women who created and sustained them. The bottlebrush trees were in full bloom, and it seemed to me that we were living in a golden age of lesbian and feminist culture and that it was a spectacular time to be alive and that I was very, very lucky to be a part of it.

city of innocence and plague

fenton johnson

let history lie
and lie light as the ashes
surrendered to the air off Golden Gate Bridge.
—Andrew Jaicks , *City of Innocence and Plague*

I NEVER KNEW A CITY before San Francisco. At seventeen years old, not knowing how to take a bus or use a pay telephone or order from a menu, clutching a scholarship underwritten by a bourbon distillery, I came from the Kentucky hills to the Bay Area. I was drawn by the hippies whose images and stories had made their ways into the remote hills and hollers of my childhood. I was drawn by the hope that someone would help me avoid the war in Vietnam. It was 1971, a peculiar moment of transition when the most powerful empire in history was in the midst of being shown the fallibility and impermanence of all human creations, especially empires. The nation was on the verge of anarchy.

By the time I arrived the hippies had fled the Haight and I had to engineer a conscientious objectorship on my own, but even so I was in California, a word that still carries a frisson of promise and magic. I saw the place in the waning moments of its glory, before the onslaught of real-estate madness. Every drive from Palo Alto to the beach was a mystical journey, climbing mountains higher than I had ever seen on a road more crooked than any I had driven to enter a forest taller and deeper than any I'd known— and then at the road's end the cold and restless Pacific, free for all, where on a crowded day one might encounter four or five people on the beach.

Then the draft ended and the young white men who then as now had ready access to the reins of power went back to the business of making money, lots of money. The sixties died on the morning in 1973 when Defense Secretary Melvin Laird stood before a bank of cameras and microphones and announced the end of the lottery for compulsory military service. And so ended the nation's most extraordinary experiment in democracy, real democracy, where the sons of the privileged were almost as likely to be called on to defend their privilege as the sons of the poor.

Thirty years pass and more, and the city is gussified and prettified and many of those who made it what it is are dead, and of those who remain few can afford to live here. Real estate and microchips dominate every conversation. Almost no one smokes tobacco. People take drugs not for illusions of revelation but for illusions of power—we have gone from marijuana to meth. In these dark days for the republic anyone who's not depressed or angry isn't paying attention, but antidepressants stand in nicely for the soma of Huxley's *Brave New World*. The future is now. We have dug our graves and we lie in them, complacent.

All the dead are present to me in these streets. I find the possibility and promise of progress not in the City's perennial protests against the American empire's latest adventures in imperialism but in the stories of the men and women who cared for our own at a time when many of those paid to do the job shirked the task. In the middle of a nation hell-bent on making money, we were a throwback in history, a microcosm of medieval London in the midst of the plague. Scorned by our president, vilified by our ministers and priests, men and women walked into rooms and cared for the dying and the dead. Much has been written of those times, but no one has yet captured their extraordinary alembic, the transformation of terror and anger into love, the cool gray city of love.

I confess I do not believe in time. I confess I do not believe in death.

•

AS MUCH AS ANY OTHER QUALITY self-obsession enables San Francisco to consider itself in the league of larger, more powerful cities. New York, Mexico City, Los Angeles, San Francisco—these are the North American cities where as often as not dinner-table conversation centers not on politics or culture but on the city itself. This is very different from, say, Louisville or Tucson, to name smaller cities I happen to know intimately. Residents of those cities think of themselves first as fathers, mothers, children, rich men, poor men, beggarmen, thieves; only later, much later, do they consider place as part of their identities—perhaps because many of them live where they were born and raised and so take place for granted. "You don't have a home until you leave it," writes James Baldwin in *Giovanni's Room*, "and then once you have left it you can never go back." Residents of New York, Mexico City, Los Angeles, and San Francisco count being a New Yorker, a *Chilango*, an Angeleno, a San Franciscan, high, even

chief, among their ways of establishing a sense of who they are—
perhaps because more often than not they came from someplace
else.

I know this because I came from someplace else and then I left.
I lived in San Francisco for most of my adult life and expected
that I would call it home until, to use the vernacular of my childhood, I passed on to that greater City on a Hill. In those days
when I traveled and told people I was a San Franciscan, they'd get
this dreamy look. "Oh, I've always wanted to live in San Francisco," they'd say. Then dissatisfaction and a lost apartment took
me to New York, an easier city in so many ways. Opportunities
knocked, doors opened. During those years when I told people I
was a New Yorker they'd get jazzed. "Gee, that must be really exciting," they'd say. These days, when I tell strangers I live in Tucson, Arizona, there's a rich pause as they search to say something
affirming or at least polite. Invariably, they resort to, "Gee, it's
really hot there, isn't it?"

What surprised me, a reasonably self-realized gay man: how
much I had invested my sense of self in my interrogator's response.
I *wanted* that dreamy look, that jazzed response; I *wanted* to be en-
vied on the basis of the place where I'd chosen to hang my hat.

I have lived away from San Francisco for ten years, a figure that
astonishes me even as I write it. I have never gone more than a few
months without returning, often for long visits, but despite the
glamour attached to the phrase "divides his time between," the fact
is that only the rarest and biggest of souls can be a responsible citizen of more than one place. Being a good citizen takes time, and
there's only so much time. It requires living with a place through
its troubles as well as its glories. In Tucson, that means staying
through the summers, but I don't stay through the summers, I flee
the brutal desert heat for the cool gray city of love.

Long and happy experience has taught me that interesting, engaged people are to be found all over the world, in the hollers of
Kentucky as well as the hills of San Francisco or the canyons of

New York, though the cost of living in the latter is slowly draining them of all but the fortunate and the money-grubbers. All the same, I am finding it hard to lay claim to Tucson—dusty, sprawling, scrappy, enchanting Tucson—in the way that I once claimed San Francisco and New York.

•

IN A MEMOIR set largely in San Francisco, I wrote, "Places shape people rather than the other way around." With moderation born of experience, I amend that sentence to read, "Places shape people *as well as* the other way around." The steep hills divided the City into neighborhoods isolated from one another so that each developed its peculiar character. The vast supply of redwood that lay within a stone's throw, the relative paucity of brick and stone, and construction techniques arising from new technology contributed toward ensuring a new and different kind of city from those of the East and of Europe. After the balloon frame house and the coping saw, could drag queens be far behind? From permanence to transience, from stone and brick to insubstantial wood, from reality to illusion. Boston sits ponderous on the earth; San Francisco is poised to rise with its famously steep hills into the airy fairy clouds. "Shocking in its obstinate abstraction," Simone de Beauvoir wrote of the city. "The blueprint seems to have been put on paper without the architect ever having seen the site." Drop a lighted match in the wrong place at the wrong time and it might be gone tomorrow, and in any case, the earth's nap has gone on too long for those living on her sleeping body to live elsewhere than in delusion.

The city is the synecdoche of the West, the expression in gewgaw-covered wood of people who came here because they wanted to leave reality behind to create and inhabit a myth. Inspect the back side of a Boston Victorian and you find patterned brick and filigreed stone that complements the building's public face. Inspect the back side of a San Francisco Victorian and you find a plain wooden box. Did gay people—of necessity students of deception—settle in San Francisco because it is a fantasy city? Or has it become a fantasy city because we settled here? Which came first, the chicken or the egg, the fantasy city or the drag and leather queens and dykes who call it home?

San Francisco is vain to the point of narcissism; like all narcissists, it exists to be loved and has only a dim idea of what it means to give love back. So much about the city is better now—why complain? In a little more than a decade, the vile Embarcadero Freeway is gone, to be replaced by a farmer's market. The new baseball stadium has made South of Market a happy, civilized logjam. Light rail reaches parts of the city that have never seen it. There are new palaces for art and performance—each a bit sterile for my taste but handsome all the same.

But few artists and performers can afford to live in a city that worships less the grueling, transformative, transcendent process of art than the social scene that accompanies it once it is finished, dead, pinned to the wall or the page. I write this not as complaint but as observation—better a new deYoung Museum than a new freeway—but San Francisco is not as interesting a city as when I first set foot in it. Money, which has so much power to corrupt, has done its work, and then there are all those fine people dead from the plague. The young bohemians who once congregated in the Haight, then the Mission, have scattered to the fringes. San Francisco will always be more interesting than Dallas or Columbus—the San Andreas Fault will see to that—but I find it sad to watch from afar as it sells its haecity, its thisness, its soul. Once people came here because they *wanted* to live on the edge, the literal, precarious, teetering edge of the West. Now, driving across the Bay Bridge, returning from one of my absences, I glanced at the jumble of skyscrapers and thought helplessly, *Manhattan*, and though the comparison is hardly original, I was troubled by the spontaneity with which it came to mind.

At the same time, the struggle of those to make and keep San Francisco edgy is richer because the more challenging and, in any case, if the train is speeding toward the broken trestle, the more interesting seat is on board. For is this not the place where we were meant to live: In the present, on the cusp, in the corporal flesh, here and now? The Russian émigré Vladimir Nabokov wrote that reality is the only word that ought always to be enclosed in quotation marks—"reality"—and he would know, having had his reality upended and destroyed in his teens. San Franciscans' only flaw—maybe our fatal flaw—is to misunderstand the object of our adoration. We style it the City—not even New Yorkers are so fixed on the habit—but in fact it is only another of the infinite names of God, the word we use to name this present moment, this here and now.

In Flannery O'Connor's short story "A Good Man Is Hard to Find," The Misfit says of the grandmother, "She would of been a good woman, if it had been somebody there to shoot her every minute of her life." The Misfit is a philosopher whose observation explains the phenomenon of this city, which once made it the butt of too many jokes, one of the nation's favorite escapes, and perhaps a metaphor for the rest of the planet: Once we were all artists and philosophers here, living with the gun we, ourselves, had loaded and making it up as we went along. *That* is what the city is losing—its delight in living on the edge of the Western world. Perhaps only the San Andreas Fault can bring it back.

tales from the casa

victor j. banis

I BEGAN WRITING AS A TEEN, and began to write professionally and to see my books published in the early sixties. By 1985 I had penned in excess of a hundred books and shorter pieces as well, in large part by having written nonstop for more than twenty years. I had grown weary of my trade, however, and perhaps owing to that, had gone through major quarrels with two different publishers. I felt that I was burned out, but I saw no alternative. Writing was all I had done for the greater part of my adult life, and it appeared that a writer I must remain; I had nothing to put on a job résumé.

It was at this time, and through a chain of circumstances far too complicated to go into here, that I found myself in San Francisco, residing in an apartment complex known as Casa Sanchez. Within a matter of months I had befriended the building manager and was helping out in the office. This very pretty woman—I shall call her Helen—had an unfortunate habit of reading a book as she walked, and would even step off the curb into the street with her nose still buried in her book. She used to joke that one day she would get run over on Van Ness Avenue or one of the city's other major streets, and so she did.

The owners attempted to hire someone to replace her, without much success, and I was already there, and eventually, and despite knowing nothing about property management, I found myself the manager of "The Casa," as we called the old girl, and so began a couple of decades of adventures, sometimes hilarious, sometimes eerie, and rarely dull.

•

THE CASA was both old and new, the "new" built from the gutted shell of an old laundry building. They had been intended as luxury apartments, it was said, and when I first came there nearly ten years later, the building still had a certain charm.

It also had ceilings that leaked. Badly. "The rain is falling all around," the tenants chanted laughingly to one another in the winter season. "It falls on land and sea. And when we live at Casa, it falls on you and me."

The fountain in the courtyard missed its basin and spit water derisively at passing tenants. The floor around it was always wet and slippery and green with moss, and you had to walk carefully to avoid landing in the fountain itself.

The fire-alarm system, perhaps haunted by some shade of the establishment that had once occupied the space, went off periodically for no discernible reason, usually in the wee hours of the morning, rousing everyone from sleep. As if to compensate, it had stubbornly refused to ring for the one fire that had occurred in the building.

In the process of remodeling, the owners had added an elevator, not within the building proper but one that stood off by itself in the parking lot, where it served no evident purpose that I was ever able to fathom. There were catwalks that connected it to the building proper, but they were impractical for, say, moving purposes, since even if movers used the elevator, they would find themselves at one remote end of a block-long complex. To reach all but the two apartments located in the proximity, it was still necessary to negotiate a veritable maze of corridors that twisted back and forth and were punctuated with endless flights of stairs, going up and down and up again. Even then, when the elevator was new, most movers shunned it and carried things up and down whichever of the flights of stairs were nearest the intended apartment, usually grumbling all the while.

Anyway, when I got there, the elevator hadn't worked for years. Nesters sometimes occupied it, until they got worried about the cables holding it somewhere between the second and third floors. In time, the elevator structure was torn down, and the entryways where the catwalks used to come into the building were left to gape like ugly wounds.

Tiles that were probably once beautiful were chipped and covered with grime that made it impossible to guess what their original color might have been, and wooden beams sagged threateningly. There was a tennis court over the garage, with cracks that grew noticeably larger each passing year, until tenants joked about chasing down a ball and landing on a parked car underneath.

People left, of course. Some, the hardier ones, remained, and over the years they began to develop a perverse affection for the building. "It has character," they said when chided by their friends. "It's not like anyplace else."

They began to feel as if they shared with their neighbors, the ones who had remained and the newer ones who found themselves drawn to the Casa's peculiar charms, some particular secret that the others had failed to glean, and when they met in the hallways or the lobby the greetings they exchanged were oddly conspiratorial.

It was true that when one entered the building, when the heavy wrought-iron gates closed after you, it was like leaving one world behind and entering another. The old, thick walls muffled the Castro's din. It was peaceful inside. The dwellers felt sheltered, cosseted. When, on a summer's evening, they sat on their balconies or their patios and sipped their tea or their wine, when they watched the fog roll over the hills like the ghost of some ancient ocean, they felt at home, as one didn't usually feel at home in the Castro, in the ghetto.

Some of the people who had lived at the Casa before and moved away drifted back, homesick, it seemed.

This was the eighties. Some of them came home to die. Some of them, it seems, were already dead.

•

"YOU MUST DO SOMETHING about that baby next door," Simon said, appearing at the door to my office. "He never stops crying. All day, all night. It's driving me crazy."

There were two difficulties with this demand. First, there was no baby next door. There were no babies in the complex, and in any event, the apartment next to Simon's was empty.

Second, to put it in proper medical terms, Simon was already bananas. For instance, he liked to hide under the stairwell in the atrium, leap out at people as they passed by, and cry, "Boo!"

I suppose you are thinking that we should have tried to evict him, but the reality is, in San Francisco the eviction ordinances make it difficult, almost impossible, to evict anyone for any offense short of multiple ax murders, and in any case, everyone knew he did this, and that he was harmless, and no one paid him the slightest attention (which may have been what got him into lurking in the first place).

"I'll look into it," I assured him that day, which is the apartment manager's catchall response to difficult complaints.

It was a little more difficult, however, to ignore him when he came to my office the second time a few days later, to declare, "I killed the baby next door."

Hmm. "Why don't you tell me about it," I suggested, truly puzzled.

"I just couldn't bear that endless crying any longer," he said, genuinely tearful. "So I took up my big butcher knife, and I stabbed it through the wall, and this woman screamed, 'You have killed my baby!' "

Oh, dear. The best I could do was take him upstairs and show him that the neighboring apartment was in fact unoccupied, which left him mystified, and I called his family to suggest that maybe Simon should no longer be left on his own.

The family did indeed come to fetch him, and I shrugged all this off as Simon's delusion—until one day a month or so later. It was Simon's apartment that was empty now while we refurbished it, and a new tenant had moved into the unoccupied one next door. And that tenant, who gave every indication of being of sound mind, came down to see me soon after he had moved in—to complain about the baby crying endlessly in the neighboring apartment—which is to say, the empty apartment that had previously been Simon's.

"I will look into it," I told him—such a useful phrase—and I went to Simon's old, now empty apartment, and stood in the middle of the living room, and I said in my most managerial voice, "Listen, I want no more of this nonsense or you will be evicted without further ado, every single one of you, and don't think the city eviction ordinances will help you either, because they do not cover ghosts."

I am happy to say, the baby's crying ceased.

•

DOG MAN'S LETTER BEGAN, "I had taken my Fancy for a walk," an opening line I have longed to use since.

I should explain that one of the staff dubbed him Dog Man because at one time he walked no fewer than four miniature schnauzers on leashes. Health issues, however, had necessitated simplifying things, and now it was only one, named, as you may have surmised, Fancy.

Our leases, in fact, forbade pets, but I had developed the knack of looking the other way when they wagged past. Dog Man was not so generous. He complained almost weekly about the pets of other tenants. In particular, he took umbrage at the rotweiler who lived with a lesbian neighbor next door. The two of them—that is to say, the lesbian and Dog Man—waged an ongoing battle, in which I was expected, however reluctantly, to be the referee.

The battle reached its apogee with Dog Man's letter: "I had taken my Fancy for a walk," he wrote, "and we stopped at Cup of Joe to pick up a coffee, which I brought home to drink with the Sunday paper. When I got to my door, I realized that I had locked it, though I usually leave it unlocked. I had Fancy's leash in one hand and the coffee in the other, and my keys in my pocket, so I took hold of the coffee container in my teeth while I fumbled in my pocket for the key ring, and while I was so engaged, my neighbor came out her door with that beast of hers, and he barked threateningly at my Fancy, and I turned to give her a good tongue-lashing, but I must have lost my presence of mind, as I forgot I was holding that coffee container in my mouth, and when I opened it to speak, the hot coffee spilled all over me."

Hmm again. The problem here is that one must reply to such a letter, and doing so diplomatically was certainly a challenge.

A challenge that I apparently failed, at least in Dog Man's opinion. His response to my response was to declare, undiplomatically, that I "should be shot."

After that, he began a barrage of letters, some of them to me, most to the owners of the property, berating me in purple prose, which often made little or no sense. It was a relief, of sorts, when he was admitted to the hospital and it turned out that he had a brain tumor. When he came home, he was subdued. Fancy was gone, adopted by a friend. Dog Man was obviously lonely, and I made efforts to be kind to him, most of which he ignored.

Some months later, when I had not seen him for several days, I took the chance of letting myself into his apartment, and found him naked and prone on his kitchen floor, the victim of a stroke. He had apparently been there since the previous day, unable to move or to get help.

I had always assumed that he had forgotten much of that presurgery period, but when I saw him briefly for the last time, now out of the hospital and on his way to live with relatives, he said, "I'm glad you weren't shot."

I thought it was a pretty good apology.

●

THE CASA PROVIDED no end of stories. There was that married couple, for instance, both of them attractive, young, very sweet, and—there is really no polite way to put this—both of them very dumb. If matched against a well-educated philodendron, their combined intellects would have come up short.

They were nice kids and mostly they caused me little grief. But there was the Saturday night when I had friends in for dinner, and while we were eating, the phone rang and I let the answering machine pick up the message, as I usually did off-hours, and I heard the young wife say, "This is an emergency. Could someone please come check our refrigerator? It isn't running, and we think it might be unplugged."

Ah, yes, that would do it, leaving only the mystery of how the refrigerator might have unplugged itself. Since this did not seem particularly urgent, and certainly not cogent, my laughing guests and I continued with our asparagus vinaigrette, and segued from that into very pleasant medallions of beef in a Madeira sauce. We were just tucking into a frothy mousseline au chocolat when the phone rang once again. It was the same young lady, this time informing me, "Never mind about sending a repairman, we fixed it ourselves. It was unplugged." That one, at least, required no letter.

•

YOU CANNOT, of course, have a large apartment complex in the Castro without dealing with a certain amount of sexual high jinks, and the Casa was no exception. The nude sunbathers were easy: I could banish them to a section of the roof that was ostensibly off-limits, and where they would be unlikely to startle unsuspecting visitors and families with children.

The Midnight Marauder came from outside the building and prowled at night, tapping on tenants' windows—not with his hand, you understand. Mostly, the tenants did not seem to mind, but he did intrude on one individual who was at the time engaged in solitary pleasures and did not appreciate discovering that he had an audience, and who took umbrage and chased him about the building with a baseball bat, and so discouraged his visits for a spell.

Window Man was a tenant who liked to display himself au naturel in his window, and sometimes assured himself of an audience by slipping notes under other's doors, suggesting that they look. Some complained to me. I suggested that they close their blinds, and made what I think were some discreet hints that seemed to alleviate that problem.

Exhibitionism was not all that rare, to be honest. One or two couples entertained their neighbors regularly with what I heard were delightful shows, though I missed the performances, sometimes to my disappointment, and once or twice to my relief. Some of my tenants were hot. Some were not.

Increasingly, as the eighties became the nineties, drugs became a problem. Now and then a tenant would complain about conspiracies and people lurking outside his door at night. One of them asked me to come into his apartment one evening, closed the door, and asked me to look through the peephole and tell him what I saw. What I saw was an empty hallway.

"Darling," I said, facing the young man, "you haven't by chance been doing a bit of drugs lately, have you?"

"Of course not," he insisted, his eyes rolling in his head.

"Then, I think you had better see a doctor," I said.

He was a doctor.

I told another tenant, in between some serious bouts, that he had reached the game show stage. It was time for him to pick door A, which was rehab; or door B, which was prison; or door C, which was the Great Beyond. He laughed at my humor. A few weeks later, I had the unfortunate experience of discovering his body. I think the door picked him by default.

•

I MANAGED THE CASA for the better part of twenty years. Along the way, I made many friends, some of them very special friends indeed, and my life would certainly be poorer without them. Joseph Chaikin, a legend in New York theater circles, was a frequent guest, and we became good friends as well. We often got performers in town with various stage shows, not generally the stars but supporting players and often stage managers. When Faye Dunaway was in town with the play *Master Class*, her stage manager stayed at the Casa. I have a friend who is genuinely starstruck, and I asked the manager if he could get an auto-graphed picture for him and, while he was at it, one for me as well. At the end of the run, just before he left, he brought me the two signed stills. Knowing that Ms. Dunaway had a reputation for being difficult, I asked him if he'd had any problem getting her to autograph them.

"No, not really," he assured me. "What she said was, 'Oh, give me the fucking things and I'll sign them.'" *Hmm.* Gracious indeed. I might add that one of my tenants was, at the time, concierge at her hotel, and he informed me that she had been asked not to stay at their chain in the future. Perhaps he had asked for a picture as well.

•

I STARTED AT THE CASA, as I said earlier, knowing nothing about managing apartment buildings. I learned that job over the years, and while I was at it, I learned a great deal about human nature. You see people in a way you don't often get to see them in other work, and share their lives in a way you might not otherwise. So I learned about people, and in the process I learned a great deal about myself. As a training ground for a writer, I thought it was terrific. And in time, I found that I must, after all, go back to writing; it is a disease for which there is no cure. I retired and, because San Francisco is too expensive for the writer's paltry earnings, I decamped from the city as well as from the Casa.

Not long before I left the company, however, a young man came to work with me in the office. He had been hired to manage another of the company's properties, and had been sent to me for a bit of training. It was quickly clear that his heart was not in it.

"I want to be a writer. I want to be out somewhere where I can meet people, have adventures, experience life," he declared passionately when I asked him about it. (I had not told him that I had any experience as a writer.) "I'll never learn anything about life in a job like this!"

I told him I thought he was probably right—I doubted that he would learn very much.

where the queer zone meets the asian zone

helen zia

I WAS AS SURPRISED AS ANYONE when my significant other and I got married after being together for twelve years, during that historic Valentine's Day weekend of 2004 at San Francisco's golden-domed City Hall, with thousands of other lesbian, gay, bi, and transgender couples.

In choosing to join the same-sex marriage revolution, Lia and I had no illusions; our civil marriage in no way affected our critical view of this patriarchal marriage institution. We wanted to get married to declare our commitment to each other and to express our defiance against the war-mongering, fundamentalist regime in Washington. But ultimately, we made it to the altar because of the Asian-American women we knew at the San Francisco marriage bureau in City Hall.

I am referring to the people who were in charge of the marriage license bureaucracy at San Francisco City Hall. Mabel Teng was elected city assessor-recorder after a nasty and close citywide contest for that decidedly unromantic-sounding job. A former San Francisco Supervisor and longtime community activist, Teng hired two other women: Donna Kotake, who also had a long history as an activist in San Francisco's Japantown, and Minna Tao, a well-known leader in the Castro for her work on LGBT causes. After Mayor Gavin Newsom took his courageous and historic stand, allowing gays and lesbians to apply for marriage licenses, the task fell on these women to make it so.

Mabel Teng, Donna Kotake, and Minna Tao were the city officials who, overnight, mobilized an army of unpaid city employees and volunteers to transform the archaic operation that handled only a few dozen marriage licenses a week into a machine that could process several hundred marriages a day—as many as they could before the anticipated court injunction would shut the operation down. Had it not been for the leadership of these three straight Asian American women, the lumbering machine might have cranked out a few hundred marriages in the two-week window before the courts shut them down. Instead, they brought together a rainbow of yellow, black, brown, and white, queer and straight supporters to process some four-thousand-plus same-sex marriages, including my own.

Initially, Lia and I were hesitant to join the other marriage license applicants because we wanted to include my elderly mother in the ceremony, and the long lines that snaked from Polk and Grove streets around City Hall discouraged us. Then our friends at City Hall called to ask if we could volunteer to help out with the deluge of paperwork on that three-day holiday weekend. As a writer, I could type, and Lia too had office skills. That day, we helped process licenses for several hundred other gay and lesbian couples who had traveled from all over for the chance to be married. When the line of couples came to the end, Lia and I seized the moment and were married by Donna Kotake, with several other friends who had volunteered looking on. We went home that night trying to grasp that we were *married*, so unimaginable only a few days earlier.

One thing that Lia and I couldn't have known was the impact our marriage would have on our families. Perhaps most opposite-sex couples expect to be taken in as family by their prospective in-laws, but that is not so for most LGBT couples. Lia and I have always felt lucky to have family members who tolerated, accepted, even welcomed us, but we still could not assume that they would respond to our nuptials with the same enthusiasm had we married partners of the opposite sex. We are among the very fortunate. In fact, it was my mother who suggested that we get married after she saw the news about San Francisco's gay weddings on KTSF-TV, the Chinese-language station. She was excited, happy at the prospect. "Helen, gay people can get married in San Francisco now," she said. "Why don't you and Lia go?"

Lia's father had been a state district court judge in Hawaii, one in the first wave of Japanese-Americans to seek elective office before statehood. As a retired judge, he is authorized to perform weddings, and when it appeared that a window for same-sex marriages might open in Hawaii in 1993, we asked him gingerly if he would marry us. The first few times we asked, he didn't answer. Then one day, months after our first query, to our surprise he agreed, and we all laughed at the imaginary headlines: "Local Judge Marries Daughter to Daughter-in-Law." But that was not to be; the window for same-sex marriage did not open until Mayor Gavin Newsom's revolution in San Francisco.

A few months after our marriage on the rotunda of City Hall, we held a small wedding party at the Silver Dragon restaurant in Oakland's Chinatown. Family and friends came together from all over the country, from New York City and Hilo, Hawaii. It was the first time in fifteen years that my five siblings and I were assembled in the same place. Six of our young nieces and nephews formed a wedding procession as Lia's brother and my mother "gave us away." Lia's father dusted off his retired judicial robe and performed an affirmation ceremony. Our Hawaii friends and relatives brought beautiful leis, and each of our siblings made moving toasts.

In honor of our marriage, friends performed hula, sang romantic standards, shouted "Banzai!" three times, and toasted us. We served the traditional roast pig as well as a wedding cake; we laughed and cried. By all accounts, it was a wedding party that far exceeded our wildest imaginations. It served another purpose, too: the melding of our extended family and friends. Our respective families, already so supportive of us, suddenly transformed their relationships to each other to reflect the more intimate "relatives" status: Lia's father and my mother now see each other as related, and my five siblings and Lia's brother have become family. This subtle yet profound shift, this joining of families, has opened my eyes to another aspect of making family. Our niece Emily, the sixteen-year-old daughter of my brother Hoyt, cannot remember when Lia and I weren't together; after our affirmation ceremony, she put her arms around Lia and summed it up this way: "Auntie Lia, now you're really my auntie."

Among activist types, an axiom holds that social movements involve moving people and changing minds, one person at a time. Queer folks have long known that homophobic attitudes change when people get to know someone in their circle who is gay. The same is true for Asian-Americans and others who dwell in the margins of society, in every corner of this land. We stop being one-dimensional cartoon characters; we get to be fully human. With each individual who comes to realize that there are Asian queers and queer Asians, that space where the gay zone meets the Asian zone opens a little more.

•

WHEN I WAS WRITING the book about nuclear scientist Wen Ho Lee, the Los Alamos nuclear scientist who was falsely accused of being a spy for China, I wanted him to know that I am a lesbian, to be sure that my sexual orientation would not become an issue in our book collaboration. During one of our first meetings in his kitchen, I told him that Lia is my spouse, just as Sylvia is his spouse. At first he said nothing, then made himself busy, bustling about the kitchen. Finally he said, in matter-of-fact physicist fashion, "That is your domain. It is not my domain." It was my business, not his, and that was the end of it.

More than a year later, on the last day of our book tour for *My Country Versus Me*, Wen Ho called my hotel room in Los Angeles—from his own room just down the hall. He had a question he had wanted to ask me. "Helen," he said, "I've met your brother, and he seems one hundred percent male. Is there anyone else in your family like you?" I answered no, not that I knew of. He wanted to know how I ended up gay. I explained that sexual orientation isn't a choice or an absolute, one hundred percent this or one hundred percent that, but it is a spectrum, like light, where people may fall closer to one end or the other, or somewhere in between. "Yes, a spectrum," he said. "That makes sense."

Then I had a question for him: "What is your feeling about gay people?" Wen Ho replied, "Before I knew you, if I met someone who is gay, I would not want to have anything to do with them. But now I think it makes no difference if they are gay."

As the enormity of the San Francisco marriage revolution began to register, it also dawned on me that this was a movement that has had Asian-Americans at its center from the beginning, ever since the first lawsuits in Hawaii in 1993. The Japanese-American Citizens League was the first (and perhaps only) national civil-rights group of people of color to support same-sex marriage; their convention voted to do so after Congressman Norman Mineta flew in for the sole purpose of arguing that support for same-sex marriage is a matter of fairness, equality, and justice. In three of the states where lawsuits by lesbian and gay couples were challenging the marriage bans, Asian-Americans were among the chief plaintiffs. Two San Francisco Asian/Pacific-American couples rode the marriage equality bus that toured America, bringing lesbian and gay married couples to Wal-Mart parking lots throughout Smalltown, USA.

The sheer out-loudness of the Asian-American presence in this round of same-sex marriage stood in contrast to the first same-sex marriage showdown that took place beginning in 1999 in Hawaii, where, in spite of the heavily Asian and Pacific Islander location, the connection between race and sexual orientation was often denied. In spite of the Japanese American Citizens League's valiant attempt to draw parallels between the injustice of the internment of Japanese-Americans with the marriage ban for gays, the mainly Asian and Pacific Islander electorate in Hawaii voted two to one to prevent same-sex marriage. Some Asian-American leaders asserted that "This is not our issue," as though queer APIs simply don't exist in the Asian-American community. At the same time, some white LGBT advocates insisted that the first lawsuits just happened to be in Hawaii, that this battle could have been filed by anybody, anywhere. According to some observers, it was simply happenstance that the first ruling for the same-sex marriage took place in Hawaii and so many of the players happened to be Asians or Pacific Islanders.

Hawaii was the first state in the nation to ratify the Equal Rights Amendment, in 1972, through the leadership of Congresswoman Patsy Mink. When the national ERA effort failed, the people of Hawaii adopted a state Equal Rights Amendment—assuring that "equality of rights under the law shall not be denied or abridged on account of sex." The Hawaii ruling in the 1990s that the denial of same-sex marriage is unconstitutional came out of the lived history of Hawaii's people, who had forged their Hawaii state constitution out of blood and tears. Native Hawaiians had been colonized and subjected to genocide, while Asian immigrant laborers were brought to Hawaii's plantations as chattel.

The inability of LGBT advocates from the mainland to recognize the lived experience of Hawaii's Pacific Islanders and Asian-Americans was a missed opportunity to forge a link in the common quest for equality and justice. This failure also made it easier for the Fundamentalist Christian Right to appeal to homophobic beliefs that gays and lesbians are somehow separate from Asian and Pacific Islander communities. After the 2004 Valentine's Day marriages in San Francisco, Korean-American churches organized rallies against the "evil of homosexuality" in southern California, while seven thousand members of Chinese-American Christian churches mobilized against same-sex marriage in San Francisco's Sunset District. From Christian friends, I've learned that ministers of some Chinese-language evangelical churches not only preach that gay children are sinners who transgress God and Nature, but that *their parents* are also damned—a special cultural twist of the knife for Asian families, where parents are revered.

Asian-American queer activists do not all agree on what political stand to take toward same-sex marriage. To some, fighting for same-sex marriage is too petty bourgeois, too much about the nuclear family, cocooning, property rights, and all the negative patriarchal things that marriage stands for. It's rather like fighting for equality in the military when you're opposed to war, as I am. There are so many other pressing issues that also inhabit this queer and Asian zone—hate crimes and violence, immigration and asylum, Patriot Act detentions and deportations, government surveillance of "suspicious" people, the disease and stigma of HIV/AIDS, to name a few. Indeed, a man from Thailand was among the couples whose marriage licenses I processed—and he had to file for an annulment when his change in status exposed him to possible deportation.

But there are no perfect battles. Same-sex marriage might not be the political battleground any of us would have chosen, but this fragile space where queer meets Asian belongs to us, not to those who attempt to use us as a wedge to extend an agenda that is harmful to our diverse and largely immigrant communities. Our lived experiences in this space are an inseparable part of our communities, and that includes the historic roles that gay and straight Asians have played to make same-sex marriage possible.

I am reminded of the adage: "None of us is free unless each of us is free." Each of us—no matter what our particular "orientation" in life—will face choices that offer the possibility of reaching beyond our own selves and self-interest. By choosing to stand up for the humanity of others, we all become more free. As the space where queer meets Asian continues to grow beyond the Castro, so too does the space for everyone, even when it happens one person at a time.

castro theatre

f. allen sawyer

"THE SMOKING SECTION IS ON THE RIGHT," I say, pointing right with my left hand. I've had this job only a few months, but it has already messed up my perception of bilateral symmetry. Whereas some people have to mime the pledge of allegiance to determine which is their right hand, I have to pretend to tear a ticket.

It is 1976 and I am nineteen years old and tearing tickets at the Castro Theatre. Several hundred times a day I stand at the front door and point right with my left hand.

It is the dawn of the Castro Clone, and I'm a tall, skinny kid with big hair and bad skin. It is before the era of gym bodies and big dicks (okay, big dicks are never out of fashion). I have one asset to exploit, and that is my youth. I have the whole ephebe thing going, and I try to work it for all it's worth. The Castro Theatre is the perfect stage set. The people working behind the concessions counter do the real work, the doorman has it easy (except for that whole right/left dysphoria), but my favorite position is selling tickets.

The box office is a separate kiosk, standing out on the sidewalk, and it is the perfect spot to cruise and be cruised in return. The only drawback is that in your little fishbowl, you are prisoner to all advances, wanted and un. I can only imagine the shades of red I turn as I sit there, the captive audience of filmmaker and film buff Artie Bressan, who is serenading me with the Nelson Eddy half of an old Victor Herbert duet, taunting me to answer with the Jeanette MacDonald refrain.

The Castro Theatre was built in 1922, and though it was ornate, compared to the grand palaces of Market and Mission streets, it was just a neighborhood theater. Until now, 1976, it had been showing third-run movies. Films would open "first-run" at the large downtown houses, and as their potential to draw crowds diminished, the films would move out to the different neighborhood houses. The Castro was a last stop. After more than fifty years of continuous operation, the theater was considered not classic but just old-fashioned. In a misguided attempt at interior decoration the lobby had been painted green and orange. But it is 1976, and the theater has been leased by Mel Novikoff for his Surf Theatre chain. Back when foreign films meant just the oeuvre of Bergman, Truffaut, and Fellini, buffs would travel out to the far end of Irving Street in pilgrimage to the Surf Theatre, where the concession counter sold apples and, I believe, coffee was served for the first time in any movie house. The Surf chain included the Clay and Lumiere, and now the Castro.

Mel and his business partner, Hal Slate, have set about to restore the theater to its former glory. But it isn't just with a fresh coat of paint and the refurbished chandeliers; their great contribution is the programming. The Betamax and VCR are too new to be ubiquitous, and there are only a dozen channels on TV. (Queens who want to memorize the dialog to a Bette Davis movie

pray for its appearance on *The Million-Dollar Movie* where it is repeated all week.)

But now on Castro Street they are presenting monthlong tributes to stars and studios of Hollywood's golden age. There had already been repertory theaters in San Francisco, most notably Jack
Tillmany's Gateway Cinema, but with the revenue potential of
the fifteen hundred seat-Castro, studios are suddenly willing to
strike new thirty-five-millimeter prints or lend archive copies of
films that might have previously only been available in sixteen-
millimeter cut-for-TV versions.

Most of the Castro Theatre employees are aspiring artists,
writers, drug addicts, or filmmakers. Ostensibly, I am a theater
major at San Francisco State, but I've come to realize that working at the Castro Theatre is what I really want to do with my life.
And it's not for the cruising, not just for the cruising. It's also for
the movies. I love movies. Growing up, I had a Saturday-morning
ritual of television viewing. First would be the Shirley Temple
movie, then a Tarzan, and if I was lucky an Astaire-Rogers musical
from RKO or a Warner Bros. gangster drama. It wasn't until my
teen years that I learned that the best old movies were being
played in the middle of the night. Luckily, my parents were fast
asleep by eleven o'clock, so at midnight I'd sneak into the family
room and, sitting very close to the set, with the volume way down
low, I discovered Mae West and Marlene Dietrich. Thank God
for UHF. Now I'm being paid to watch movies. Well, not watch
them exactly, but they are just behind the big red double doors
into the theater. I could earn more money if I took the closing
shift, but I prefer to get off after the last intermission and catch
the late feature. On matinee days, I come in before or after my
shift so I can see both pictures. I've dropped out of school, and
I'm spending all my time at the theater (earning $3.25 an hour).

My obsession, misperceived as initiative, has now led them to
promote me to assistant manager. Thus begins my "showman"
phase. I carefully select which music plays between the movies,

and I start bringing LPs from home to play on the projection booth turntable. I badger the projectionists to cut the rating certificates off the heads of all the trailers. There may be a federal law against this, but I find it disconcerting to watch a black-and-white double bill only to have the screen flash a bright green announcement that "The following film is rated G." I even have opinions on exactly when to open and close the curtains.

It is not uncommon that we change double bills daily. A film reel holds twenty minutes of film and the average movie is five reels long, so every day the projectionist has, at the least, ten new reels of film to deal with. In the booth there are two carbon-arc projectors side by side, and every twenty minutes a bell rings to warn you to watch the upper-right-hand corner of the screen for the cue marks that tell you when to change over from one projector to the other. You then have twenty minutes to thread the next reel and rewind the previous one for the next showing. Needless to say, the projectionist has enough to do without worrying about the small finesses I am asking for.

•

IT IS SUNDAY MATINEE, and we have a Lerner and Loewe double bill of *The Little Prince* and *Camelot*. I've selected a special LP to play as preshow music, but in the booth, Joe has put on one of our generic instrumentals. I try to assert my authority to this septuagenarian projectionist—hierarchy needs to be established—to no avail. The audience is seated and the movie begins—but twenty minutes into *The Little Prince* the screen goes blank. As the audience begins the obnoxious rhythmic clapping that frustrated audiences always do, I run through the balcony and up to the booth, sure that Joe has fallen asleep and missed his changeover. I throw open the door and yell, "Wake up, you old fart!" —only to find Joe dead on the floor, the loose end of the film slapping his body as it spins. He has had a heart attack.

My first call is for an ambulance; then Mel, who is not home; then my manager, who is not home; and down the phone list until I reach the company's financial officer, whose sole advice is to call the projectionists' union. I am amazed that the replacement projectionist sent by the union arrives only minutes after the paramedics.

•

THE HAVING-SEX-WITH-MEN part of being gay is a no-brainer, and my coming out basically coincides with the Castro neighborhood's birth as a gay community. I find my place within the new queer community at the same time the theater finds its identity as the symbol of that community. The first benefit I remember at the theater is a fund-raiser for Jeanne Jullion, a lesbian mother who lost custody of her sons in a heated battle with her ex-husband. The plight of lesbian mothers brings home the real consequences of living as a second-class citizen, and it isn't long before legislation introduced across the country specifically denies us our rights. At the theater, benefits for individual cases give way to large-scale fund-raisers to fight state and national anti-gay initiatives. More than Harvey Milk or Pat Norman, I believe we have to thank John Briggs and Anita Bryant for getting us organized. It is these bullies who inspire us to combine our strengths and fight back.

There is also fun on Castro Street. The Halloween parade has moved from Polk Street to the Castro. The annual children's costume parade in front of Cliff's Variety store has ceded the street to queens and fairies of a different kind. No one has taken out a permit, no safety monitors are trained, but the revelers take over the street all the same. Harvey Milk comes into the theater to escape the crowd, and when someone asks him why he isn't wearing a costume, he replies, "I've come as Dianne Feinstein, I've put ice-water in my veins."

•

IT IS NOVEMBER 1978. I am now the manager of the Castro
Theatre. There is a strange pall over the city as we come to terms
with the Jonestown Massacre.

At work I've fallen into a routine; I sit in every night to watch
the late feature, which means I stay after everyone's gone home to
do my paperwork and prepare my deposits. This lets me out onto
Castro Street just in time for "last call," when it's much easier to
arrange an assignation. I sleep every day till noon, at which time I
turn on the TV and watch KRON's midday news to catch up on
what's happened in the world while I've been asleep.

Tuesday, November 21. I scratch and stretch and turn on the
set. They are rebroadcasting an interview with city supervisor
Dan White. Damn, I think, I hope the mayor hasn't relented and
given him his job back. An announcer's voice breaks in: "*And that
was Dan White, last week, before he shot Mayor George Moscone and
Supervisor Harvey Milk.*" Diane Feinstein appears on the screen,
harbinger of news too terrible to be true; this clip will be repeated
over and over again for many days.

I'm in shock, but I know that in their collective grief, anger,
and confusion people will gravitate to the Castro Theatre. As the
custodian of this community symbol, I know I have to prepare it
for all the attention it is about to receive. I throw on some clothes
and walk the few blocks to the theater. I drag out the huge
wooden ladder. I can't remember if I enlist someone off the street
to help me raise it or if I've called some employee in to assist. I
take down the names of whatever inconsequential films we were
showing and put up a memoriam announcement. That night, tens
of thousands of people converge at Castro and Market to start the
candlelight march to City Hall. Film and photos shown around
the world feature the theater and its marquee.

•

TWO DAYS LATER IS THANKSGIVING. I stay home all morning and prepare a traditional turkey dinner. It takes me five trips to walk it, along with my grandmother's silver and linens, to the theater—thank God I live close enough so that nothing gets cold. I set everything up in the mezzanine. My plan is for the staff that has to work tonight to eat in two shifts, but this a night when we need to be with family, and our family is here at the theater. After the film starts, I close the box office, and we leave the lobby unattended and all gather round the table, thankful that we have each other.

•

KNOWING THAT I had already killed one projectionist, the union decides to send only their younger members. My favorite is a young dyke. If you give her a few lines of cocaine, she'll stay after closing and run any film you have. Most of my filmmaker friends get the rare chance to see their work projected on the Castro's silver screen. It's a funny thing about silver screens; most of them are actually white. Once, to prepare for a 3-D festival, we hired someone to paint our screen silver, the idea being that silver is more reflective and would enhance the effects. The brushstrokes were so pronounced that we had to replace the whole screen.

•

AS TIME GOES BY, I realize that I don't actually need to hit the bars every night. As the last film ends I just stand in the lobby and peruse the exiting audience. I choose my prey and start up a conversation, usually the offer of a backstage tour. The original proscenium is still there—the theater was built for silent films, so the screen was put up against the back wall. With the advent of sound, a hole was put in the back wall and a little wart was built to house the speakers. As sound became more sophisticated, it was necessary to move the entire screen forward to make room for the needed equipment. When I am lucky these tours end on the mezzanine couch.

It is Monday night, May 21, 1979; I am on the couch with a comely young man whose name I've neglected to ask. We are interrupted by a commotion out on Castro Street, and without putting on our clothes, we step out the tall windows and on top of the marquee. Below us are regimented rows of policemen in full riot gear. I know that Dan White has been convicted of manslaughter instead of first-degree murder; I know that a protest had been planned at City Hall; but I figured by this time Joan Baez had sung "Amazing Grace" and everyone had gone home. What I do not know is that nearly five thousand people have caused more than a million dollars' worth of damage to City Hall and several police cars. Now the cops have come to Castro Street. They have cleared everyone to the other end of the block, but here we are unseen above them. I hear something along the lines of "Now it's our turn!" and more "Fags" and "Faggots" epithets than I've ever heard before. Someone gives a signal, and so begins the second half of the White Night riots.

•

THE EIGHTIES HAVE ARRIVED, and it's great to be gay! There are rumors of a gay cancer, but that's no concern of ours. The San Francisco International Film Festival has moved from the Palace of Fine Arts to the Castro Theatre. I get to meet George Cukor, Akiro Kurosawa, and Volker Shlondorff (who gets mad at me for starting the show late and making him miss his flight home). Frameline's LGBT festival has made its home here.

June 23, 1981. Vito Russo inscribes a copy of his book, *The Celluloid Closet*: "For Allen, Can I come and live in your movie house?" Four years later, he will get his wish. After his memorial, Rob Epstein and I will embed some of Vito's ashes into the back wall of the auditorium.

I have a regular customer; he never sees a movie but he comes in all the time to buy popcorn for his dog. His name is Ron Lanza, and he has just taken a lease on a mortuary out on Valencia Street; his plan is to convert it into a combination café, theater, and community center. The next thing I know, I have quit my job and I'm helping Ron build the Valencia Rose.

It is a clean break, and I go cold turkey.

The next time I can remember being back in the theater is November 1, 1984, the premiere of *The Times of Harvey Milk*. Director Rob Epstein once worked here behind the candy counter. He will go on to win two Academy Awards. Artie Bressan finds me in the crowd and tells me to watch for an aerial shot he took of the candlelight march to City Hall; he tells me that he has dedicated that shot to me.

Artie will die in 1987, Mel Novikoff and Hal Slate are dead, as are thousands of filmgoers whose tickets I tore. The theater will survive the 1989 earthquake; it will survive the proliferation of VHS and DVD; it will survive a beloved programmer who books for cineasts instead of for the neighborhood; it hopefully will continue to survive whatever is thrown at it.

It is 2006, thirty years have passed. I am still tall but no longer skinny, my hair is shorter, and my skin is still bad. I am escorting Ann Blyth down the Castro Theatre aisle, after a screening of *Mildred Pierce*. Hired by Mark Huestes, a candy-counter alum who now produces twice-yearly movie-star tributes, I have taken this same walk with Debbie Reynolds, Ann Miller, Margaret Pellegrini (one of the original Munchkins), Jane Russell, and many others. Whichever star is on my arm, they inevitably will compliment me on how lovely my theater is. I nod and thank them. I may work here only for special events, I may only catch a half a dozen movies a year, but I still think of the Castro as my theater, I still think of the Castro as my home.

adventures in the celluloid cathedral

jim tushinski

MY LIFE HAS ALWAYS BEEN ABOUT MOVIES. So many of my memories involve movie theaters and the films I've seen in them. I'm a movie lover, plain and simple. It's usually not the box-like mall theaters of the 1970s and 80s that occupy my most cherished memories, nor the comfort and efficiency of today's stadium-seating multiplexes that inspire me. I'm not a churchgoing man, but I imagine the feelings a religious person has inside one of the world's great cathedrals are similar to how I feel when I'm watching an exceptional film in a real movie palace. I've been in a number of them—huge, grandiose, impossibly ornate, and sometimes run-down theaters from the 1920s and 30s that have survived all the vagaries of the movie business for the last eighty years. These are my temples—with gold leaf cornices, curtains that part to reveal big screens, chandeliers, haunted balconies, and aging seats—offering you the sense that when the right film comes along, you are sharing mysteries and secrets with the other people in the audience. I was fortunate enough to live within walking distance of one of the best for twenty years. It's my Saint Peter's, my Mecca, my Chartres—the Castro Theatre in San Francisco.

The first time I saw the Castro, it reminded me of a Mexican cathedral, albeit one with an enormous vertical neon sign and a marquee. I had come to San Francisco as a penniless twentysomething grad-student tourist, on a stopover before continuing my cross-country drive down to school in southern California. I'd been in love with the idea of San Francisco for many years, brought up on *Tales of the City* and *Vertigo*, and had my first glimpse of the Oz-like city as I drove across the Bay Bridge on a clear, beautiful summer day in 1984.

After parking my yellow VW bug on Howard near Sixth Street in the infamous South of Market neighborhood, I settled into my tiny room at a gay hotel called The Anxious Arms and planned my first San Francisco excursion—to the gayest place on earth, the corner of Castro and Market streets. Within the hour, I was walking up to Market to catch the Muni Metro subway, counting the three stops until I could emerge onto the streetcorner I had fantasized about since I was a dorky college student in mid-state Illinois.

I remember walking up the steps at the Castro Street Muni station, and at first all I could see was this incredible blue sky. Then I saw all the men, gay men everywhere and of every sort. On reaching the top of the steps, I was disoriented by the huge intersection, the traffic, the people. I stood on the street corner as all those gay men moved around me, and I slowly turned a full three hundred sixty degrees, feeling like Mary Tyler Moore, taking in a place hundreds of times more magical than I could have imagined. Behind me were hills holding back a blanket of fog that threatened to spill over the crest and tumble down onto the city below. And yet this corner wasn't a city at all. It was a neighbor-hood, a town within a town, with shops, restaurants, and bars all crammed together like Main Street in the Chicago suburb where I grew up.

In one direction, Market Street, looking impossibly broad, sloped gently back toward downtown, but in every other direction, the roads all went up and over formidably steep hills, each hill covered with gingerbread houses and trees. Towering over this little town was the Castro Theatre, an elaborate wheat-colored building with a two-story neon sign proclaiming not only the theater's name, but also the name of area around it. *CASTRO.* Above the marquee, to the right of the sign, was a soaring rectangular window divided into fifty or sixty smaller panes, topped by another window—a half-circle that echoed the ornate, curlicued bulge in the roofline farther up. Around and above these windows was a plaster ornamentation of garlands, alcoves, and medallions, all painted the same wheat color, except for tall accent columns of goldenrod on either side. When I came back at night, the theater was a riot of red and blue and yellow neon zigzagging and curling up and around the sign and the marquee. The walls were uplit by floodlights and under the marquee, which extended out over the sidewalk, hundreds of lightbulbs illuminated the inset entry doors of dark wood and the freestanding ticket booth.

A year later, I became a San Franciscan, moving to the City with no job, no friends, no place to live, and no money. I had spent the previous twelve months in southern California, slogging my way through the first year of a graduate program I had little respect for, dreaming of San Francisco and the Castro Theatre. Like so many gay men and women before me, I gave in to the enchantment of the City. I dropped out of school and made my way north to the place that seemed more alive and more beautiful than anywhere else I'd ever been.

Even after a few weeks of unemployment, transient hotels, cold summer nights, loneliness, and awkward one-night stands, I was still in love with the City. I ended up seeking shelter and sol-ace by going to movies at the Castro Theatre whenever I could afford it. It became my home when bad roommates, worse dates, and a perpetually overdrawn bank account got me down. If it was a choice between using my last five bucks to eat or to go to a movie at the Castro, well, missing a meal or two never hurt any-one. Escaping into a celluloid dream in the dark, magical interior of the Castro was my survival mechanism against the cold reality of the big city.

And what an interior it is. On either side of the curtained screen are faux-Corinthian columns painted gold, which are then repeated at intervals along the side walls. Below the two main columns are round paintings of mysterious women, carefully spotlit, who resemble figures from a John William Waterhouse painting. Also flanking the screen are massive organ grills, deco-rated in a golden Baroque fever dream of figures and medallions and jardinieres, and in the center of each, a small balcony, large enough for just two or three people, juts out from a curtained doorway. On each of the side walls of the auditorium are painted large scenes that resemble eighteenth-century French tapestries, depicting fountains and colonnades and reclining nude figures.

Above, the elaborate dome ceiling seems to drape over the au-ditorium like a bedouin tent, decorated with obscure mythical fig-ures. One can peer at them for hours and never quite make out what they are—is that a centaur? A wizard? In the center hangs an art deco chandelier, all jutting silver angles. The seats of the main floor are divided into three sections by two aisles, and when one walks to the front of the theater and looks back, the balcony hangs magically over the rear of the auditorium without posts to support it, and the tiered seats stretch up to the projection booth, which seems miles away. Turn around again and the grand theater organ, down in the orchestra pit, is quietly waiting for an audience to ar-rive. Before evening performances, the organ rises out of the pit while one of the Castro's professional organists entertains the audience with medleys of old standards. The final song before the organ is lowered back to its resting place is always "San Francisco," to which the audience claps along until the final bars when the organist slows the pace and comes to a thunderous conclusion.

Over the years, the interior of the Castro has gone from rundown to spectacular. When I first started going there in the late 1980s, the sound system turned dialogue into a muddle of unrecognizable words. It got so bad that I complained to friends that I would see only foreign films there—a vow I was never able to keep. The seats were rock-hard, and many of them were broken or had springs that stuck into your rear. The curtain was torn, and paint was peeling everywhere. The grand theater had seen better days, but films were shown here that you couldn't see anywhere else. The bill often changed daily—wonderful double features of classic films alternating with newer art films. Picking up the eye-catching, informative calendar outside the ticket booth every three months became a much-anticipated event. A Fassbinder retrospective? You got it. A seventy-millimenter festival? Here it is. A rare screening of Pasolini's shocking, infamous *Salo*? Yup, it's on right after a revival of *Meet Me in St. Louis* and *Singin' in the Rain*. Finally, in 2001, the theater was closed for a major renovation, and when she opened up again, the change was phenomenal—a new sound system, all new seats, new paint, a new screen and new curtains, new carpet. The Castro Theatre was back in business and better than ever.

One of the first things I discovered when going to a movie at the Castro was that the audience could play as important a role in my enjoyment of the experience as the decor and even the film itself. Castro audiences are known for vocalizing their delight or outrage. At screenings with just a few people in attendance, the grandeur of the place seems to keep the audience anesthetized, but when the crowd numbers in the hundreds or climbs toward capacity (more than fourteen hundred seats), anything can happen.

The two most frequently heard sounds from a Castro audience

are foot stomps and hisses. The foot stomps are used when applause just isn't enough. I've seen this most often when the director or star of a particularly beloved film makes an appearance before or after a screening. At first there is thunderous applause and whistles, but then a vibration begins to grow, rumbling under the applause and finally erupting into rapid, rhythmic pounding as thousands of feet stomp on the floor. The entire theater seems to shake, and many a filmmaker or actor onstage has been dumb-struck by this odd, endearing expression of public love.

The hissing, though, is what Castro audiences are famous for. No one knows when the hissing tradition started or why it continues to flourish, but it happens when something in the film or in a personal appearance disappoints or outrages someone in the audience. Whenever President Bush's name is mentioned onstage, for example, a chorus of hisses erupts. Ditto for Jerry Falwell or whoever is the latest conservative bogeyman. When an older film contains something considered racist or politically incorrect, hissing will ensue. Sometimes, the hissing is good-natured or more of a game, and I know of several filmmakers who come to screenings at the Castro hoping their films will get hissed. It's a badge of honor to some.

Much of the time, the audience in the Castro is predominantely gay or lesbian, for the theater functions as the symbolic heart and community center of gay San Francisco. Every year, the San Francisco Gay Men's Chorus performs their Christmas show to sold out-crowds. Many special screenings of camp classics are given, often complete with elaborate drag performances and appearances by aging stars reveling in the adoration of their gay and lesbian fans. For me, though, the highlight of the year is Frameline's San Francisco International Lesbian and Gay Film Festival, one of the largest film festivals in California, a two-week extravaganza of sold out screenings, gossiping with other film nuts in long lines, audience mayhem, Hollywood stars, and scores of films that will never be released in theaters or on DVD. In my first ten or so years in San Francisco, I could afford to go to only three or four films during each festival, but as I advanced in my career and made more money, I would buy a pass and save up vacation days at work so I could be completely available for the festival, taking in three or four films a day. Being surrounded by thousands of people waiting in long lines to see films by and about gay, lesbian, and transgendered people was more exhilarating to me than any gay pride parade.

As you may imagine, seeing a film at the Castro Theatre is not like seeing a film anywhere else. For someone who is as in love with film as I am, the combination of the right film, the theater's atmosphere, a Castro audience, and my emotional state at the time can result in indelible memories—sometimes exhilarating and romantic, transformative and profound, and sometimes bittersweet, ironic, and a little sad. So I present to you my most memorable Castro moviegoing experiences. Not all of them involve my favorite films, or even films I would care to see again, but all of these experiences mirror my life in San Francisco throughout the years as I looked for love, sex, meaning, and community. They each represent a moment when something inside me changed. Movies can do that, you know. Especially when seen at the Castro.

•

MOST PEOPLE have never heard of *Jeanne Dielman, 23 Quai du Commerce, 1080 Bruxelles*, a three-hour Belgian/French film made in 1976 by lesbian director Chantal Akerman, but it is generally considered one of the towering achievements of twentieth-century avant-garde cinema. I knew of the film's reputation and of its challenges, so when it showed up on the Lesbian and Gay Film Festival schedule one year, I made up my mind to sit most of a Sunday afternoon in the dark of the Castro and see what all the fuss was about.

There were no more than twenty or so people at the screening. Anyone not enamored of Cinema with a capital C would have been scared away by the program notes—the film recounted the mundane life of a young Belgian widow who, unbeknown to her son and her neighbors, moonlights as a prostitute. But the scariest part for most moviegoers: almost nothing happens in the course of three-plus hours. We see long static shots of Jeanne (played by lesbian actress Delphine Seyrig) going about her household chores, turning an occasional trick, shopping for groceries, walking around her neighborhood. In one scene, Jeanne simply sits in a chair and stares into space for what seems like an eternity. And yet the film builds intensity and a sense of claustrophobia and dread so carefully and expertly that when something does finally happen near the end—a small gesture that in any other film would have been completely ignored—the entire audience let out a gasp.

The film itself was shattering both emotionally and aesthetically: There was a different way of telling a story and making a film than I was used to. Even more remarkable, however, was sharing this experience with a small, enraptured audience who responded to this off-putting, visceral masterpiece just as I had. And I like to think it could have happened only at the Castro.

•

PICTURE THIS: you're in the Castro Theatre during the Lesbian and Gay Film Festival of 1996. It's packed with lesbians who are there to see the first screening of what is now considered a classic—the Wachowski Brothers' *Bound*, a violent thriller about a mobster's girlfriend and her butch lesbian lover who together attempt a dangerous double-cross. First, the audience starts whistling and whooping during the seduction scene when Jennifer Tilly guides Gina Gershon's hand into her vagina. Then the audience holds its collective breath during one of the most intense sex scenes between two women ever put in a Hollywood movie. As the plot twists and the tension mounts, thirteen hundred women (and a good number of men, too) begin gasping and shouting at the screen. Look out! Oh my God! Go back! A climactic shock caused the entire theater to scream in unison. At the end, the whistling and applause and foot stomping shook the house. When Gina Gershon appeared on the stage in person, pandemonium broke out, visibly stunning the actress. In all my years of movie going, I had never seen an audience respond with such enthusiasm and...well...love.

•

IF *BOUND* SHOWED ME what an audience enamored of a film can do, the infamous festival screening of Todd Verow's "gay serial killer" movie *Frisk* showed me the dark side. It was June 1995, and Mark Finch, the beloved director of the Lesbian and Gay Film Festival had committed suicide by jumping off the Golden Gate Bridge in January of that year. In a tribute to Finch, the festival premiered Verow's adaptation of Dennis Cooper's novel, in which Finch had a bit part, on the Saturday night before the San Francisco Gay Pride parade. This was a slot normally reserved for something fun and fluffy, something to put the audience in the mood for a celebration. What the festival got instead was closer to a riot.

Frisk is not an easy film to watch. It's deliberately convoluted, perversely violent, and experimental in its approach to narrative. The theater was at capacity, primarily because the film was shot in San Francisco and featured a bevy of local actors and gay community members. The lead actors were attractive and showed a lot of skin, something that usually gets the festival audience through some pretty awful films without much complaint. But the vibe in the theater started getting bad soon after the film started.

Walkouts began, first just one or two people, then entire rows.

When one character started rhapsodizing about wanting to feel the insides of a boy, the booing and hissing started. When a torture scene began, the members of the audience shouted, "Sick!" "Horrible!" Someone threw something at the screen. For the rest of the film, the walkouts were loud, usually accompanied by a shouted expletive. Most of the audience who stayed continued to grumble and hiss. When the end credits rolled, a loud chorus of boos tried to drown out the scattered applause. The majority of the audience hadn't just been bored by the film, they actively and vocally hated it. It was as if they felt personally assaulted by the filmmakers and the festival programmers.

Frisk had its supporters that night (myself included), but the toxic atmosphere in the theater made me head for the exit without staying for the Q&A session. As the remainder of the audience spilled out onto Castro Street, which was closed to traffic for the annual Pink Saturday street party, and began to mix with the already raucous crowd of revelers, there was a sense of defiance, a feeling that the world sucks and horrible things happen, but damn it, I'm going to party anyway.

•

BEING A SINGLE MAN in San Francisco was a blessing and a curse. At least that's how I remember it. I've been single for only two one-year periods during my twenty years in San Francisco, and yet I managed to pack the best and worst dating experiences of my life into those two years. And of course, the Castro Theatre played a part.

In July of 1986, I had been in San Francisco for just about a year. I'd found a job working as a file clerk at a law firm making a thousand dollars a month, just enough to afford sharing a flat with two other gay men right around the corner from the Castro Theatre. There was one key ingredient missing from my rapidly improving San Francisco life—a boyfriend. I'm one of those guys who is happiest in a relationship, and in that first year, I was having no luck. There were plenty of tricks, which were a nice diversion sometimes, but every attempt to actually go on more than two dates with the same man fizzled into indifference. After one particularly bad date, I proclaimed to a friend that I was through with men but agreed to accompany him for "just one drink" at the Detour, a loud, dark local bar that was one of our favorites. That night I met *the* man. It was a feeling I'd never had before—he seemed to be as into me as I was into him. One week after we met, I asked him to go see a movie at the Castro. It was a test. I was taking him to see one of my favorite films—Robert Altman's bizarre masterpiece *Three Women*—and I wanted to see how he would react. As Shelley Duvall and Sissy Spacek swapped personalities and the film took off into its bizarre, dreamlike conclusion, I experienced a double thrill. I was watching one of my favorite movies in this glorious theater, and I was sitting next to a man who was handsome, sweet, sexually compatible, and who would sit through this Robert Altman film just to spend the evening with me. It felt like my life was finally getting started and the future held unlimited potential.

Slow dissolve to four years later.

I was single again, licking my wounds from a messy, painful breakup with the man I thought I'd spend the rest of my life with and ready to jump into the dating game once again. It was June and the Lesbian and Gay Film Festival was in full swing. I'd met a tall, dark, and handsome man at the gym and got up the nerve to ask him out on the Saturday night before the gay pride parade. I had two tickets to see a French-Canadian film by Léa Pool called *¿corps perdu* (but presented under the somewhat less romantic English title *Straight from the Heart*), which looked like it would be a perfect date film—sexy, lyrical, and passionate. I met my date at a local coffee shop, where we chatted for a few minutes before heading to the theater for the early-evening show. He was gorgeous, with a charming smile, and was at least three inches taller than I was. As we walked down the street, I knew he was getting covetous stares, and I was desperate to make this work even as I started to suspect that the interest was less than mutual.

¿corps perdu was just what I had expected, a heartbreaking love story starring two beautiful actors. I left the theater wistful, with an ache and longing in me to find another man with whom to fall in love, and I felt that my handsome date would be just right for the part. He, on the other hand, had been less impressed with the film, commenting that it was "kinda boring and kinda sappy." I thought I had noted restlessness in him, but I bravely pushed ahead. We stood under the marquee, the audience streaming out the doors around us, couples holding hands, friends laughing and calling to each other, and I nervously asked if he wanted to go get some dinner. His eyes drifted away from me, and there was a pause before he responded.

"Look," he said, "it's the biggest party night of the year and I should be going."

I'm sure I said something like, "Sure, okay," in an attempt to sound blasé, but I stood in the festive crowd, the marquee lights shining down on my stricken face as my date and I parted ways, and I silently cursed the movie for being too romantic, me for being so stupid as to believe I could find love, and the Castro Theatre for offering a flashing neon promise that life here in the gay mecca could be just like in the movies.

I didn't stay single long. My current partner and I met on a blind date, weathered the 1990s, bought a house, endured the dot-com crash, and spent many, many hours at the lesbian and gay film festival, one of us bringing the other sandwiches as he camped out in the Castro Theatre for three-movie marathons. Eventually, though, I became dissatisfied, not with my partner or with the film festival or with the Castro Theatre, but with always being an audience member. In college, I had wanted to be a film-maker and couldn't afford it. In the days before digital video, making even a student film required lots of cash for film stock and developing, and I was always broke. I made a few films on Super 8 but decided that I would concentrate on writing fiction instead. After all, I needed only a pen and paper for that. Years of watching the short film programs at the Lesbian and Gay Film Festival, however, had made me anxious to try again. I jumped into digital video and within a year had completed a short film *Jan Michael Vincent Is My Muse*, which had successful film festival screenings all over the world, none of them, however, at the Castro Theatre.

When I started shooting my feature-length documentary, I dreamed that it would play at the Castro during the film festival. I wanted to know what it was like to be on the stage, looking out at the auditorium I had known so intimately as a filmgoer, seeing it from this humbling yet powerful perspective. In all my years of watching movies at the Castro, I had never set foot on the stage, never walked up those steps and stood before a microphone as I had seen scores of filmmakers do. Through most of my years as an audience member, the idea of presenting a film I had made at the Castro, or at any theater, seemed an absurd dream. As the documentary began to take shape and the fact that I would actually complete it became irrefutable, I knew that if it didn't screen at the Castro, then I had somehow failed.

It wasn't a rational idea. In fact, it was quite absurd.

The documentary, *That Man: Peter Berlin*, had its world premiere at the Berlin International Film Festival, a far more prestigious venue than the San Francisco International Lesbian and Gay Film Festival. I ended up traveling all over the United States and Europe with the film in the following months, and yet, as incredible as all that was, I fretted and worried about whether Frameline would accept the film into the San Francisco festival and whether we'd be at the Castro. I wanted my film to come home. Although I'd already made the transformation from audience member to filmmaker, it didn't seem real without walking up the steps to the stage and looking down into the orchestra pit at the Castro Theatre organ, knowing that hundreds of people chattered and rustled before me as I stood blinded by the spotlights.

When it finally did happen, I was too nervous to really notice. A large enthusiastic crowd greeted the film, and although I went up on stage before and after the screening, I remember only the spotlights, shining in my face and making it impossible to see more than two or three rows of seats. Yes, I felt a sense of achievement and relief that I'd made it to the big screen at the Castro Theatre, but I also felt something I hadn't expected—a nostalgia for the days when I would sit with a group of people in the Castro and watch a movie, knowing that what I was seeing wasn't real but pretending it was. Now I knew the amount of work and frustration it took to make a film, saw the numerous imperfections that no one else seemed to notice. I wondered if I could ever sit in the audience and lose myself in a film again. At least that's what I told myself was causing my sad and wistful mood in the face of fulfilling a dream.

There was something else, though. The year before, my partner and I had moved away from San Francisco, an idea that only three years before would have been inconceivable to me. I'd lived in San Francisco longer than I had lived anywhere, had built a life and found friends and work that inspired me, yet by 2003, my partner and I decided the high cost, crowded conditions, and fast pace of urban life had tired us out. We wanted something different. So when the documentary screened at the Castro, we'd been away from San Francisco for a year and a half. In that short time, so much had changed, and even though I had been back several times during that period, each time I returned it seemed the change had accelerated. Friends had moved, favorite stores and restaurants had closed and been replaced.

It was the same city, of course. And it will always have a special place in my heart. Whenever I return, I grapple with the changes and yearn, however foolishly, for the places and people long gone. But when the sky is that intense color of blue that seems to happen only in San Francisco, and when the fog spills over Twin Peaks on a summer afternoon, I can still shake off the useless cobwebs of nostalgia and look for the things that haven't changed and that still embody the San Francisco I have always loved—the enormous rainbow flag flying over Harvey Milk Plaza, the sound of streetcars on Market Street, and the view from Corona Heights, looking down at the impressive, wish-fulfillment palace called the Castro Theatre, welcoming newcomers and dreamers as it always has and hopefully always will.

new jerusalem

carol queen

WILL AND I USED TO CALL San Francisco "New Jerusalem." We were influenced more by William Blake than by anything churchy; stuck in college in Eugene, we fought churchiness tooth and claw, at least its homophobic manifestations. Will had helped organize a statewide gay rights group that traveled from one small town to the next; activists from the cities went to Baker or Roseburg to meet the people who might begin organizing queer support groups there. I went along on the trip to Baker, where two lovers just out of high school had shot themselves the previous summer. This brought secretive queers out of the woodwork like nothing else; we had an all-night party/strategy session in a double-wide on the edge of town that is still the closest I've ever come to joining the Resistance.

Will was about to move to New Jerusalem, while I was to stay on fighting churchy homophobia in the guise of the "No on 51" campaign, Eugene's own Anita Bryant-inspired ballot initiative that sought to overturn the city's new antidiscrimination ordinance. If this sounds at all arcane to you, Grasshopper, put the book down and go Google Anita Bryant. Now.

While Will got to work at the Pacific Center in Berkeley I became (at age twenty) the youngest member of Eugene Citizens for Human Rights. I attended steering committee meetings of a group too diverse to ever agree on anything. We weren't just lesbians and gay men, we were Marxists and businesspeople, too, and we had serious arguments about strategy and representation, not to mention whether the biggest donors would call the shots. One high-priced gay Washington lobbyist type, surely one of the first of his breed of gay suits, came to consult with us and agreed that it might be okay to go door-to-door, introducing Eugene to its homosexuals, but surely no one with an earring or a leather jacket should be allowed to ring a neighbor's bell, nor a dyke with a crew cut.

I had inherited the campus Gay Alliance from Will. I co-directed it with him before he graduated, and that, no doubt, is what gave me my seat on the steering committee—I represented a populous, liberal voting bloc, at least in theory. I also served on the speakers' bureau, which resulted in my coming out to my grandmother via my televised debate with Lynn Green, a young, churchy Stepford mom who supposedly just emigrated to Eugene from San Francisco so her kids wouldn't have to grow up surrounded by homosexuals. (I was always convinced that she had been trained in a special school somewhere and then posted to this battlefront—if not grown in a Petri dish in a lab.) The TV program featuring our debate got rebroadcast to Boise, Idaho, for some reason, where Granny saw it and sent me a card saying, "Well, I guess I don't have to keep waiting on you to get married," and then at Xmas she sent me a big doily she'd crocheted. (Clearly the contemporary gay marriage debate had not sent its distant early warning signals to Granny in Boise, though I had already heard rumbles from some of my fellow Eugene Citizens for Human Rights members: Maybe we'd fight for that next!)

But we lost the referendum, and after that no one had the will to fight for much of anything for a while. Eventually, the ordinance went back on the books, as it became less and less unusual for cities to have laws like it. And my old friends had to rouse themselves to fight homophobes on a statewide level, not once but multiple times, yet another reason it was wise to have held those meetings in small towns. But by the time the Oregon Citizens Alliance had reared its hateful head, I had moved to New Jerusalem myself.

What I needed in the short term was a vacation. And Will, tucked up in an art-fag Hayes Valley flat with his adopted dog, Steve, a scruffy stray he'd invited into his life back in college, invited me down for Pride.

Now, I had been to gay pride marches before. I helped organize them in Eugene, where we accommodated groups as disparate as the local Metropolitan Community Church congregation and Faggots Against Fascism. And I had taken my gay youth group on a field trip to Pride in Portland, Oregon's big city. But I had not been to the big daddy of all pride parades, San Francisco's; nor had I even been to San Francisco as an adult, only a couple of times as a kid, walking the hill down to Fisherman's Wharf with my mom and dad, petting a llama at the zoo, and finally, at about age eleven, scanning for hippies during a quick visit during the Summer of Love.

But ten years later, and with Will as a tour guide, a different city by far spread out before me.

Let me explain first that though I was a dyke, and Will a fag, I was totally in love with him, the kind of love that can exist only between a man and a woman when conversation between them usually goes like this: "The reason straight people are homophobic, Carol, is that we have a sexual orientation, and they don't." Well, if anything, I had too much sexual orientation, but I was still so young that much of it spun out in my mind rather than on the weekends…not that I was inexperienced, mind you; indeed, I had had more sex than almost anyone I knew, with gay men being the glowing exceptions to this general fact. So I idolized them, and Will as my best and most influential friend among them, and I was willing—nay, eager—to let him sweep me through several days of his San Francisco.

Art filled his big Victorian Linden Street flat, or maybe it was Edwardian, I didn't know the difference. I have a photo of him there (so young that my heart hurts to look at it, after all we've all been through since then): He's wearing a lavender sort of doily on his head, laughing, and he had been exploring a somewhat tame but fiercely literate version of graffiti art, a huge panel of which he poses in front of, an outpouring of whatever he came to be thinking of at any given moment. It featured quotes and poetry, snippets of manifesto, and at least one colored-pencil drawing, I seem to recall, of the Golden Gate Bridge, because even the queers who flocked to San Francisco in the 1970s, recognizing it as their Jerusalem, retained a streak of smitten tourist. I know I did, and have never completely lost that feeling of expansive love upon coming into the city by bridge.

Will was all over art in those days, when post-sixties surrealism had begun to merge and mate with punk, a dollop of revolutionary fervor on top. Will went on to edit what I think of as the City's first 'zine. Called *Vortex: A Journal of the New Vision*, it was actually the first place I was published. "Everywhere," said the cover, captioning an exploding house that spewed a nuclear family in all directions, "the old forms are hollow and collapsing structures."

Hanging from the hallway ceiling was a mobile made of matchbook covers, that ubiquitous one from the seventies with John F. Kennedy's picture on it. A dozen JFKs swirled when the front door opened and closed. Right inside Will's front door was NeoBoy, a graffitoed child mannequin snagged from an outdated department-store display. He had all sorts of stuff written on him and was clearly a proto-punk icon.

Speaking of punk, we went to the Mabuhay Garden where I thrilled to Pearl Harbor and the Explosions. Someone that night, maybe Pearl herself, wore lederhosen on stage, which was awesome—to date, I was the only woman I knew who ever wanted to wear lederhosen, though I could never find any that fit—and I managed not to be crushed during the midweek bout of slam-dancing that ensued.

But the first night of my stay—I think we pilgrimaged over to the Mab on the second—we had to do two things. We had to go to Will's friend Murder Boy's art opening. It was in a gallery on Divisadero, I think, and so suitably dark and art-fag and atmospheric that I remember none of it, nor any of the other artists whose work was there. But then we made it to the Castro. Sitting at the Elephant Walk drinking Blue Moons (which glowed in the dark, the effect of blue curacau and tonic water under black light), he explained the Castro's history, working-class Irish to Harvey Milk. He had sucked up San Francisco history as avidly as any immigrant, able to put it all into perspective, especially if that perspective was queer. We didn't know yet what more history the Elephant Walk would see just a few months later, the epicenter of the Castro branch of the White Night riots. Back in Eugene, I paced back and forth all night waiting for Will to call me back with further reports after first calling in to tell me about police cars burning as he threw rocks and bellowed with rage down at City Hall.

We had another reason to visit the heart of New Jerusalem: a John Waters movie was playing at the Castro Theatre. Packed in and clutching my smell-o-rama card, it was the first time I ever heard the Mighty Wurlitzer and saw it rise from the depths. I don't remember if it choked me up then as it does now: Maybe not, since what gets to me today is in part the fact that I saw it then, a queer Castro as yet unsullied by history, unless you counted speed. In fact, just a year later I was there for Pride with my new lover Natalie who had to clutch my hand as hard as she could as we made our way sliding between an absolute wall of men: The Castro was as crammed as any Halloween night you've ever seen, with almost every soul but us a sexed-up gay man in the prime of his life, threatening to part us like river rapids would part swimmers trying to stay together. I realized that day that I had never been in a place full of men where I had no fear and no need for fear: and the Castro may be dandy now, but I mourn the passing of that scrum of testosterone and naked chests. Nothing I have seen since, not even the Eagle on a good day, has been quite like it.

Will and I went to the Haight, too, just because any freaky tourist should see it, but it was in fact insufficiently queer to spend too much time on. My sole true memory of that afternoon (which ended in North Beach, far more memorable) is preserved in my photo collection: me, in a Hawaiian shirt and white navy pants, the kind whose legs bell out like crazy, in wire-rimmed glasses and a lesbo modified-bowl haircut, in front of awesome Haight Street graffiti reading "Witches arise!"—arms raised as though determined to call down the Goddess. Since then, of course, the witches have arisen very thoroughly in San Francisco; I wonder whether one of Starhawk's own buddies wielded the spray can that, let's face it, gave me one more reason to want to split churchy Oregon and move to New Jerusalem.

Will thought I should see some hot San Francisco lesbian action, in spite or because of that dykey haircut, but this proved problematic; he only knew one frisky girl, apparently, to be my guide. He tried to convince me to go with her to the women's bathhouse, a notion which brought out all my innate shyness, even more so because she worked as a stripper, which petrified me completely at the time. I managed to get out of it, instead interviewing her over tea at Will's kitchen table like a little anthropologist, and doubtless confirming any stereotypes he might have held about lesbian courtship rituals. This ranks in my memory as one of the most unsuccessful blind dates ever.

I still wonder who she was. Her name escapes me completely.

North Beach, now: it strikes me that there was far more queer-beat connection in those days, when Ginsberg was alive and plenty of people trolled the streets who might have fucked Neal Cassidy. Or maybe Will and I were just both beatniks at heart; I know I was. Going to City Lights Books was like visiting the Vatican. But Will was just as interested, in fact perhaps more so, in turning me on to Vesuvio, maybe because both of us resonated with its over-the-door sentiment: "We are dying to get the hell out of Portland, Oregon!" We had an afternoon drink there and I took photos of Will and our other Eugene expat friend, Roan Pony D'Arc (rest in peace, Roan: the first AIDS death I ever knew), with my dad's old circa WWII camera. It gave me the most splendid double exposures, maybe inspired by the double allegiance we had to the neighborhood: home of the old Black Cat Club, and the place the Oregon conscientious objectors fled to after getting out of the Waldport C.O. camp as World War II drew to a close. If I understand my queer/beat history correctly, that's what brought Ferlinghetti and the boys south to North Beach.

Roan was the tiniest man I have ever known, as small as me or smaller, and he had been far too big for Eugene, flamboyantly artistic in a way no one else there was. He stenciled ponies everywhere, all along whole city blocks, and called himself Roan Simone Pony until he got inspired (or maybe, who knows, visited) by Jeanne d'Arc and changed his name.

In San Francisco Roan went on SSI, which I gathered was what all the druggie art-fags did to make ends meet. I wonder how much of the queer fabulousness of that fabulously queer decade can be laid at the doorstep of some friendly caseworker down at SSI, giving all the boys the means to live a carte blanche life of artiness. There were men like this everywhere we went, filling up the Stud (on a Saturday afternoon in 1978, the single best dance club I've ever visited, packed like writhing, shirtless fag sardines into the glow of true deejay genius), spending all their time at the baths, developing intricate drag personae (Will's was Kitty Left-overs; Roan did not need one, being a proto-genderfucky godling as it was). These drag personae seemed equally important for drag performers (the impersonators at Finnochio, the culture-jammers of the Cockettes, and the Angels of Light) and everyday art-fags who never really took a stage except, well, the everyday. If you didn't have a drag name, at least, to Will and his friends you were suspicious, a Castro Clone not in touch with his feminine side.

Roan and Will and I went up to Coit Tower. We didn't do any-thing else touristy, really, on this entire visit—not traditionally touristy, anyhow—and I wonder whether the famously dick-shaped structure was my consolation prize for not being able to accompany them to the baths.

Will and I dropped acid. It was my first (and second-to-last) time, because the second time was as whacked-out and distressing as the first time was glorious. We drank jug wine, Almaden or something, and went joyriding around the city as the acid came on. Many, many years later I was shocked to realize that he had taken me driving through the Presidio, where our howls of mind-expanded glee probably woke a few petty officers. (I somehow spaced this part until the next time I drove through those winding streets, at least a dozen years later, and realized I had been there before.)

Nicely toasted, we queued up on Market Street. *The Rocky Horror Picture Show* played at midnight at the Strand, and we were in line, tripping gently, for at least a half an hour, maybe much longer. Will found a bunch of his pals (or maybe made some new ones), and I was accosted by two cute-if-sun-wizened swingers from the Central Valley. They noticed I had a tattoo. Perhaps the biggest difference between then and now, besides being pre- ver-sus post-epidemic, was that not everyone had a tat, especially one that showed; mine, a little red Commie star, peeked out whenever I wore a low-cut top. Later that was how I figured out I was femme—my propensity for cleavage, not the ink.

Successful swingers hitting on dykes know that the woman of the twosome has to be the most forward, at least at first. She cooed and stroked down my breast in the guise of admiring the art. I was petrified. Finally she said, "He has a tattoo, too! Do you want to see it?" I stammered, "Sure," at which he began to take his pants down! I expected something either lewd or super-butch, a tag from a military night gone wrong but there, just below the band of his tighty-whities (he demurely pulled them down just enough for me to peek), was a femmy little rose. From my vantage point today, the swingers would have maybe been a good time. Then, though—still too young to know a nice kinky adventure when it came on to me—I squeaked and fled back to Will's side.

In the Strand the main attraction—the Sweet Transvestite's pansexual seduction, then downfall—was preceded by a Betty Boop cartoon, the one in which she plays Snow White. The acid fully on, I watched it with the dawning, fascinating realization that all the cartoons that had ever been were crypto-drug documents. What else would have inspired a cartoonist to make the Mirror, Mirror on the Wall into a hand mirror that turned inside-out and walked away on its handle, sprouting another leg to speed its ambulation? At least that's what I thought I saw.

And don't get me started about *Rocky Horror*—this was 1978, remember, very early in its cult, and though people were already dressing up like the movie's characters, you could still hear the dialogue back in those days. I had actually seen *The Rocky Horror Picture Show* back when no one shouted back at the screen—yes, that's how old I really am—and one of these days I intend to do a cultural study of its many changes through time. Then, I just gazed at Frank-N-Furter through eyes as big as saucers, still unaware that my future would hold a man who looked just as good in drag as Tim Curry. "Don't dream it, be it"—I wasn't the first, and wasn't the last, little queer for whom that line was as much a prayer as anything a churchy person might intone.

Pride Day arrived, though I do not remember sleeping between our night at the Strand and Stonewall Day's dawning. As a result I remember slightly less of the parade itself than I might, in my historian's heart, wish. We watched it from the sidelines, and I have to say I think it was almost as huge back then as it is today, and every single kind of queer seemed to have a contingent. One of the elements that catches people's imaginations, newcomers to Pride, whether gay or straight or some other flavor, is the way diversity marches past, a kind of diversity you rarely see spelled out, laid out before you—and this was certainly true back then, when the community had already sprung as many facets as a jewel.

So the Golden Gate Business Association, sort of the LGBT chamber of commerce, marched past in droves, everyone holding a sign saying what kind of business they ran and there was everything! Even though most of my money was still with the Marxists at home, this was truly impressive, and helped flesh out what Will had spent several days showing me: that San Francisco had developed queerness into a true (and strong) minority population, with neighborhoods and every kind of cultural and social structure to support people's development, well-being, and safety. In the ensuing years, of course, this development has if anything increased, though you could argue that AIDS decimated some of these social structures, too, and queer integration in San Francisco has continued and affected the need for separatist institutions. But Will and Murder Boy and Roan Pony and everybody else had flocked there specifically because it was safer than anyplace else, a place that made a place for queer folk like no place in the world. It was New Jerusalem, a refuge-cum-24/7 art happening.

And no time more than on Pride Day. After the church congregations, the drag troupes, the disco-thumping floats with hunky men, the few politicians already reading the electoral writing on the wall, Will and I strolled over to the Civic Center. It was not nearly the clusterfuck it is today, with booze booths and barely relevant vendors; it felt more like Sunday in the park, albeit a park full of the most splendid, huge drag queens, many of them with glitter-sprinkled full beards. One sailed by on roller skates. I realized with a thrill that many of them had on more than two wigs. (This was news to me; drag queens were smaller back in Oregon.) There were great thrift shops in the 1970s, and these queens had taken full advantage, decked out and taking up at least four peoples' worth of personal space in their vintage platforms and crinolines.

We passed two hippie drag queens, proto-Radical Faeries really, with their own long hair ratted and their beards glimmering in the sun. One carried a protest sign: "US out of San Francisco!"

Those were the days when that seemed possible. And even today, I think, we are the place in the United States in which the United States has the least firm toehold.

notes on the castro

kirk read

SEPTEMBER 11, 2005: It's been one hell of a week on cable television, what with Hurricane Katrina and all. My new favorite word is *lawlessness*. We will not tolerate lawlessness by hoodlums. I'm completely obsessed with Nancy Grace, the former prosecutor turned anchor on CNN. "I'm Nancy Grace and I am locked and loaded." She's my new Patti Smith. Very vice principal. Asking the tough questions. She never closes her eyes. I think they're glass. As she talks she nips at the camera "Let me get this straight, you mean to tell me" and then at the end she gets all nice nurse: "Our prayers are in the Southeast. Good night, friend."

•

BARBARA BUSH is back on the scene with her fist-sized pearls. She told one reporter at the Astrodome, "Churches are taking people in and giving them a decent, respectable life, putting them to work!"

Something I'm wondering about a lot this week is how sexual culture is developing at the Astrodome and all the other shelters. Where are people masturbating? Do the bathroom stall doors afford enough privacy, or is there a quarter-inch strip of empty space where the door closes? Are they making noise? Are men cruising in the bathrooms? Are single mothers sleeping together for the first time? Are men and women waiting until lights out to fuck under a couple of large blankets? There ought to be provisions for the erotic in the Astrodome. It's as important as eating. It's as crucial as a lost-and-found room for children. I'm not trying to be provocative. I bring this up because I don't think you can understand the Castro unless you're willing to consider the way neighborhoods and communities organize their collective sexual norms. The Astrodome is our newest American neighborhood. And these are people who lived in New Orleans. Which means either they understand pleasure or they at least live in close proximity to some of its various manifestations.

This Castro had its hurricane twenty-two years ago. And it took more than a few days for the government to show up.

The first few years I lived in the Castro, I had sex everywhere I could. I'd find myself in doorways and airwells with men who were individually and collectively welcoming me to the neighborhood by sucking me off with the rapacity of a Shop Vac. With the crevice attachment. They taught me to use the muscles in my throat like five baby hands squeezing. Welcome Wagon: Where I grew up in Virginia, the thing we did instead was make mint jelly, apple butter, and peanut brittle, then take it to new neighbors in a wicker basket lined with a fabric remnant. And no, I'm not making this up to give you some quaint vicarious southern nostalgia. Sexual generosity begins in childhood.

When I first moved here from Virginia, I used to take long

walks through the Castro every day. Earnest, A-student walks. I read up on the history—where Harvey Milk's camera shop was, which protests involved police brutality, how Twin Peaks at the corner of 17th and Castro was the first gay bar with a bare glass storefront. But there's a way in which the culture of the Castro is ethereal and can't be located in the physical realm. This has become more apparent with the advent of the Gap and twenty-four-hour fitness and all the other strip-mall yuppie kudzu. It's first and foremost a community of lovers. With any given partner you're six fucks away from everybody else. I always chase the slutty men in their forties and fifties who survived by some extreme miracle of natural selection. It's a rush to think that the man I was playing with had probably been with someone who'd been with Sylvester and Kevin Spacey (not as thrilling), back to Allen Ginsberg, further back to Walt Whitman. An Army of Lovers and all that. This is less true these days. Monogamy is making a big comeback, and everyone's got a marriage fetish. Whatever.

Being an artist and living in the midst of such affluence forces you to be creative. You're not just inheriting all the mythology of a place, you have to be feisty about how you live.

I found all the clothes I'm wearing on the streets of the Castro. It's the best trash-picking I've ever experienced. Even Manhattan doesn't come close. Too much competition there. You find a beat-up bookshelf on the streets of SoHo and a woman will stab you with the pointy end of her umbrella to clear you away from the area. A well-heeled woman who doesn't even need more furniture. She'll cut you. In the Castro I've found dressers and futons, boxes of books, bags of clothes, dish racks, CDs.

One of the best things I ever found was called an Aqua Vulva. It looked like one of those plastic inflatable bathtub pillows, but it had additional features. Like a tiny raft—you lube it up and go.

•

IT WOULD BE EASY to write a rant about being poor in a gen-
trified quasi-shtetl, how the only way I could really afford to live
here and keep my soul intact is being a hooker and dealing drugs
and doing marketing focus groups and having lots of first dates
and lunches with people who'd buy me a meal. But if I had a
condo and the job that goes with it, I'd be way above going
through free boxes and I would never find the Aqua Vulva.
Which, to me, is the sort of surprise we all came here for, whether
we're in touch with that or not.

When my boyfriend and I started dating, I was just about to go
on a book tour. But not like a tour where you fly back and forth to
twelve cities. This was not a Belle and Sebastian tour. This was a
Bon Jovi tour. A different town every night for months.

Before that, I'd given up my apartment and was going from
house-sit to house-sit. I was walking a friend's dog named Armistead, and my boyfriend Ed and I at that point were on our third
date. We walked down to Dolores Park and passed this couch that
someone had put out. There were clothes all over it. It was the
end of the month, and someone just couldn't deal. We kept walking to the park, then on the way back, Ed saw me eyeing the piles
and said "Do you want to look?" And I said, "Yeah," and immediately we were trying on clothes, sitting on the couch, testing
whether it sagged in the middle. Neither of us had room for a
couch, but when you're a trash-picker to the core of your being,
it's just what you do. Third dates are when things start getting
mentioned. People who want to have children figure out a way to
drop it into conversation just in case it's going to be a dealbreaker.
For us it was that we both trusted the street.

One time we were walking to Castro Tarts, the cheap Viet-
namese breakfast place, and before I left the house I cast a spell
for lamps. I'd just gotten home from a pagan witch camp and I'd
spent the week dancing around bonfires and eating spelt and making altars out of redwood needles and dried mushrooms, so this
did not seem like an odd request. I said, "I need lamps." Ed goes,

"Where do you want to go buy lamps? Community Thrift?" And I said, "No, I'm going to get them free on the street."

Ed is very patient with me. We walked about half a block and these two circuit queens were finishing up a yard sale early. It was only noon, but they were bickering. I saw two perfect metal lamps and said, "How much?" and one of them said "Just take 'em. We're done." And he closed his garage door and I could still hear them full-on screaming. And I thought, *Man, that's what happens when you share a garage.*

My first apartment in San Francisco was a six-by-eight walk-in closet under the stairs in Richard Labonte's flat on Clinton Park at Dolores. I did dishes and other chores, and he let me live there free for a year. His lover, Asa, is a folk artist who turns old Victorian windows into light sculptures. Asa is from Mississippi and dips Copenhagen and had a German shepherd mix named Percival. Again, this is why you move to San Francisco. To meet your future characters.

Richard was the general manager at A Different Light since the early eighties but then the store sold to someone with no book background and they turned Richard loose without a pension and started cutting back everyone's hours. People with AIDS who worked full-time were getting cut back to thirty hours, just enough to kill their health insurance. All of us part-timers were relieved of duty.

•

THIS IS GETTING BITTER, but I'm just being honest. You stay in heaven long enough and you realize how God treats the workers. And then you turn to Satan, which has its own set of problems. It's the tension of magic and commerce. It's an old fight.

May Day of this year I danced around a Maypole with hundreds of other witches in Golden Gate Park. Little kids were coming up to people putting date and fig bars in their mouths and saying, "May you never go hungry." Afterward, Ed and I drove into the Castro to run some errands: Pick up mail, get photos developed, go to the bank, play Ed's Lotto numbers.

I'm walking down 18th Street in a gold-and-magenta peasant skirt and my face is painted with simple red warrior lines which I thought was elegant. We walk past Starbucks, which is where all the HIV-positive bears on disability go for lattes. People are staring at me like I have kicked over a bucket of paint in the galleria, like I'm some sort of blight on their masculine landscape. You know that episode of *The Brady Bunch* where it's girls against boys and they're building a house of cards? Marcia is putting up the last card and her bracelet is dangling perilously close—Marcia's bracelet is about to ruin everything. It was like that. All these guys with protease-inhibitor bellies and tribal tattoos and uniforms courtesy of Abercrombie are looking at me quizzically. Slurping their frappuccinos in brand-new work boots. Cuz blue collar is just drag here.

Ed says he got a weird hunch that he was back in the high-school locker room. I just tune these children out anymore. They park their cars in handicapped spots and go to the gym. Nobody's telling the truth, and I've had it.

The Castro is the land of the dinosaurs. Pharmaceuticals and crystal meth have given way to the new clone. The brontosaurus. Men whose rear ends ache from the kiss of steroid needles. They hug each other like prizefighters, and the mating calls have changed. So many people are supersized, and I'm convinced that all this emphasis on physical enormity is crowding out the possibility for ephemeral magic. Twenty-two years into an epidemic that promised to make us a more spiritual, elevated brotherhood, and we're still dressing up like the fucking Village People. That's disappointing.

I don't really know how much gay laundry I should be doing.

I think the gist of it is we're doing the wrong drugs. I think this neighborhood could really turn a corner if we'd stop doing speed and take up mushrooms instead. Bulldoze Pottery Barn and put up a community garden of free psilocybin mushrooms.

But there's still magic here. We're in the middle of a war and we're sitting and listening to each other. That's a start.

Did you notice how some memos went out this week in the media? *Shhh*, they're not refugees from Hurricane Katrina, they're evacuees. The other memo was that it was time to kick it with the survival stories. Something uplifting. Black people are *happy* to be in Texas.

So on that note, I'll close with hope.

I cohost an open-mic night in the Castro, which is something akin to being a licensed clinical social worker. One of our regulars is Marvin, a sixty-something heavily tattooed nudist who does interpretive dance. He was right in the middle of "Total Eclipse of the Heart." He's buck naked, and his genitals have been vacuum pumped within an inch of their lives and he's dancing from side to side, putting his arms up and down like he's shaking out a rug. In walks Jello Biafra from the Dead Kennedys. When I was thirteen I used to memorize vast stretches of his spoken-word albums, and he is not a concise man. Jello Biafra is the reason I started doing spoken word, and one of the reasons I started writing. Of all the moments for him to walk into my world, this wasn't necessarily the one I would have selected. When Marvin finished his dance, the room was uncomfortably silent. People just didn't know how to receive the information. We've got to be patient and make more room for freaks. They're saving our city. They're saving our lives.

I said to them and I say to you, "When I sing 'Turn Around' you sing 'Bright Eyes.' "

There's still magic here.

Good night, friend.

a brief history
of the blue house

michelle tea

THIS IS A STORY ABOUT 251 14th Street, known far and wide, in legend and myth, gone down, down, down in history forevermore as the Blue House. When I moved into the Blue House I was, um twenty-three and had only just moved into this other flat over on Harrison. A house full of bitches, political ones, the worst. So self-righteous in their attitudes, so smug about the cucumbers submerged in their home-pickling juice in those big, rustic jars with the little cockroaches scuttling over the glass. Despite a lifetime of poverty I had never cohabitated with cockroaches, a point of pride in my family—we were broke, but we weren't gross. It wasn't the cockroaches that drove me out. As you will soon learn, I can roll with the roaches fine if I must. It was Joe-Ellen, my political roommate, telling me in that voice that we

must learn how to exist alongside other species and so that was
why the roaches ran rampant over the smugly home-pickled
pickle jars and elsewhere. Flicking on the lights in the kitchen after sundown was such a terror, the awful leap of the bugs beneath
the sudden glare. Oh, fuck Joe-Ellen. Joe-Ellen, who said I
walked too heavily up the stairs each night as I returned home
from the bar. Who was so intense about her pirate radio broadcast
that my aforementioned footsteps could disturb the recording of,
was so goddamn pleased with the possibility of being arrested for
her pirate radio broadcast, who breathily informed me of what I
should do if the FCC ever came for her, who taped a printout of
the instructions by the door. Joe-Ellen, who scolded me for keeping my bedroom door closed too much, saying that I wasn't allowing my energy to enter the home. But I came home only to mas-
turbate, write in my journal, and wait till I could go over to my
girlfriends' house where everyone was fun and talked shit and
drank 40s. Which was also a problem—I wasn't home enough, either, she said.

  "Well, I'm Working A Lot," I said. "At Forests Forever," I
hastily added, "Saving Headwaters Forest From Pacific Lumber,
Whose CEO Looted The Pension Funds Of The Workers
And…" I launched into my nightly telephone script, but Joe-Ellen
wasn't impressed. "Do You Really Have To Work So Much?" she
challenged. I was saving up to go on a road trip with my girlfriend.
Plus, I was poor. "Yeah, I Do," I snapped. "I'm On GA," she
bragged.

  I gave my notice and found, at the very last minute, a room on
the second floor of 251 14th Street. A shitty little stretch of the
Mission. Run-down homes on one side, shifty late-night carjack-
ing operations in the warehouses across the street. All night long
the car alarms on the stolen vehicles sang. Next door was a crappy
little corner market reselling cigarettes that plainly had *do-not-re-
sell* stamped on the cellophane. Possibly they also ran a lottery
scam of sorts. I got booze there, and those cigarettes, and big or-

ange jugs of Tampico, for nutrition. Farther down the block was a legit auto shop, an old Latino guy who fixed classic cars and kept big, dreadlocked junkyard dogs chained up and barking behind the chain-link. A little laundromat on the corner. That was it. All around us, the Mission roared—the hippies selling produce at tiny Rainbow on 15th, the homeless selling stuff on blankets across the street, drugs another block down by the 16th Street BART hole.

But on our little stretch, nothing. Just the first floor's crack-addicted cousin who would occasionally sit on the steps, obsessively sweeping the crumbs from the cement, an occasional band of teenage boys who would select our ungated stoop at which to drink their bottles. No big whoop, really. It was home for seven years.

When I moved into the Blue House, in 1994, the primary tenant was a quiet straight girl who was obsessed with Aleister Crowley and the Civil War. She had spells in Italian written on her ceiling. She stayed up late watching sci-fi programs in the dark living room, her mean cat nestled into her pajamas. You'd think it was nice that a cat wanted to sit on your lap, but this cat would settle down and when it was time for you to get up and go about your life, it would try to scratch your eyes out. I avoided it. The Crowley girl ate meat, amazing, I didn't know any people who ate meat and naively thought maybe most people had stopped. The other roommate was from another country, maybe Holland, and she did Egyptian belly dancing at a Middle Eastern restaurant and naked pole-dancing at a North Beach strip club. She was straight, too.

The best thing about the Blue House was the Bearded Lady café, located two fast blocks right up the street. The Bearded Lady was the dyke cafe. A trio of very cute butch dykes owned it and served up endless coffee and sandwiches and vegan soups. I lived there. Everyone did. The back patio would be packed with lingerers and loiterers, people who apparently had no jobs, no responsibilities, no ambitions outside wasting away another gloriously sunny San Francisco day sitting at the metal tables, smoking their hand-rolled cigarettes and getting all hopped up on coffee. Some folks brought their pipes and did hippy speedballs, exhaling their moldy smoke up into the fluffy white flowers that hung about the fence that separated the café from someone's backyard, where kids kicked balls around and hollered. Stevie, who ran the Bearded Lady, used to live in the Blue House, too. Amazing. Yeah, she said, it was this big dyke household. Stevie lived there when she was a broke outlaw, and everyone else who lived there were broke dyke outlaws, too, pulling scams to make the insanely cheap rent.

Stevie told me that Liberty lived in my room and put those bolts and metal rings into the floor, to tie her lovers down and fuck them on the hardwood floor. Oh, I said. Wow. Liberty was a sort of famous sex worker, a prostitute, and I saw her in this documentary about all the dyke strippers and prostitutes. There was like a million of them, and there was Liberty, but that was the only time I saw her, on the big screen, though now I lived in her room. Marty, who I had been in love with had lived there, too, crashing in the back room we didn't even rent out now, it was Crowley girl's office, with her computer and more Italian hocus-pocus on the walls. A girl named Scream had lived there—she was a stripper, too—maybe she'd been Marty's girlfriend and they both lived there with Marty's dog that she'd rescued, and they didn't pay any rent cause they didn't have jobs, they just found ways to illegally procure money, and before that they were living down in a van somewhere.

Marty was hot. Her outlaw sheen was totally real, unlike those pirate radio poseur bitches from the other house, and I was glad she had lived in mine. Marty wasn't on GA, either, she was on SSI, which was serious, you had to go to court and convince the judge you were nuts, and Marty and all her friends would take turns going into court and testifying how fucking crazy each other was, to get these piddly checks from the state, which went far when you lived at the Blue House. Lana Little lived there, too, and made a film in the bathroom.

Oh, I should explain the bathroom. There were three. One had a shower, a rusting tin box that was scary to use with the ragged, gangrenous holes in the center. Later, the landlord replaced it with a regular cheap plastic one. That shower room also had a little sink, and that was it. Next door was a water closet, just a toilet, and across the hall was the big, marvelous bathroom where Lana shot her film, a takeoff on the sort of lesbian culture that these girls defiantly were not. It was called *Women Loving Women* and it featured a bunch of granola-esque lesbos getting gangbanged by a crew of ferocious, dildo-wielding SM dykes. It was shot in the big bathroom with the claw-foot tub and the toilet and the sink. Marty's last girlfriend, who perhaps had had a million girlfriends, had also lived there, a radical femme stripper who placed personal ads in the paper looking for butches for her and her radical femme stripper girlfriends to group-fuck in the bathroom at the Stud. Tour updates from Ani DiFranco's mailing list came in the mail for her for years after I lived there, as did calendars from the local SM lesbian organization for Stevie.

Shortly after my arrival, Crowley-girl and the belly-dancer moved out, allowing me to revert the flat to its destiny as a glorified crash pad for fucked up queer girls incapable of living a normal life and paying a normal rent.

First came Jan. A punk girl with bleached, teased hair and bright, synthetic clothing, she was a referral from a friend who had neglected to mention her huge IV drug habit. Her first weekend there, she fucked her best friend's girlfriend in the water closet after shooting them both up with Ecstasy. Ecstasy? Can't you just swallow that? A couple times I worried that Jan might die, like when she called me into her bedroom and said, "Check in on me off and on to make sure that I don't die." "Okay," I said. I wondered if I should ask Jan to leave. I didn't. She cut her hair

like a boy and got rid of the bright clothes, wearing mostly black
jeans and booze-themed T-shirts. Jan was butch under all that
new wave. She switched from shooting up to pounding beers,
with some routine drug binges. Like normal, I thought. After she
quit the needles and all the shadiness that goes with them, we became the best of friends, and one night in her room, both of us
manic-drunk like we got, both of us wanting to get it on with
some girl that wasn't there, I let her cut into my arm with her X-
Acto knife. A little asterisk on my shoulder. She begged me to do
it and I liked it afterward, a little raised tattoo-like thing for me to
run my fingers over. Jan had lots of places like that on her body.

Eleanor was British and sort of muscled her way in. She'd been
crashing platonically in Jan's bed while Chantal lived in the other
room. Chantal was a deejay who moved in with her underage runaway girlfriend. *Hot*, I thought. The girlfriend would tie up the
phone, lying on the couch in the living room all day. *Not so hot*. She
and Chantal would fuck in the shower, leaving behind little
grenade-shaped big mouths of Mickey's. Once again, hot. Eleanor
had a huge fight with her. Not over the girl, or the booze. Over the
Buddhist meditations Chantal was doing in her room. The kind
Tina Turner did. Where you meditate for a car, or more money.
They pissed Eleanor off, and then Eleanor punched a hole
through Chantal's door and Chantal moved out and Eleanor took
her room. She made it beautiful. Sponge-painted red and yellow
with gold paint-pen illustrations because Eleanor was an artist.

Then Wendy moved in. I used to be in love with Wendy, too.
She was tall and skinny, a butch from Texas, and sang in bands, or
she used to, but now she mostly smoked tons of pot like everyone
who lived in that back room, the old office we rented to bring our
rent down. Wendy dated Lana Little, who had outgrown the Blue
House and encouraged Wendy to outgrow it, which manifested as
Wendy poking her head into my room at ten o'clock at night
while I was applying eyeliner for a night out and yelling, bad dad
style, "You need to clean the crumbs off the table, I need to live

with people who have got their shit together!" This from someone who had spent the previous night smoking speed and playing
hangman in the kitchen with Jan.

Jan was wicked smart. She had math equations tattoos and was
vegan. A vegan drug addict. Anyway, Wendy had a bad back, and
she would lie in her bed in tons of pain, expecting us all to take
care of her, but we couldn't take care of ourselves. Like when Jan
was sick for a week and I went out every night getting wasted and
tossing her the errant bottle of Odwalla, and it turned out she had
like strep throat or bronchitis and a fever that could have brain-
damaged her. She didn't hold it against me, though. It's not like
when I had that awful kidney infection and she suggested I lay off
the sauce and quit being such a whore. That's not how we rolled
at 251. I resented Wendy resenting my inability to fix her ramen
and bring it to her in her bed where her mangy cats had peed and
she was in too much pain to change the sheets. The whole scene
was too grim. Eleanor would soon drive her out with her psy-
chotic mood swings and love of picking fights. An evening of
Eleanor banging her head against the living-room-door jamb as I
attempted to write the great gay American novel was enough to
make me want to move out, if I thought I could survive outside
the Blue House, which I doubted.

After Wendy was Lou, who thought the Blue House would be
a great place to get sober. I can barely address this folly. Lou
would lie on the couch watching PBS all night while me and Jan
were out sucking down cocktails. We would return and she would
look at us and sadly talk about how crazy her life used to be, how
wild and drunken, and how she'd flirted with death and whatnot.
Now she had an environmental disorder that required visits to
herbalists in Chinatown who sold her a great mass of herbs and
other things, like the casing of certain beetles, of which she would
make a great stinking tea, the steam hanging malevolently in the
kitchen among the roaches Jan wouldn't let us kill because she was
vegan and loved all life. But at least Jan, unlike Joe-Ellen, made it

fun. She painted their backs with blobs of glow-in-the-dark paint, so when you walked into a darkened room, you saw them first.

Lou had been a vegetarian, but her herbalist had told her that her body needed meat, and so she kept a little altar with paper images of cows and pigs and chickens on it, so she could give them proper thanks for offering their lives to her own. I had mixed thoughts about this like, 'did she think the animals felt better about their slaughter just because she made some barnyard paper dolls and propped them up on a box?' but more than anything I didn't like to judge, so I left Lou to her animal worship and her other, more exciting back-room activity, channeling.

Lou channeled and was working on past-life stuff. She channeled the archangel Michael, who had answered her question "What is the meaning of life?" with a number, delighting Jan, the mathematician, and also myself. I'd stolen Crowley girl's Crowley book before she'd left, and had moved on to a bunch of books about the kabbalah, and it sounded cosmically correct that the meaning of life was a number. Lou, a Taurus, eventually could no longer deal with the utter grossness of the house, and moved out.

She was replaced by Tanya, another Taurus who would not be able to deal with the utter grossness of the house. The house was really, really gross. Bookshelves were thick with dusty books belonging to people none of us had ever known to live there. There were the roaches. A damp towel under the leaking sink in the shower room had sprouted an otherworldly fungus that looked like conical lasagna noodles. Jan adored them. She tried to identify them with the help of several fungus picture books but came up blank. Perhaps we had nurtured a new sort of fungus into existence. I finally threw it into the trash, then tied up the trash and threw it off the back stairs. It was so exhausting, walking it down to the "yard." Alas, I missed the trash can and the bag exploded on impact, releasing the fungal spores into the atmosphere.

I had had the briefest of affairs with Tanya when she was visiting San Francisco during Pride. She was so cute with her mohawk and her turned-up nose and exotic accent. I fondly remember her tying me up with rope she'd purchased especially for that purpose. Then she went off to Reno, sent me a postcard, and when she returned, I didn't want to sleep with her again. I felt tied down very easily, generally, if someone wanted to fuck me a second time. I felt suffocated, no matter the ardor with which I may have pursued that initial fuck. So after getting that postcard I was like, whoa, I'm a free agent here, and Tanya went back to London, only to return again as the back office's low-low-rent occupant.

Poor Tanya. She had arrived here during Pride and thought the city was like that all the time. She always wanted to go out, but I was writing more now, and doing most of my drinking at poetry events, which bored the shit out of her. And so Tanya fell into a depression. She got medication for it, and then she fell asleep. All the time, everywhere. She would come home from her job at the Humane Society, snuggle down on the living-room floor with all the animals she kept bringing home despite me and Jan saying no to every one of them. With her dogs and cats and frogs, she would pass into a narcotic slumber on the floor.

Poor Tanya also wanted a clean house. After what we'd been through with prior roommates, Jan and I made it a point to tell potential inhabitants that we didn't clean, ever, and we didn't believe in chore wheels, and we didn't have house meetings. If you could handle it, our tough, mocking tones suggested, you could live here. Everyone, no matter what their better judgment told them, wanted to give it a try. Because it was so cheap. "Would it be okay if I cleaned?" Tanya asked hesitantly. "None of you would have to. I'd do it myself." I thought it was cute that Tanya thought our reluctance to clean was borne of a hatred of cleanliness, rather than a side effect of alcoholism and deep laziness. I also thought it was cute that she would take on cleaning the Blue House like it was her own little art project.

The Blue House was so toxically filthy it had recently almost killed Jan and me. We both got staph infections in our noses. A regular nose picker, I thought the thin scab of staph up inside my nose was just an especially dry booger. Jan thought the same about hers. We had just returned from a poetry festival in New Mexico, which dries your boogers out so bad the scuzzy hotel we'd stayed at had a row of dry boogers stuck to the headboard by the last guest. Really, the Southwest was famous for dry boogers. Weeks later and the scab/booger situation was starting to creep me out. One of us went to the doctor, Jan with her medical insurance she got from her office job at SF General, then me with my sliding scale status at the local clinic. The scale slid all the way down to free for me. A staph infection, living up our noses. We figured it happened when Jan was wrestling with her boyfriend in the kitchen. The area around the trash can was especially thick with grime, a tacky mat of organic mess stuck heavily to the stone floor. Jan's boyfriend, a handsome boor named Franklin, shoved her face into it and held it there. It's not what it sounds like. It wasn't, like, abusive. Jan loved nothing more than to instigate impromptu Fight Club-style activities; her love for Franklin no doubt bloomed in the face of his violence. They kicked the shit out of each other, drunk, on the scuzzy kitchen floor, and Jan's face went into the diseased muck and we both somehow got the infections up our nose. Probably sharing cocaine dollars or something.

Tanya cleaned up a little and we swiftly trashed it back to normal. This cycle repeated a bit until the resentment in the house was palpable. Tanya snuck yet more feral cats into the house, and then her dog chewed up my wings, you know, those real-feather wings that you wore like a backpack that were so magical in the nineties. Those wings were a splurge. Sweet Javiar the deejay that worked at the shop that sold them let me have them for cost. Now there were feathers hanging from the pit mix's square jaw.

Tanya left. But before she left, she transformed the big bathroom. She painted the walls red and the trim a gleaming gold and installed a real-candle candelabra to hang from the ceiling. Who knows what Tanya could have done if we wouldn't have blocked her. Perhaps we were against the concept of cleanliness, generally. If we allowed standards, we'd have to uphold them. I for one couldn't handle the pressure.

The next roommate was Becky, also from Texas. Becky's parents paid her obscenely cheap rent. She wasn't the last roommate to have the parents footing the bill, and it always pissed me off, no matter how much I liked the roommate, and I loved Becky. But it triggered all my class issues to live with someone whose parents weren't abusive to them. Okay, that's not true, Jan's parents were nice to her but they didn't pay her goddamn rent. My parents could barely pay their own rent. As broke as I was, I never missed a rent payment, though our phone got shut off regularly. But back to Becky. She had a little cat whose name was "pussy" in Croatian. Becky was into techno and wanted to be a deejay. She had twin turntables and a drug problem. At first we thought she had a manageable, fun drug problem like everyone else. Then Jan found syringes in her room. They were stuck in her Tampax box, and Jan was scavenging for plugs and found them. *Fuck.* Jan wanted to maybe kick her out, which was rich considering her own past as the resident junkie. We confronted her, and Becky, so cute with her tomboy spiky highlighted pixie cut, said they were a friend's, and like so many suburban mothers we believed her 'cause it was easier than the alternative. I would come home from wherever and Becky would be stretched out on the couch, passed out, a cigarette in her hand and an ashtray balanced on her belly. *Becky?!* She'd start, knocking ashes onto her Diesel jeans. Becky was on heroin, but when she told me she was on pills, I believed her. I didn't know from heroin, I only knew she was high. And getting mean. And really, really messy. Me and Jan didn't realize we had any standards until Becky wrecked them. I tried leaving friendly notes by the towers of filthy dishes lolling on the kitchen table. *Wash Me.* Or, I thought, at least leave them in the sink. Becky flipped out, she hated the note. So I threw all her dirty dishes into the bathtub. I don't know who I was punishing with this. They stayed there forever, and then I emptied the cat box into the tub, to clean it, and that didn't work, so the tub was clogged with litter and that was the last time I saw it. Anyway.

One night Becky came into the living room holding mirrors around her head so she could see the tiny police officers that were busting her. They were flashing red. She made Jan and her girl-friend get up and look under the couch cushions, checking for miniature flashing red narcs. The Blue House has historically been a tolerant and accommodating place for people bottoming out on drugs. That was Becky's real break. She wound up locked in a closet in a hotel room in the Tenderloin, and then her parents came from Texas and took her to rehab.

Who am I forgetting? The people who crashed for free, like the runaway from Washington state, fifteen years old with the stinkiest feet I ever smelled, who I let stay in my room. The sub-letter I slept with, ruining our burgeoning friendship. The two shameful trust-fund stoner girls who stayed in the back. Noreen also stayed in the back room but then she was a roommate. A pretty great roommate, really, though she too illuminated the ex-istence of housecleaning boundaries I didn't know I had. I mean, ashing your cigarette on the kitchen floor? There are overflowing ashtrays for that, or grab one of the many empty booze bottles rolling around with butts clotted at the bottom.

Noreen moved her girlfriend in, and she was a person who liked to live in a clean house. Jan had left, and I was a relic from another time, a time of glorious entropy, when nature's devolu-tion into chaos had been revered. Noreen's girl, Moira, snapped on rubber gloves and cleaned with a vengeance. And Doreen, a new and depressed girl living in the back office room, smoking lots of pot and painting the walls black, she liked the place clean, too. Passive Noreen went along with the new guard, and one day I came home to find the living room painted a hideous, mental-hospital shade of pale, bile-y green. It was leftover institutional paint. It had to be. And our living room had been so wonderful. Some girls had shot a movie in our house, they'd paid our rent for the month to have it, and painted the living room a fabulous bright purple, with mango trim. I loved it. "I think I died in a room like this," Doreen said darkly. And they all painted it, without even asking me how I felt about it. I knew my reign had come to an end. It was time to find a new place to live, real-world rent to pay.

I moved out. But the girls kept moving in. Tracy, from Olympia, who continued with the cleaning, and when I returned to shoot a music video in the big bathroom, I was shocked at how great the place looked. I could have lived in such a cute place, I thought, too late. Another girl from Olympia lived there, and Merry, who was a singer, and Melissa, who took great pictures and was so super-hot with her big-haired mohawk and thrifted finery, drinking beer all day and taking pills to clean the house. Veronica, femmy and sexy and always making out with people in public.

It was Veronica who sent out the e-mail when the Blue House got sold. Everyone was evicted. The last roommates had gathered everything that had been left behind by more than a decade of roommates and piled it all in a room. If you have ever lived in the Blue House, come and get your stuff, it said. There was a giant mound of abandoned belongings and my birth certificate, apparently, was sitting on top of it all. I remembered, vaguely, shoving a giant box of papers and other shit into the water closet and shutting the door. This was after the toilet there started its mucky brown leak and we stopped using it to pee in, and used it instead for "storage."

I haven't even got to the parties, like my last one there where I truth-or-dared a girl to put leftover rice in her ass crack and dared someone else to pour soy sauce on it and eat it out. I haven't got to the ghosts, the nightmares I had all the time, how terrible the long hallway felt in the middle of the night, the feeling that someone was behind you in the stairwell, the shadow Moira saw moving

into rooms, how thick the big bathroom would feel with something that felt like evil. I didn't get to how I would throw all my
dirty clothes out my window to the street below and then lug them
over to the laundry. I didn't get to that time I found a cockroach in
my hair as I was falling asleep. I didn't get to Cort, our landlord,
who lived downstairs and sang sad songs on his personal karaoke
machine, how his heartbreaking warble would drift up to our flat
and kill us. There's so much I didn't get to, and so much that will
never be gotten to, because that house, on the dumpiest street of
the Mission, just sold for six hundred thousand dollars, and whoever moves in will never know everything that happened under
their very own roof.

the hothouse

charles q. forester

IT WAS A TIME OF EXUBERANCE. Part of an entire generation of gay men coming out, I was thrilled to hold hands in public.
We were discovering Eastern religions and organic food, and
were no longer embarrassed by how we threw a baseball. We were
shucking tradition and becoming the people we never dared
dream of becoming and eager to meet a thousand men who were
eager to meet us. Amazed that hundreds, possibly thousands, of
wholesome, good-looking men sucked dick.

    With everyone in America experimenting with sex and drugs,
smoking dope and taking LSD were my drugs of choice with
MDMA (today's Ecstasy), quaaludes, and psilocybin mushrooms
easy to come by. I didn't take drugs to sidestep reality; I wanted it
altered and trimmed with rainbows, and in those days rolling
joints was proper etiquette at dinner parties.

Sex was the new democracy, our shared language and the community's chief form of bonding. I had few friends I hadn't slept with, and sex was fast becoming the favorite indoor sport for men like me.

It was a time of optimism. We were men who grew up fearing for our lives if we'd been exposed. We had known ostracism and abuse, but in San Francisco all that disappeared and we were freed from old restraints. Our joy was unbounded. We did not have a president destroying the nation, the economic base was stable, and no pandemic of deadly proportions had reared its head. We had been set free, nothing went wrong, and we were loving it. The only worrisome diseases, gonorrhea and syphilis, were easily treated, and a trip to the VD clinic might get you a date. For those of us who had been involved in the Vietnam anti-war movement and civil-rights movements, sexual liberation was the next frontier. We were evangelists of openness, believing that lowering inhibitions would make the world a better place.

In a time when walking to the corner store might get you a blowjob upstairs from someone sitting on his stoop, the bathhouse was uniquely suited to the times. No longer simple saunas, San Francisco bathhouses were designed for gay men, safe spaces entirely ours. If ever there was a treehouse that barred girls and parents, this was it.

Going to the baths replaced joining tennis and country clubs. By the mid-seventies there were close to twenty bathhouses in San Francisco, most clustered South of Market with one in the Mission. Ritch Street Baths featured a large hot pool, tanks of tropical fish, a steam room maze and café. My memories are of clean white tile, men in towels, and a sex-positive staff. This idea of a clean well-lighted place for sex was a revolution; in them you could fuck yourself silly, gossip over granola and yoghurt, or cuddle in a carpeted video theater. Sex no longer meant lurking at truck stops; it was clean, healthy, and plentiful. The Club Baths at 8th and Howard was newer and bigger, but I stopped going when the man in front of me in line was refused admittance. Was he too ugly, too fat, a minority? I don't remember but sex for me was about inclusion and fun, not discrimination. For a community that had grown up as outcasts, that kind of discrimination was incredibly hypocritical.

Some baths served a rougher crowd. The places were dark, one a health hazard. My favorite had a floor without music, just the sounds of men having sex. It was a South of Market SRO hotel that had been converted into The Hothouse as a venue strictly for sex and your imagination, no hot tub and no steam room. On entering, you checked your clothes in lockers separated from the main room only by a chain-link fence. You had no secrets; you were part of the show. A maze hulked in one corner, and a massive hammock made from tires and chain dominated the room. Upholstered couches and armchairs on Oriental carpets offered a place to sit. Rooms on the second floor were beige and music was piped in. The third floor, painted black, was silent, the only lighting the neon green exit signs in the hallways. It was a scene set for serious sex and exhibitionism; two rooms had chain-link doors for those who wanted to be seen but not touched. Several had slings. It was a place of abandon, a place to be with other men. But it was also becoming a place for men on speed, casting shadows on my pleasure.

•

ONE EVENING AT THE HOTHOUSE stands out as quintessential San Francisco, with rain coming down so hard the windshield wipers on Michael's truck couldn't keep up as we headed South of Market. We'd brought sushi for dinner, and when Michael went into the shower to mix the wasabi, a kid swabbing the room asked what it was. When Michael joked, "some new drug," the kid probably believed him and tried all night to track down a hit.

Our favorite rooms were on the building's interior light well. If we were lucky, men in the room across from ours had not closed the shades, providing us with a private show. Or you'd invite them to come over. One room featured a changing collection of apparatus, like a pelvic-exam table, a parachute harness suspended in one corner, or a Saint Andrew's cross. The most sought-after fantasy room was in a corner with a round bay window. The glass in the windows had been replaced with strips of mirror. There was a sling in the middle of the bay. In it you could see your ass from forty-odd angles, none of them bad. Another mirror hung overhead.

With the room always reserved on weekends, I played in it only once, a Tuesday when things were slow. The man in the room was a big guy still wearing dress pants. I never asked but wanted to believe he was a closeted husband from Modesto or an accountant from Milwaukee in town for a conference. As I passed the door, he nodded and gestured toward the sling. I nodded back, came in, and closed the door. I climbed into the sling. I had never seen my crotch from so many angles. It was all there and all quite ready.

In another circumstance I would have not been attracted to this man, but there was something so weird and unexplained that it turned me on. I doubt that we exchanged more than five words. He slipped on gloves and we went at it. His face was impassive, but his eyes were alive; the man knew what he was doing, and he knew he was good at it. After almost an hour of pleasure, I smiled and said thank you. I never asked his name; the episode was one-of-a-kind and oddly exciting. It was best kept as memory.

Michael and I ate our sushi, dropped some windowpane, and rested before we began to play. Michael was the finest man I have known, my perfect partner. A handsome man with curly black hair, a ready smile, and a loping gait. We met when he was a bartender at Toad Hall, one of the busiest bars on Castro Street. When we played at the Hothouse that night, he had just started a landscape business that would soon grow into one that was re-spected and popular with the ladies who lunch from Piedmont and Pacific Heights.

Michael was a child of gay liberation, working on the earliest community projects—a cheerleader for the first softball team and in the court of the third Empress. He was a sexual athlete, with his high-school years spent in tearooms at the Pier in Long Beach. Everyone who met Michael liked him; he was an easy guy to be around. And everyone remembered him. In Europe, strangers would approach us and recall talking with him at Toad Hall.

As a cook Michael had no equal. He was an adventurer with exquisite taste and a sophisticated nose. Every dinner excited my tongue, and his food looked as fabulous on the plate as it tasted. Most important for us, Michael wanted a home, and together we created a gracious one where friends felt comfortable. Michael had no artifice; what you saw was what you got, and part of him believed that his role in life was taking care of his partner. Even as he was dying, Michael worried about me. On his last night, our dear friend Rochelle suggested that I leave the room so that he could die without worrying about me. From him, I came to know the meaning of unconditional love.

That night at the Hothouse our sex was strenuous and generous. Michael was vital and moved seductively, his simple gestures always true. With both of us Pisces, we intuitively knew what the other was thinking and responded with a touch, a kiss, the roughness of feet. We were top and bottom, lover and child, strong and giving. We loved being naked and making out, his kisses formidable.

When we went to the baths, we played together and with oth-ers, sometimes singly. We saved our lovemaking until we'd come home. Our bed was sacred.

After playing that night, we had rested, then gone our separate ways. Michael was likely playing in the glory holes, and I was walking the halls. An incredibly handsome man walked past on one of my circuits. If only....Later we found ourselves standing against a wall at the end of the hall. I was surprised he didn't walk away when I stopped.

There he was in front of me, an intelligent being with freckles and red-blond hair, a man more beautiful than any UnderGear model because his eyes knew the world was both joyous and sad. At that moment, the most attractive man on the planet was standing next to me, not looking at me but not looking away. I was really stoned and knew surfaces were overly important to me, but I was certain this man had substance as well as good looks, his head that of a Greek god, his body strong. There I was, trying not to stare and trying to figure out what had I done to deserve such amazing grace right there, not looking at me but not looking away. I picked up an empty paper cup on the shelf behind me, miming indifference, certain of rejection if I said a word.

"Are you here with your partner?" he asked. He knew me! In the bruising world of recreational sex, it's best to learn your place, your sexual strata, the best place to fish. At least those who succeed know these things, and I knew I was not in his league. How could he possibly know me? Was I that stoned? Was I that jaded? If I'd not been so excited, I might have stopped to consider my failings. I did not.

I invited him back to our room. He said he'd cut off his ponytail and spent some time at the gym since we'd seen him a year ago. Through the haze, memories finally emerged of that evening at the Hothouse and the many perversions we had shared. The three of us celebrated with an uncommonly hot reunion fuck. I lay back and held him in my arms. Michael went down on him, and then we switched positions with Michael holding him. I pleasured as much of his body as I could reach with my mouth and hands, hopefully touching his spirit. Memories of both encounters with him remain warm and almost as strong as my embarrassment.

What I remember of the rest of the evening is sitting on couches in the main room, probably drinking a Dr Pepper. Two men were jostling in the tire/chain hammock. The hammock was eight feet square and these two were using all of it, slipping into the tires and pushing each other to the edge. The play of athletes, testing their bodies and balance, finding each other's limit, showing off and then rocking, wrapped together as the hammock swayed. One was in his forties, with a muscular body and a flash of silver at the temples; the other was young, lithe, and playful. They wrestled lovingly but hard. How lucky to be witnessing them holding and twisting, almost falling and being raised up. They were tender and grinning, aggressive and receptive. As yellow pin spots lit their bodies moving through the smoke of the room, I was returned to Sparta with heroes coming through the mist, men of another culture to inspire ours. If this was the coming of the age of gay men in San Francisco, I would be content with our future.

Going to the Hothouse was like playing on the jungle gym at the Franklin School as a kid; mine had no equipment. Michael and I had climbed around each other, tested our balance and used most of the muscles in our bodies, and played with a gorgeous man. We came home happy. Back in our flat, Michael and I fell into each other's arms. We made sloppy, tender, and passionate love, soaped each other down in the shower, and fell asleep, exhausted and complete. I loved him so much.

first days

k. m. soehnlein

WHEN I ARRIVED IN SAN FRANCISCO, I had, in the years just past, lived through a violent mugging, an attack by gay bashers, the rapid death of my mother from cancer, a messy breakup with a long-term boyfriend, a new relationship full of moody storms, two lonely semesters of graduate school in Tucson (as close to "living in the middle of nowhere" as I'd ever experienced), a root canal botched so thoroughly by a dental student that I was forced to pay several thousand dollars to a reputable, actual dentist to fix the damage, and an aggressive case of venereal warts that had shocked me into temporary celibacy. I felt as though I had endured more than my share, and also that I still had so much to learn. I was wary and hungry, all at once.

I wanted to be a writer; that's why I had come to San Francisco, for a creative writing program. My previous attempt at earning a degree, in Tucson, was clouded by a sadistic workshop instructor, who sat at the front of the room in dark glasses, dangling my story between her fingers like a soiled rag, provoking the class with, "What are we going to do about this?" Offsetting her cruelty was the news that a literary journal wanted to publish one of the first stories I'd written, a story about a guy much like me breaking up with a guy much like my ex, against the backdrop of a mother dying from cancer. I had stories I was ready to tell, and I wanted to tell them well. And so, hungry and wary, I was trying again.

When I arrived in San Francisco, I was twenty-seven. I didn't know if that was young or old.

•

AUGUST 1993. I was subletting in the middle of the Castro. On my first morning, I walked across the street and signed up at the Market Street Gym.

The trainer at the desk flirted with me. In the small back room where the stretching mats were laid out, a guy folding himself into crunches looked into the mirror we both faced and locked his eyes on mine. As I sweated my way along rows of metal machinery, I was amazed to realize that two hunky guys, working out together, were both glancing my way.

Working out was something I'd once disdained as only for the shallow, but in Tucson, gym membership had been part of my university tuition. Battered by criticism, far away from home, I took solace in focused exertion. My body was quick to respond, as if I had tapped an underground well and was suddenly oil-rich. I tore the sleeves off my shirts and flexed my freckled arms in the sun.

Now here I was in San Francisco, getting attention for this rebuilt body. I didn't know if that made me shallow, but I understood that I would be fresh meat only for a limited time. To be noticed but unknown is the privilege of the urban newcomer.

I concentrated on the two hunks. One was tall and brown, wearing shiny sweatpants; the other was about my height, pale and wearing the briefest of shorts. They looked like a set of salt and pepper shakers. I played the stare-and-look-away game while they whispered to each other.

At last the shorter one nodded gravely. I ventured a hello, offered my name.

"Rolando," he said, his Spanish accent thick, the *r* rolling like a melting ice cube between his pouty lips. Rolando's circular pecs, stretching a yellow ribbed tank top, beckoned like two buttercream-frosted cakes. His waist was minuscule. When I stepped close to shake his hand, he blinked elliptical feline eyes at me. He smelled of sex. "I have not seen jew," he said.

"I just started working out here."

"You been working out before," Rolando said.

The taller one stepped up. His boyish face was shadowed by the brim of a baseball cap, beneath which black eyes, wet and still as a cartoon puppy's, appraised me. From the neck up he looked sixteen, but he had a man's body—broad back, long limbs, epic shoulders. He introduced himself as "Oscar," his accent a mellower version of his friend's. "You just joined this gym?"

"Yeah. But also, I just moved to San Francisco."

"When you come here?" Rolando asked.

"Yesterday."

A meaningful glance passed between them. I wondered if they were more than workout partners. They communicated with the silent code of a long-term couple.

At the end of the workout, standing outside, I saw Oscar exiting the gym with no sign of Rolando, and I called to him. Hit by the afternoon sun, he was sturdy and shiny as bronze. I asked where he was going. He said he lived in Diamond Heights, indicating somewhere above the Castro. "It's my friend's place," he said. "Not Rolando, a rich friend."

"Is Rolando your boyfriend?"

"No. We're from the same city in Colombia."

I told him I'd love to visit South America. "It's not so good," he said, pressing his lips together and changing the subject. "Where did you move from?" When I told him, he replied, "I'm going to move to New York next." I waited for him to finish with "month" or "year," but it was just an indeterminate "next."

"I'll tell you everything I know," I offered. He returned me the first smile I'd seen on him so far; I forged ahead. "I'm subletting, right over there." I pointed across the street to a massive three-sided cement building coated in chipped, dingy paint. Its details lent it the feel of a neglected palazzo: decorative pillars and faux balconies, shutters painted brown, a turret capping the sharp-angled intersection of 16th and Market.

I dropped my voice flirtatiously. "Can't get much closer."

He didn't take the bait. He was heading home to change his clothes, he said, then turning around to go to work. But just as I was saying a resigned farewell, he added, "I finish at ten. You can meet me after if you want."

He named a Mexican restaurant on 17th Street, a couple of blocks from this spot. Spitting distance. The half-smile Oscar flashed as he departed was encouraging. "See you later," I called after him, taking care to not let my voice ring too brightly, too eager. It seemed I had my first date in San Francisco.

•

MY SUBLET WAS SMALLER than a studio apartment. One room plus a bathroom, no kitchen save a hotplate and a dish rack that drained into the tub. It belonged to an acquaintance named Jan, whom I'd known since my time in New York. Back then, Jan sported scholarly glasses and let his prematurely thinning hair grow unfashionably to his shoulders. Once in San Francisco, he shaved his scalp, bulked up his frame, and began running an escort ad in the *Bay Area Reporter* featuring his photo under an all-caps headline: THE TOP. One wall of Jan's apartment was lined with portfolio drawers that held mockups of his 'zine —stories about his sexploits and clip-art collages that championed his life as a "pro-sex sex pro."

I had his room for the month he was out of town, at a hundred dollars a week. It seemed as good a place as anywhere to begin reinventing myself.

I had arrived with a couple of suitcases. Everything else was in storage, including my Smith Corona word processor, a machine that allowed me the luxury of eight lines of correctable text memory. I'd rung the bell for the building manager; it rang and rang with no answer. At last someone exited, a woman in a shapeless coat, her head down. I grabbed the door before it swung shut. "Hey!" she barked, pointing to a sign next to the buzzer that I'd already seen: DO NOT ENTER THE BUILDING UNLESS LET IN BY A RESIDENT. I pleaded my case. "Second floor," she grumbled.

The elevator never arrived, so I carried my bags up a flight of stairs covered in trampled carpeting. Down a long hallway and around a corner, I found the manager's apartment, knocked, waited again.

The door swung open suddenly. A wraith of a man stood before me, his haggard face scrutinizing. His age might have been anywhere from forty to sixty. He was lit from behind, so it took a moment to see that his flaccid mohawk was tinted electric blue. "Hi. I'm staying in Jan's apartment? You're supposed to give me a key?" He waved me into a second room, where another man was zoned out on an unmade bed, flipping indiscriminately through cable TV. He was the mirror image of the first, except his mohawk was pink. The room blurred with smoke that smelled of tobacco and something else, more acrid and chemical. From somewhere, unidentifiable, dirgelike music played.

In Manhattan, where I'd lived prior to Tucson, my building manager had been a Puerto Rican with the unlikely name of

Washington who was extremely helpful until noon, when he began drinking and quickly became useless. This seemed like a Castro version of the same phenomenon. Which is simply to say that
I skipped all my questions—like, Where do I put the garbage?
And, are you aware that the intercom doesn't work?—and simply
took the key. I was pretty sure they'd forget all about me as soon
as I was gone.

•

I WORE A FLANNEL SHIRT, the sleeves ripped off, under a
zip-up jacket, and loose, faded jeans in the grungy style of the day.
The fog had moved in, and the night sky was shaded pewter and
dotted with moisture. The air held the smell of sea salt. I left the
building at nine-fifty-five to meet Oscar at ten, and I still got
there early.

The restaurant, Don Jose's Cantina, was at the corner of a
tree-lined alley. A CLOSED sign swung in the window. I spotted
Oscar, wearing a white taqueria smock and a different baseball cap
from the one he'd worn that morning, covering the remains of an
industrial-sized tub of salsa. I rapped my knuckles on the glass.
During the moment it took him to register my presence, I held
my breath, wondering if he'd forgotten me, or worse, just hadn't
counted on me showing. He unlocked the door.

"I found it," I said, meaning the restaurant, trying to be funny
because it would have been nearly impossible not to find it.

The joke didn't register. Oscar said, "I'm still cleaning up," and
headed into the kitchen.

That's when I noticed the willowy fellow leaning against the
Plexiglas shield that protected the food line. I figured he was a
customer, but he turned an eye on me as if taking in a rival. "How
do you know Oscar?" he asked.

"We just met today," I said, "at the gym." From the gentle turn
of his lips I figured he'd witnessed a string of Oscar's gym tricks at

Don Jose's after hours. If so, the good news was that I'd likely get laid tonight; the bad news was that in this equation, I wasn't anyone special. "I just moved to San Francisco."

"What's your plan?" he asked.

"Whatever Oscar wants," I said.

He laughed magisterially. "I meant a plan for living in San Francisco, honey."

"Oh! I'm working on a master's in creative writing."

"Really?" His voice warmed with genuine curiosity, so I told him about leaving New York for grad school, how when I'd told a friend of mine that I was moving to San Francisco he'd dubbed it "the elephant graveyard." I was instantly sorry I'd used the metaphor; this guy was several years older than me—who knew what death he'd seen? But he laughed, a wicked, smoky cackle, and said, "That's good." He introduced himself as Richard.

Oscar returned, his smock replaced by a sweat jacket. On the sidewalk, I stood by while Oscar and Richard gossiped about a mutual friend who had a lead on a job at a restaurant where Oscar wanted to work. Richard related anecdotes about the place in a theatrical, queeny manner: male pronouns substituted with female, problems referred to as "drama," doubts dubbed "issues." His storytelling voice had a performer's cadence, an assertive upswing for the subject of every sentence, a dropped, nearly hushed delivery for the object. I saw that he wasn't treating me as a rival but as a member of his exclusive audience.

He finished by asking, "Do you want to get stoned?"

"Richard lives across the street," Oscar said, indicating a three-story house, pale blue with white trim.

"Definitely," I said. I had wondered how easy it would be to find pot in San Francisco. I needn't have worried.

The house was what I'd later identify as Edwardian, with fewer gingerbread curlicues than the older Victorians but with the same wood siding and elaborate windows. This house had been renovated; a granite staircase with cement walls on either side rose from the sidewalk to a door that featured an art deco stained-glass window. "You know who used to live here?" Richard asked. "Anne Rice."

"I thought she lived in New Orleans," I said.

"She lived here when she wrote *Interview with the Vampire*. I'm told she wrote the whole thing at Café Flore." He pointed back toward Market Street and added, "Longhand."

The only longhand writing I did was in my journal, which on inspired days drew out anecdotes and images that might wind up in my stories. An entire novel in longhand seemed impossible. Hell, any novel at all seemed impossible. And yet that was my intention, in San Francisco, to write a novel. I would be taking notes about tonight, for sure. If I got lucky, I'd be taking them in the morning.

We climbed to the second floor. Richard's room was a narrow chamber at the front of the house, above the stairwell. Like all small, dark rooms, it had a childlike quality; its scale evoked secret hiding places, tree houses, wardrobes. He'd built a loft: mattress on top, sofa beneath. The ancient wallpaper, a busy pattern with gold leaf mostly rubbed off, was adorned with dozens of vintage album covers. Chanteuses like Peggy Lee and Julie London gazed down in soft focus, a portrait gallery of patron saints. I marveled at the collection.

Oscar said, "I don't know these ladies."

"Julie London was on a seventies TV show called *Emergency*," I said.

"We didn't have that show in Bogotá," Oscar replied.

"You're too young." Richard sighed, lighting up a pipe and passing it to me. He had to show me how to cover the hole on its side as I inhaled, then remove my finger to empty the chamber of smoke. In New York, we'd always smoked pot rolled into joints.

Richard put Peggy Lee on his turntable and sang along: "If that's all there is, my friends—"

I joined him: "—then let's keep dancing." I didn't normally

raise my off-pitch voice in front of others, but the pot made me brave.

"You have a good voice," I told Richard.

"He's a drag queen," Oscar said. "He's on stage as Bette Davis."

Richard pressed his fingers to his temples as if to ward off a headache. "Not a drag queen. An actor."

"An actress," Oscar said, grinning.

I realized I'd seen a review of Richard's play in the weekly paper, which I'd flipped through while searching the classifieds for an apartment. The show was playing at a Castro cabaret called Josie's, also within spitting distance from everywhere I'd been today. The review had commended Richard's "star quality."

Oscar wanted to know about New York. I warned him how expensive it was to live in Manhattan, but he said he had a friend who would help him get work modeling. "It's such an unfriendly place," Richard sighed.

"I have great friends there," I countered, insisting that I'd be moving back once I finished school.

"Lots of people say that," Richard said. It sounded like a dare.

Oscar eventually roused us to walk to a bar called the Detour. The night expanded and softened around me, as if we weren't outdoors at all but inside a vast, airy ballroom. Richard and I gabbed; I pointed out the building where I was staying.

"Oh, that place," he said knowingly. Thinking of the mohawked managers in their smoky room, I had to wonder what my residence at this address was telegraphing about me.

The Detour was down the block, painted black from sidewalk to awning. A bassline thumped against the walls. Richard stopped at the door. "I'll leave you two alone," he said, pressing a tiny Ziploc Baggie into my hands. In it was a round, green marijuana bud. "Welcome to San Francisco," he said.

Inside, smoke floated in beams of pinpoint white light and red-tinted shadows. The bar ran the length of one wall; three shirtless bartenders kept busy behind it. A chain-link fence bisected the room, creating a simulated danger zone on one side. I bought Oscar a beer, and then followed him to the far side of the fence, where a huddle of three friends enfolded him. One of them demanded of Oscar, "What took you so long to get here?" I felt my face flush.

The guy nearest me asked what I did. "I'm a grad student," I said. He told me he was "superstoked" because he'd just been hired by the Detour as a barback. "I'll move behind the bar after, like, a couple months probably."

"Good work is hard to find," I said.

"Yeah," he said with a kind of sigh. "I'm also a social worker at a group home." He wrinkled his nose, as if it was too tedious to discuss.

I tried to puzzle this together: The job that sounded weightier and more accomplished was the one he was treating as the necessary evil. The one that would put him on display in the midst of a loud, smoky room, shilling for tips from drunken strangers, was the one he was proud of. Well, if Richard could shed "drag queen" for "actor," why couldn't this "social worker" aspire to "bartender"? Maybe I'd find my own way to drop "grad student" and allow myself "writer."

Oscar and the others were laughing over some shared intimacy, talking so fast, with so many insider references, I couldn't keep up. After a while, I spotted Rolando. He walked straight to Oscar, who, after a greeting, nodded toward me. Rolando's eyes widened for a fraction of a second, then returned to their usual catlike composure. I waved and smiled, probably appearing too eager for a player like Rolando. He stepped closer, and I felt his breath on my ear. "You will be at gym tomorrow."

"Sure," I said, though I hadn't planned on going to the gym every day, and I hadn't planned anything past this night.

"I work out most in mornings," he said. "Before noon."

"Less crowded then," I offered.

He nodded and then stood silently at my side. Had I just agreed to meet him? Were we making a date? Though I was pretty sure by now that Oscar's interest in me had simply been friendly, without romantic intention, I wasn't sure what to make of Rolando.

"I need another drink," I said. I'd finished the first without realizing it.

At the bar, Oscar approached from behind to announce that he was leaving—something about "a friend in Daly City." As the bartender delivered my pint and I fumbled for money, I caught sight of Rolando near the door, eyes focused on me so intensely I had to look away. His communication style was more than just a struggle with a second language. He was so deliberately cryptic, it was spooky.

"Sorry we can't bring you along," Oscar said. "Save my number." I would indeed save it, even call him once more, though we'd never again go out. Our relationship would be limited to hellos at the gym, usually with a flicker of acknowledgment just shy of true flirtation. Oscar would come to mind a few weeks later, when I was again at the Detour, talking with someone I'd just met. "You know what I hate about the men in San Francisco?" this guy would ask, quickly providing his own answer: "They don't follow through." His tone was pure bitterness, but he had a point. I would learn soon enough that this was a city where you regularly exchanged numbers with the guys you don't plan to call.

But that night, I couldn't be mad or upset with anyone. Sure, I'd had my hopes raised and then dashed; sure, I'd been abandoned in a bar, drinking my beer too fast and failing to read the signs or make sense of the values everyone else took for granted. But I'd also met a local celebrity who got me stoned in the house of a famous writer, all of it only a block from where I was staying, all of it on my second evening in San Francisco.

And anyway, a night in the Castro isn't over until it's over.

•

HALFWAY DOWN the half-block walk home, I caught sight of a guy in tight jeans and a motorcycle jacket heading my way. When he got closer, I saw he was about my age and, most striking, that he was offering up a friendly smile.

I turned around after I'd passed him; he had turned, too, still smiling. It was the first clear signal I'd gotten in hours. "Out for a stroll?" I asked.

"I was going to check out the Detour," he said.

"I was just there."

"Leaving so soon?"

"I thought I was on a date, but the guy met up with a friend and left without me."

"Bummer."

"Well, I understand now why they call it the Detour."

He laughed, which was a great relief. He had deep-set eyes and a commanding nose, a narrow, handsome face with a strong chin. He asked, "So now you're buzzed and horny?"

I smiled. "Yes, and yes."

He giggled. "Where do you live?"

"Right there."

"That place?"

"Why does everyone keep saying that?"

"It has a reputation. Tweakers, transients, people coming and going." I was debating whether or not to ask him the meaning of "tweaker"—a term I'd never heard before. Then he said, "I've been in that building before," his bright expression darkening for a moment. I decided not to pursue it.

Instead I made an offer: "You want to visit it again?"

He ran one hand across his dark buzzcut and moved the other to the front of his jeans, adjusting a notable mound of flesh. "You're giving me a soft-on," he said.

We began kissing in the creaky old elevator, our tongues tussling in each other's mouths. The doors opened onto my floor and then shut before we pulled apart; we laughed at our mutual greed. Entering my room, I paused to give him my name. He replied with his, Andrew, and we went back to making out.

Naked, Andrew had what a personal-ad writer might term a "natural body"—a torso that was fit, without gym bulk. His cock was as sizable as the outline in his jeans had promised. One of us tossed the other on the bed and we enacted something like wrestling, if wrestlers were allowed to end in a sixty-nine.

"It's good to meet someone who's as horny as I am," I said. I hadn't realized just how frustrated I'd been by my unconsummated flirtation with Oscar.

"You're fun," he said appreciatively. "I'm so sick of those guys who only want to play feelie-meelie." He patted his hands gently across my skin, laying the back of one on my cheek, a romantic-movie gesture. Then we both burst into laughter. No tender caresses for us.

I pinned him down and put a condom on his cock, but he turned out to be bigger than I could easily accommodate, and he lost his bone. "Flip?" he asked, and I pulled the condom off him and put one on me. I didn't last long, either; fucking seemed somehow too intense for our playful vibe.

Afterward, he asked, "So what exactly are you doing in this building?" He was impressed to discover he'd been my first San Francisco fuck; he even asked if he would wind up in one of my stories.

"Absolutely," I said.

I produced the Baggie of weed, a portion of which Andrew pinched off and loaded into a pipe he'd been carrying in his pocket. "You're here only one day and you've already got a pot dealer?" I told him about Richard. "Oh, I've heard of him," Andrew said. "I want to see that show."

"Maybe we can go together," I suggested, adding hurriedly, "It doesn't have to be a date."

Before he left, we took a bath. The tub was next to a bare window, and once we realized we were probably putting on a show for someone across the air well, where three floors of apartments were stacked, we began to giggle our way through another round of sex, for anyone to see.

The next morning, in my journal, I wrote, "He's someone I could be friends with."

•

A COUPLE DAYS LATER, I ran into Rolando at the gym, working out alone. As soon as he saw me, he summoned me with one of his looks. I joined him at the bench press; with a minimum of speech, we began to alternate sets. I don't think I'd ever done anything as macho as this: "spotting" a partner through weight lifting, grunting competitive encouragement. Though, really, how macho is it when your actions are a prelude to sex?

Midway through, Rolando asked, "You want a massage?"

"Um, sure," I said. "But I can't afford one."

He looked at me thoughtfully. "I give you," he said.

We left without showering—I wouldn't let him wash that musky smell from his skin—and walked down Market, around a corner onto one of the numbered streets. He stopped in front of a nondescript, street-level door painted the same shade of gray as the house above it, and turned a key. Inside, we went down three steps to the concrete foundation, and then moved along a dark, narrow alley and through another door. I had no idea what I'd find inside.

It turned to be a converted garage, running deep under the house, filled with bolts of fabric, racks of garments, long tables covered in sewing supplies, even a headless mannequin, the type designers use to construct clothes. Every wall was papered with glossy pages from fashion magazines, the supermodels of the day—Linda Evangelista, Christy Turlington, Naomi Campbell—

striking a hundred stunning poses. I was a bit of a follower of fashion myself, but Rolando was clearly more than a mere enthusiast.

"Is all of this yours?" He nodded. "Can I see what you've made?" Reluctantly, he flashed a few pieces—a black minidress, a tweed skirt, a shiny evening gown, still in formation—then just as quickly laid them down and maneuvered me toward a curtain, which he slid aside to reveal a single bed, backed into a corner. Here he had tacked up the Calvin Klein underwear ad that had made Marky Mark a star.

He peeled off his shirt, then mine. I was soft compared to him, though I was in the best shape of my life. He began rubbing my shoulders, less a massage than a way to position me for a tumble onto the bed, on top of him. Within a minute our gym shorts were gone, too. He wrapped his solid legs around me and lifted his hips so that his asshole was grazing the tip of my cock. No feelie-meelie, no laughter. No condom, either.

"Like this?" I asked.

"You want?"

"Well, I mean, shouldn't we—" I stammered, as he inched himself toward me. He was so warm and slick, it was as if he had already lubed up. In I went.

I knew better than to fuck without protection, and until recently I'd been only safe. But in the past year, I'd "slipped" several times, both receiving and giving, letting the so-called heat of the moment overrule good sense. After each time, my partner had assured me he was negative—though a couple of them were strangers to me, and one of them did indeed pass on an STD. I thought I'd left these mistakes behind, that in San Francisco I would clean the slate. (In San Francisco? How preposterous it sounds now.)

Above Rolando, thrusting, I hit a spot that sent his eyes rolling. Within that glaze of temporary surrender, I imagined I could see the vulnerable boy he had recently been: a wispy teen in a Bogotá apartment, flipping through *Vogue* and dreaming of America. Now he was here, a muscle-toughened man who exuded sex appeal but had, perhaps, no sexual smarts. I couldn't believe I'd ever seen him as cryptic or sinister. In this intimate moment, he was as fragile as anyone I'd ever met. I ached to talk to him in his own language, to be fluent enough to communicate the risk of what we were doing, to communicate anything at all: what it meant to be new in a city, to feel new in your body, to dream and aspire when your life feels half buried underground. But language is complex; sensation is simple. The fucking went from warm to hot, and I let it last in silence. He had a large, wet mouth, lovely to kiss.

Afterward, he asked, "It's okay like we done?" I hadn't come inside him; perhaps he wanted assurance that raw fucking was fine as long as the top didn't ejaculate.

"I'm negative," I said, "last time I tested. You should—we should have used a rubber to be safe." My intentions were hollow echoes against the hard facts of what I'd chosen to do.

"Don't tell Oscar," he said.

He walked me out, along the concrete corridor to the street. I wasn't sure if this anonymous passageway seemed less mysterious or more, now that I knew about the life being lived within.

The air had changed in the twenty minutes we'd been at it. Already, fog was spilling down over the hills, invading the sunny street. Saying good-bye, Rolando patted me on the ass. "I fuck you next time," he said, though I was pretty sure neither of us would follow through.

•

IT TOOK ME MANY YEARS to write stories of San Francisco.

I finished grad school, got my degree, and wrote a novel, though not a novel set in this city. Not yet. That took time. I wrote about San Francisco only when it seemed I would lose the

San Francisco I knew. I needed to stick around long enough to understand what had disappeared, and what remained.

The Detour changed hands and then closed. Don Jose's became a Hawaiian restaurant. The Market Street Gym has long been owned by a national chain, though it hasn't lost its reputation as a pickup place. The "palazzo" at 16th and Market got a fresh coat of paint; a sign on its front door now advertises rents double what they were back then.

I haven't seen Oscar or Rolando in years. I recently told a friend the story of meeting the two of them, and he asked me, "Were they sex workers?" Certainly the clues were there: Oscar living with a "rich friend," Rolando coming on with an offer of a massage, the two of them departing the Detour for some mysterious encounter after midnight, in suburban Daly City of all places. But do sex workers toil away in taquerias? Do they fuck without condoms, no questions asked? I wonder if Oscar made it to New York, if Rolando made it as a designer, if either of them, but especially Rolando, is still alive.

Andrew is still here. He did indeed turn out to be a good friend—a great friend, an indispensable ally. I can't help but marvel that I met someone so important so soon after arriving. The city slips away in fractions, but a friend who can remind you who you were a lifetime ago, this you hold on to at all costs.

For years, if I thought back to my first days in San Francisco at all, I saw them simplistically, a brief transition before I discovered my actual life. But I see now how my arrival set up everything that was to come. From the start, San Francisco gave me quick access to whatever I sought, then showed me, either gradually or suddenly, what I was really looking for.

uneasy street

jess wells

DUBOCE TRIANGLE is a magnificent little village on the left side of the Castro, diverse and welcoming. In the 1980s I had a tiny condo in a building built after the Great Quake of 1906, all bric-a-brac and crown molding, just four rooms with good light and high ceilings in a railroad configuration so small one should have said caboose. As in a village, the banker would call to tell me that my girlfriend had written another check in pencil, and the greengrocer would warn that she had already picked up milk. The drag queen bar on the corner was our living room, where we'd meet each night after work and talk with the dapper, silver-haired bartender who called breasts "bazoomy-booms." Walking to the Castro, I stopped in bookstores and coffee shops filled with people of every gender, orientation, and ethnicity, every age and income level. There was everything you needed right there:

laundromat, thrift store, bakery, bookstore, everything. It was Europe, it was Manhattan. To me it was the best of San Francisco.

Best in part because within two blocks of my door my girlfriend and I were stepping over the imaginary line into the Castro, where we were suddenly free to hold hands, confirmed in who we were, with the world's biggest gay flag above our heads. Our lesbianism didn't draw attention there, it was a nonissue, it was invisible. I had a friend in from New York who exclaimed, "In the Castro, even the beggars are gay." And there was an allure about the place that was stronger than Valencia Street, which at the time was the lesbian version of the Castro and reflected everything that we knew about the differences between men and women. Valencia was a downtrodden street, raggedy and poor. The bookstore was blocks from the bar, which was blocks from the bathhouse, and there were no boutiques or curio shops in between. It was treeless and dangerous, overhung with a depressing gray color. The Latino residents made it clear that they didn't want us there. The lesbian bar, Amelia's, was eventually replaced by a straight bar named Elbo Room which was replaced by a bar called Amnesia. You couldn't write that progression in fiction, because no one would believe you.

But in fact elbow room was something we were jockeying for in the eighties, not just queers in a straight world but gay men and women with each other. If you weren't six feet tall and a potential trick you just weren't seen in the Castro. Men looked at a man's eye-level and didn't see anyone or anything that wasn't an upright, able-bodied, male sexual target. The not-tricks were something to be navigated around like dumpsters or newspaper kiosks. And at that time, several bars in the Castro made it clear that they just weren't going to let women in, queer or not. One evening my friends and I were strolling down the street and a black woman was being denied entrance to one of the bars on 18th Street, so we did what any good rabble-rousing band of radical lesbians would do and we started castigating the patrons. Sure enough, they took us up on it and the punches started flying. A gay man grabbed my wrists and steered me into oncoming traffic. At that point I vowed that no man would ever control my hands again, and I joined the San Francisco women's boxing team, sponsored by the Police Athletic League (which is a whole story in itself). Why did I become a boxer? people asked. Because a gay man tried to kill me in the Castro.

In 1994 I became a single lesbian mother, living in a little condo with my son. If I felt like a dumpster to be navigated before, imagine how it felt to push a baby carriage through the Castro. When you're a new mother, the hormones racing through you make you terrified over potential danger to your baby, and so I strolled through the Castro gritting my teeth (as in stroller not as in easygoing walk). Men nearly fell on top of my child because they couldn't detect anything that wasn't at their shoulder level. Especially at that point in the gay baby boom, lesbians with children were somewhat rare, and especially since I'm a femme, I was assumed to be a "breeder" and so an interloper in the neighborhood. I was scoffed at and scorned, clucked at and sighed over, not just a useless woman but a member of the oppressing class.

Soon afterward, I wanted to live with a new girlfriend and the condo was too small so we rented a huge house that was right in the middle of the Castro. What a difference a few blocks can make. Suddenly, it wasn't the multicultural experience of Duboce Triangle. There weren't any old people, there were hardly any people of color, or women or straights, punks, disabled, or poor. The shops weren't stores for the lives of the residents: The neighborhood was a gay theme park filled with T-shirts, rainbow flags, and twenty-four-hour bars. It was all drunkenness and proclamations stamped on cotton.

A decade later I developed a new manifestation of my queerness—I'm bisexual (which is a whole story in itself!). Going to dinner with a man in the Castro was a new adventure of being on the outside of the inside (or is that the outside of the outside?). It was a strange feeling to be perceived as straight, with a gay waiter camping it up for us as if we were there for a floor show with our tuna on radicchio. I wanted to holler, "I'm queer, too, can't you tell?" but I'd gotten used to being misunderstood in the Castro.

My twelve-year-old son and I both feel pretty comfortable there now. The neighborhood is still predominantly male, but it's more inclusive and I guess if I'm seen as a fag hag, a dyke, or a mom, I don't care. It has a good Italian deli, a great place for buttons and quality household items. The ice cream's good, the bookstore is excellent, the movie theater is a national treasure, and the outdoor dining is the best. It's festive, it's irreverent. And every summer when I see the tourists, I remember how important it is that there's a place where someone from a farm in Idaho can come out and try on a new identity for a few days. The rest of us can manage our struggle with our uneasiness over the subtleties of queer, of outcast, of in crowd.

changing revelations

andrew ramer

I WAS STILL IN HIGH SCHOOL in 1967, so I missed San Francisco's Summer of Love—but it rippled down to me, newly transplanted from a Jewish New York suburb to Orange County, California.

The first day of school one of my new teachers said to me, "I know about you and I know about your kind. You're sitting in the back row and I don't want to hear a single word out of you." That was a Friday. Monday morning, the boy from the Howdy Committee assigned to show me around met me at my bus and told me that his father wouldn't let him spend time with me. Another classmate asked, "Which side do you wear your tail on?" My life in New York had not prepared me for daily acts of anti-Semitism, which I dealt with in silence. But I knew that up in San Francisco, at the opposite end of the state, I'd find a cure for all of that.

In 1969, in my freshman year of college, I hitched to San Francisco for the first time with some friends, my hair not yet down to my collar, my first wispy mustache starting to grow in. If Jerusalem was the center of the world for my ancestors, the place Jews turn to in prayer, San Francisco was for me the New Jerusalem, the revelatory source of healing and change for the entire planet.

Streets apulse with sexy young men wearing love beads and long hair, bell-bottom pants and granny glasses, the City was a far cry from the middle-class suburbs of my youth. I spent hours in City Lights Books, pouring through Hindu, Taoist, and Buddhist texts, which awakened me to spiritual possibilities no one had ever talked about in the sterile synagogue of my childhood. A rock concert at the Fillmore, and the drugs that I imbibed, taught me about altered states of consciousness and plugged me in to a vision of a new world—one I was as yet too timid, too closeted, to touch or taste.

One weekend my girlfriend and I flew up to San Francisco to visit her brother and his girlfriend, real hippies in my estimation, their every word and action worthy of study for self-improvement. I remember waking beside my girlfriend, early one morning, in two sleeping bags zipped together on the floor of her brother and his girlfriend's flat. Light streaming in through yellowed lace curtains. Guitar propped in a corner. Plants cascading from macramé hangers. Psychedelic posters on the walls from rock concerts. Enthralled, I said to myself, *Someday I will live in San Francisco with all my friends, in our own flats in this same building*. That to me was the picture of heaven on earth. But when I came out as a gay man, I turned my back on all my old fantasies, of marriage, nice Jewish children, and living in San Francisco. Applications to rabbinical school sat on my desk, filled out but never sent in. No way could I go back in the closet. Instead, I moved to New York City, to a building with strangers who, for a time, became friends. We had house parties in our chopped-up brownstone. A directory when you first came in read: "Coats—parlor floor. Food—first floor. Dancing—second floor. Conversation—third floor. Drink and drugs—top floor."

For more than a decade, New York was my shared Eden. Capital city of the planet. The place where I loved and loved again, grew, learned, became a writer. Easy to feel Jewish there without doing anything about it; my spiritual teachers were Hindu, Buddhist, Taoist, Native American, Sufi. But gradually the city that had welcomed me became a haunted one. There was nowhere I could walk without Memory choking me. Memory woven of failed love and AIDS deaths twined together like the two strands of DNA. The corner I made out on with Dan. The walk in Central Park I took with Seth the week before he died. The Chinese place Nick and I ate in every week. The church in midtown where George's memorial service was held. Then I met Wally, a southern boy who charmed me into partnership, moving to New York to live with me in my tiny two-room walk-up. But New York was too big, too fast, too noisy for him, and he began to hunger for the West. When he was accepted into a PhD program, I had no hesitation. We packed our possessions in the back of his truck and drove to California, settling an hour south of San Francisco, in a large, sunny apartment where he could study and I could write.

In those first years I avoided San Francisco. Too loud, too gray, too cold, too scary. I needed the safe nest and silence Wally and I created. Our vegan life and shared Buddhist practice sustained me. But after seven years of living in the Peninsula, the pain of New York washed out of me, Wally and I realized we wanted very different things and we split up. More pain. More healing. Then, two years later, realizing that the suburbs were no place for a single gay man, I called the three old friends I had in San Francisco and asked if they knew of a place to live. One, who I've known since I was twelve, was looking for a housemate in his railroad flat in an Edwardian built two years before the 1906 quake. I took the train up. Then a bus. Walked several blocks to his building, on the edge of the Castro. He showed me around the flat and left me to sit alone in the large, empty dining room at the back of the building. The light filtering in awakened the long-forgotten certainty that someday I would live in this amazing city. And it's from that no-longer-empty room that I am writing now.

But the wide-eyed boy who knew that he was living at the beginning of the Age of Aquarius woke this morning to news about bombings in Lebanon, Iraq, Israel. I remember my college roommate yelling at me because I used an aerosol deodorant. "Don't you know that they destroy the environment?" No, I didn't. Today I read that carbon dioxide concentration in the air had increased from two hundred eighty parts per million in pre-industrial times to three hundred eighty-one parts per million today. And the trees that could remove this from the air are disappearing at the rate of 100,000 acres of forest a day. I can still hear our chants at marches and rallies back then, which I knew would change the world: "What do we want? Peace. When do we want it? Now!" But at the last antiwar march I attended, in front of San Francisco's gold-domed City Hall, those same words screamed through a bullhorn sounded hollow when they came back at me.

Perhaps it's the belief of every younger generation that they will live to see the coming of the messiah. But at fifty-five, I feel lucky each day that I wake up. And the San Francisco that meets me has changed, too. The real hippies I emulated, vagabonds, émigrés from a stifling middle class who seemed to be ushering in a brave new world, have been replaced by the homeless men on their cardboard pallets who live on my street, four, five, or more at a time. One roars like a lion, terrifying passersby. Another sleeps all day beneath a warm-air vent at the back of a restaurant. And AIDS—it never really went away, and friends are dying again, their bodies burned out by the same drugs that kept them alive. Crystal meth and other substances, the children and grandchildren of the drugs we took thirty years ago to attain enlightenment, destroy minds, bodies, communities.

And yet San Francisco is still a revelation for me. But it's a revelation traveling in the opposite direction. I left the world of Jewish practice when I came out, certain that there was no place for me in it, and never would be. True, I have a BA in Jewish studies, but that was a secular journey, about history, archaeology, texts, images. I considered myself gay before I was Jewish, and my communities were all gay ones. After eight years with non-Jewish Wally, I wanted a Jewish husband, but I expected to find him in one of the city's gay Buddhist groups. Then, at breakfast, on the first Friday that I was living here, my housemate asked me if I wanted to go to services with him. I was about to say, "No fucking way," when I saw the look of disappointment organizing itself on his face, in response to the way that my face was already puckering. So I said yes, and sat through the entire service with fists clenched, breathing in and out slowly, trying to gain access to my battered Buddhist nature. Although Congregation Sha'ar Zahav was founded in 1977 by three gay men, it felt like all the parts of Judaism I'd left behind. But I noticed in the weekly handout that there was Torah study in the morning, which appealed to the lover of texts in me. So I went, looking for friends in a new city, and found more than that.

The San Francisco of my earlier years was external, rich in street life and appearances. The San Francisco of my middle age is internal, with time spent praying in community, studying in community, and teaching in community, with a lesbian rabbi and queer friends of every age, gender, persuasion, many of them Jews by choice—none of which I could have imagined when I was in my twenties. That old San Francisco shimmering at the dawning of the Age of Aquarius is met by a city in the midst of poverty, war, pollution, violence, which seem to be getting worse and worse.

But the me of now remembers these words of Rabbi Tarfon, written more than two thousand years ago: "It is not your duty to complete the work. Nor are you free to desist from it." I don't believe that I will live to see the coming of the messiah. When I walk the streets of this city I know that in my own small way I am doing something concrete to make the world a better place. The teens I tutor in writing their bat and bar mitzvah sermons, many with two moms, will step out into the world with deeper insights than I had, more self-knowledge, and a sense of community that I could have only dreamed of. The people I tutor on their journey to becoming Jews will step into the ritual waters of the *mikveh* with a dedication toward *tikkun olam*, repairing the world, that uplifts all who meet them.

•

SHATTERED GLASS from a bus stop around the corner glitters in the morning sun as I head to work. A homeless man sleeps beneath a tattered gray blanket. On the bus, a young man of seventeen or eighteen, sitting across the aisle from his girlfriend, slams his hand so fiercely into the seat in front of him when she calls him "Stupid, stupid, stupid" that his skin shreds. Turning to the youth beside him he says, "That feels better." The two young men talk about how good it feels not to be making their child-support payments. I am sitting next to the girlfriend, who continues taunting her boyfriend. My heart is pounding and continues to pound for the next twenty minutes, as we get off the bus, the two of them shouting at each other. A toothless woman younger than me staggers past, clutching a small bottle wrapped in a paper bag. A slight bent woman pushes her walker in front of her, the green tennis balls stuck on the bottom of the legs dragging on the sidewalk. A little girl in a pink frilly dress clutches her mother's indifferent hand. Three drunken men sprawl on the sidewalk, one in a puddle of urine. Up Fulton Street, the golden dome of City Hall shines. I expect no miraculous intervention. No stunning revelation. These moments of real life lived on these streets come toward me, alive, sometimes too alive. This is my San Francisco now, the one I knew that I was destined to find all those years ago, long before I was ready for it, perfect home for my aging Jewish queer body.

a diamond is forever

michael nava

THE LAST TIME I PLAYED BASEBALL was in high school, under compulsion, and the position I played was called, I think, "throws like a girl," deep in right field. I remember sitting out there in the dandelions with my mitt on my head to keep from getting sunburned, furiously plotting my escape from the stultifying Central Valley town where I lived.

Somewhere in the distance, the game was proceeding; a pitcher lobbed the ball, the batter swung, the boys in the infield jumped to their positions, the other outfielders moved in or backed up. I sat in the warm grass, worrying about SAT scores and scholarships. I may also have been thinking about one of the books I read secretly in the stacks of the main library downtown, which had titles like *The Sixth Man* and *City of Night*. I had known since I was twelve that I was homosexual, and I constantly monitored my behavior for manliness in the way I walked, and talked, carried myself, where I looked, what I allowed myself to notice.

By the time I was seventeen, I had very nearly perfected my disguise. Only my lack of athletic ability betrayed me. Sports represented exclusion. That hour of humiliation in right field reminded me that no matter how well I honed my act, it was still an act; I was terminally different. In the fall I went off to college—the first person in four generations of my Mexican immigrant family to do so—and never returned. The dandelion field and the high-school jocks faded into irrelevance as I launched myself into the all-consuming enterprise of becoming a grown-up.

Twenty-five years pass. It is 1998 and I am forty-three years old, a lawyer, and a writer. I had moved to San Francisco from Los Angeles three years earlier, seeking in the city poised at the edge of the continent, like so many others before me, a fresh start. Los Angeles had become for me an apocalyptic city, where every streetcorner seemed haunted by the ghost of another friend or acquaintance who had perished in the epidemic. San Francisco was the Oz of my childhood, "the cool gray city of love," as one of its many laureates, Herb Caen, pronounced it. It was also the place of my sexual coming out, during the years I was at law school at Stanford in the late seventies. After the Angeleno megapolis, the human scale of San Francisco—the wedding-cake Victorians, toy-like trolleys and cable cars, sudden profusions of rosemary and roses spilling over fences and retaining walls—was disorienting. I had become so acclimated to whizzing through Los Angeles in my vehicular bubble that I had forgotten what it felt like to walk from one place to another and to experience the human respiration of a city.

What does a fresh start look like? It looks like a tiny flat on the top of a hill with a long view of the towers and spires of downtown crowded against the sunlit waters of the Bay; that it is simultaneously filled with possibility and empty of actuality. Nothing that I had planned when I moved here worked out as I had expected it would—the relationship broke up, the reputation-making book was rejected by one publisher after another, and ultimately I was even evicted from the hilltop flat when the owners decided to reclaim it. I was, in the most profound and most fortunate way imaginable, *disillusioned*. I came to see that those things that I had believed gave life meaning—relationships, reputation, and achievements—were capable of delivering only the most transient satisfactions. The greater and more lasting satisfaction was simply being alive to the world, moment by moment, guided only by my curiosity. Curiosity is the greatest of spiritual and intellectual gifts; it is, I am convinced, the very spark of life. To walk through the world in wonder inevitably yields the wonders of world, even in as unlikely a place as Candlestick Park, where I saw my first baseball game.

So, back to July 1998.

An acquaintance calls me one Sunday morning; he has tickets to a Giants game. Will I come? *Baseball?* I don't think so. But he wears down my resistance and promises that if it's too boring, we'll leave. To be on the safe side, I pack a book and the brief I have to file the following week.

The stadium is surprisingly beautiful. I have never seen a green as green as the diamond at Candlestick, and it feels good to sit in the sun. The game begins. Whatever I once knew about the rules I have long since forgotten, but then, in the bottom of the first inning, Barry Bonds hits a home run. And in that moment, I get it: What he has done is breathtaking. He has stood his ground as a very fast, very hard object comes flying at him, and, using only his physical strength and a pretty slender piece of wood, has slammed the ball across the field and into the stands and made it look easy. It is an iconic male moment, combining courage, power, and nonchalance. I toss my book aside and stand up and cheer.

I fell in love with baseball that year. Of course, I was not the only American enthralled by baseball for the first time or all over again that summer of 1998, the home-run race between Mark

McGwire and Sammy Sosa. In this innocent, pre-steroids scandal year, for a few weeks baseball captured a nation's attention in a way reminiscent of an earlier time, even more innocent in some ways, and now relegated to film clips of Babe Ruth and Lou Gehrig and Joe DiMaggio.

I was fortunate in having the Giants as my home team; they win enough to get your hopes up and then find ways to lose that seem calculated to twist the knife in your heart, but they play, always, as if it really matters, and for a moment you can forget you're watching nine rich guys engaged in a child's game. I watched games on TV with the phone in my lap so I could call my friend Katherine, a longtime fan, during commercials and parse the previous inning. For the first time in my life I read the sports section, slowly educating myself about ERAs and RBIs, just as in law school I had once worked my way through the eighteen exceptions to the hearsay rule and grappled with the Rule Against Perpetuities.

Baseball seeped so far down into my psyche that I replayed the games I watched on TV in my dreams. What I didn't do was get to many games, because I was skittish about going alone, and it soon became clear to me that finding other gay men who liked baseball was like looking for ice cubes in Death Valley.

I was not the only gay man who had done time in dandelion fields. Many of us had had a troubled relationship with sports, even those who were athletically gifted. Athletic prowess is only a part of what straight guys love about sports: Sports also provides virtually the only language they can speak to one another that touches anything like the full range of human feeling—joy and happiness and sorrow and loss as well as competition. Sports affords them almost their only emotional release. Sports is the *lingua franca* that unites straight guys into a tribe, the last vestige of the Eden of boyhood. It was an Eden most gay men did not share. Of necessity, we invented another language, formed a different kind of tribe. Much has been said about the tribal pursuits of gay men. Baseball is not among them.

I have never belonged to either tribe, completely. As a law student at Stanford, I would come up to the city for weekends. The Castro scene was then at its most frenetic. I was a boy from a working-class, Mexican, Catholic neighborhood, and what I saw excited and repelled me. The exaggerated masculinity of the clones on the one hand projected a male sexuality in a way that today is as familiar as a Calvin Klein underwear ad but was startling then.

On the other hand, this masculinity was also as two-dimensional as a billboard. I guessed that many of these boys had simply exchanged their mother's heels for their father's boots, that these masculine poses were mostly a matter of drag. The men in my family were cannery workers and construction laborers, and from them I observed that manhood was more than flannel shirts and facial hair; it meant hard work, deferred pleasure, heavy responsibilities, and no complaining.

I'm not saying theirs was the only legitimate model of manhood or even the healthiest one, but they had a gravity—perhaps even a melancholy—of which I, too, am made. To be a man meant you lived for something greater than the satisfaction of every passing impulse, whereas the gay men I saw seemed to be making careers out of instant gratification. Standing in the Stud in my button-down shirt, a beer sweating in my hand, I felt as much a misfit as I had on the baseball diamond.

Yet I never tried to hide that I was gay, not at school or later on when I worked as a prosecutor and then in a private firm or for an appellate court judge. When I wrote my first book, it never occurred to me that the protagonist would not be homosexual. Whatever it cost me to be out was worth it, if only because it is difficult to live an authentic life when all your energy is being consumed in the elaboration of a lie about something as basic to your identity as your sexual nature. I no longer worried about whether I appeared "normal," but well into my thirties I still believed, in some recess of my heart, that I did not measure up as a man. This self-doubt was evident in the way I said I was a gay man; the emphasis, slight but telling, was on *gay*.

My gender politics also contributed to this. Many of my closest friends have been fierce women, like the band of radical lesbians I knew in college, who, though officially committed to destroying the patriarchy, took me on as a kind of mascot. At a poetry reading, one of them read a poem that urged women to strangle their male fetuses with their umbilical cords. After she read the line, she paused, looked up at me, smiled, and said, "Except Michael."

I came to believe that women were better humans than men, and to feel guilty about the destructiveness of my gender. I felt, for a while, almost apologetic for being male. As I approached the end of my thirties, though, something in me changed. I began to feel that men were more than despoilers of civilization. There was a masculine power and energy that, at its best, showed up as a kind of bravery—"grace under pressure," that old fraud Hemingway called it, but he was onto something. Somewhere along the line—in the sickrooms of friends, in the rooms of recovery, sitting at the blank screen of a computer—I was forced to recognize that even I possessed a measure of this masculine grace, this bravery. By the time I reached forty, when I described myself as a gay man, the emphasis had shifted: gay *man*.

So, finally, at forty-four it was okay for me to love baseball for the same reasons other men loved it when they were twelve. Baseball players are the physical symbols of this elusive, mysterious quality of bravery that most of us men are looking for in ourselves. The game is a kind of theatricalized battle in which the players struggle, suffer, prevail, and go down to defeat, and no one gets killed. The spotlight shifts from player to player, sometimes to cheers, sometimes to groans, and in every game at least one of them has that shining, unambiguous moment of glory. This is a moment few men can extract from their own ambiguous struggles through life, but what man doesn't dream of it?

Older, jaded fans assured me that the Giants, like most other baseball players, were a collection of tetchy millionaires with egos the size of opera divas. Maybe so, but from where I sat in the upper reserved stands, the Giants, circa 1998, embodied the male virtues. Veteran outfielder Ellis Burks radiated dignity and class; Stan Javier, another outfield *veterano*, leonine self-assurance. J. T. Snow at first base and Jeff Kent at second had the self-confidence of boys who were always bigger and stronger and better at games than anyone else; outfielders Marvin Benard and F. P. Santangelo, shaped like fireplugs, made up in grit and shrewdness what they lacked in stature. Rich Aurelia, the shortstop, and Bill Mueller, on third, went about their jobs with unflashy competence.

Brent Mayne, the catcher, seemed to beam rays of calm intelligence to the skittish pitchers. On the mound, leftie Shawn Estes was a golden boy who worried his doubts like a man who has lost a filling and can't stop touching the place with his tongue; Russ Ortiz, a great young pitcher, draped himself in an older man's gravity to compensate for his youth, like a boy wearing his father's suit; Jay Johnstone, a relief pitcher, was a lug of a guy who must have spent his adolescence being asked to get things off shelves that no one else could reach, which turned out to be good training when you come into a game with two men on base and no outs; and Robb Nen, the closer, was as precise and serious as a surgeon.

And Bonds, out in left field—Bonds was the athletic equivalent of a genius. A show-off, visibly self-absorbed, he walked in a golden glow that compelled attention even when you didn't like him, and when he played well, he was transcendent. I didn't know what he or any of the rest of them were really like, but the boy in me worshipped the men they appeared to be.

The fact that I'm gay, of course, adds an erotic tinge to my fandom, but the homoerotic quality in baseball is not only well documented but also pretty obvious if you pay attention for long. It's also not new: from Gilgamesh to Gary Cooper, the hero has often been romantically beautiful, and part of his charisma has always been sexual. Many baseball players are handsome men with bodies like something out of Michelangelo's sketchbooks. These bodies are inescapably the center of attention—how they move, what condition they're in. Sometimes you hear the anxiety about all this male pulchritude in the nicknames that players are given, which often seem like a tittering put-down. The players themselves seem to have no such anxieties. They smack one another's butts and weep in one another's arms with alpha-male self-assurance. The game is steeped in male physicality; it's really the only occasion in which straight men are permitted to notice another man's body. In this way, too, it's a throwback to the Eden of early puberty, before the fear of being labeled queer sets in, when boys are openly curious about their own and one another's bodies. For me, obviously, it's a label that's lost its power to terrify.

The older you get, the more settled in your habits you're supposed to become. That's why this late-blooming passion for baseball makes me so happy. It reminds me that there is so much in the world left to fall in love with. It also brings me around full circle in a way, back to the dandelion field where, unbeknownst to myself, as I fantasized about the life wanted, I was taking my first steps toward it. Now that I'm a grown man, I can watch the game I hated as a boy and understand finally what it meant to other boys, how it gave them heroes, models, examples of the bravery that they—and I—would one day be expected to exhibit on much tougher fields than a baseball diamond.

evolutionary changes

jamison green

IN MY EARLIEST MEMORIES, San Francisco was always there, always glistening across the water. Both my parents would remark on it without fail whenever we would round a particular corner in the Oakland hills near our home: "Look at the city; isn't it beautiful?" It always was. Then the road curved again and descended behind pine, redwood, and eucalyptus trees, and the city vanished. But it was always there, promising, promising what? Energy? Adventure? To me, San Francisco represented potential, it was the world beyond me.

My father was a furniture wholesaler, and he had a space in the San Francisco Merchandise Mart on the corner of 9th and Market. He went there every Friday, when the buyers would come, while Monday through Thursday he visited the stores that bought from him, and potential new customers, too, from Eureka to San Luis Obispo. The mart itself was a special place because it wasn't open to the public, and that exclusivity appealed to me as a child. I coveted special secrets, and I loved knowing something others didn't know, or getting to do something others couldn't do. Sometimes I'd go to the Mart with my father in the summer when I wasn't in school. He would show his pass to the security guard in the lobby, obtain a temporary pass for me, and then he would pick up his mail from a box beyond the security desk. We rode up in the elevator—I think it was to the eighth floor—and he would stride the long hallways, looking at his mail and calling out greetings as we passed men and women inside showroom after showroom, while I ran along behind him, looking at all the different styles of furniture, extravagant and homely lamps, dinettes and bar stools, impressed that so many people would call out my father's name when they saw him, and that he knew all of their names, too.

Outside on Market Street, the streetcars and jitneys and taxis competed with private cars, surging forward when the lights changed, filled with people with important things to do. Businessmen always wore hats when I was young. You rarely saw a man on the street downtown in the city without a hat. And women wore gloves. My mother said there was a rule about not wearing white after Labor Day, but she recommended never wearing white in San Francisco because one wouldn't want to appear to be a tourist. I loved the intersections in the financial district where pedestrians could walk diagonally across, rather than have to wait through two traffic signals to negotiate the right angles. Those intersections still exist today, but the jitneys are gone. They were cars that resembled black London taxis that ran only along Market Street, and you could wave one down from anyplace along the sidewalk, and ask to be dropped off anywhere else within their range. I don't remember whether they cost anything. San Francisco seemed to be designed to serve the people who gave the city its life.

When I was young, the toll on the Bay Bridge was twenty-five cents, and the bottom deck of the bridge carried no automobile traffic but was striated with railroad tracks. Passenger trains snaked through the neighborhoods of the East Bay, and came together to rumble and clank across the bridge in the grime-coated steel girder half-darkness that ended at some terminus from which they may have fanned out to explore San Francisco neighborhoods far from downtown. But I was unaware, as a child, of anything beyond the urban center and the waterfront, from China Basin, where the warehouse storing my father's inventory was located, to Aquatic Park, where we flew kites on spring weekends. My family also frequently visited Golden Gate Park and Playland-at-the-Beach out on Highway 1, and we went to the homes of my parents' friends in various quadrants of the city. But I had my bearings best in North Beach or Chinatown, along the Battery-Sansome corridor and the Embarcadero, around Union Square, and in Civic Center. I felt part of the world in those places, part of the history that had played out there, like a tiny red blood cell traveling with a purpose in the bloodstream of the world, along with all the other people striding or strolling or gliding in some vehicle from place to place, though that purpose was unknown to me.

In the summer of 1966 I was earning money for college by working at a high mountain camp in the northern Sierra, so I missed the riot in the Tenderloin district, just a block from Glide Memorial Church, a disturbance of order that would become known as the Compton's Cafeteria Riot. Like most people, I didn't even know it had happened until almost forty years later: it was ignored by the press, and all the San Francisco Police Department records from that era have been lost, but historian Dr. Susan Stryker found writings about it from the queer press of the late 1970s and spent years piecing the story together, culminating in an award-winning documentary released in 2006 entitled *Screaming Queens*, and I served as master of ceremonies that June 22nd at the installation of a commemorative plaque in the sidewalk at the corner of Turk and Taylor, where the riot had occurred.

Granted, in 1966, had I been in the vicinity, I would not have known what to make of it all. I was seventeen, and unconnected to queer culture. I didn't identify as "homophilic" (a term in common usage at the time) because I was convinced I would never have an intimate partner. As a transgendered (a term *not* in common usage at the time) teenager, I felt I simply couldn't choose to act on my attraction to either girls (who had bodies like mine but genders that were quite opposite my own), or boys (who had genders more like mine and bodies that had some muscular similarity but were genitally opposite my own) so I believed that I should just mind my own business.

I went to Eugene that fall to attend the University of Oregon, where I quickly became friends with a group of young men and women from California who were interested in art and politics, and I became a fixture on the local "hippie" scene, playing rhythm guitar and singing with several rock bands, discussing gender-bending with long-haired graduate students and resisting the Vietnam war. By the time I was in graduate school, 1970-1972, when I was the only female-bodied person working on an MFA in fiction at the U of O, women were inviting me to join their consciousness-raising groups, but I was much more interested in hanging out with my male friends, playing music or working on theater or art projects.

I had finally figured out that I liked having female lovers, and I was struggling with the label "lesbian" ("dyke" was much more comfortable as a label for me then). But still I missed San Francisco, and as often as I could, I commandeered friends' cars and talked even more friends into accompanying me for the eight-hour drive each way, just to spend a day or two in the "real" city, hanging out in the Panhandle, riding the cable cars, roaming the waterfront, even just going to the zoo. I needed the cool bay fog; I needed the creosote smell at the piers. I needed the expansive views and the dynamic, varied architecture. I needed the sense of liveliness that San Francisco imparted to me, day and night, rain or shine, in burning heat or chill winds. Out of sight on a daily basis, San Francisco became a magical place, with restorative powers that could replenish any mental or physical drain that my academic (or later, workday) world had created in me. And I wanted my friends to understand how it made me feel. I wanted them to believe in San Francisco the way I did.

I moved back to the San Francisco Bay Area in January 1978. My partner, Samantha (who had also grown up in the East Bay, though closer to Hayward than to Oakland), and I set out to build our life together centered on lesbian and pagan social circles, and we also socialized with a few straight friends and gay male couples who also lived in the East Bay. I worked in the financial district for the first couple of years after we settled in, and I loved my commute on BART, reading *One Hundred Years of Solitude* and books by Gregory Bateson and Steven Millhauser. I loved walking through Embarcadero Center early in the morning, before it was filled with shoppers, taking a circuitous route to my office on California Street, outside of which I would often pause to watch people on the cable cars for a few minutes, anything to prolong my exposure to the smell of the Bay, the sounds of the traffic, the sight of the busy, mostly well-dressed people with places to go.

It struck me as funny to think of myself as a businessperson, and I struggled with what kind of clothing I should wear, since it was virtually impossible for me to wear feminine attire. I wore loose men's trousers, man-tailored blouses from the women's department at Macy's, a tweed blazer on cooler days, and suede oxford shoes. I probably looked awful, and I clearly confused people who frequently would ask whether I was a man or a woman.

I didn't want to be a man or a woman; I wanted to be a writer. That was all I ever wanted to be, since I was seven years old. That was why I got an MFA in fiction writing: to prove to my parents (and myself) that my interest in writing was valuable, maybe even important, but at least worthwhile, not just a technique for indulging my fantasies, a glorified indolence. But I hadn't yet figured out how to make writing work for me as a career. It was through my desire to write, though, that I first visited Castro Street.

I had submitted an assortment of my fiction to a literary agency with an office on Castro Street, and one of the two women who ran the business invited me to meet with them. I was doubly thrilled: first to be invited to the gay mecca, and second to think that I might actually be on my way to making a living as a writer. A small independent press in Oregon had published a few of my short stories in a book called *Eyes* in 1976. I'd had some good reviews, and a distributor was handling sales and marketing, but there was no money in it for me, really. If I could get an agent, I thought, that would be all it would take. Especially a San Francisco-based agent, one who would champion the West Coast literary sensibility that I felt infused my work. I was certain that my agent would understand me; my agent would love me and encourage me and fight with editors for me, and make sure I got rich.

I had sent to them what I felt was a representative sample of the full range of my work up to that point. I had stories that had elements of fantasy like those of Donald Barthelme or Richard Brautigan, stories that were very mundane on the surface but still emotionally powerful (reminiscent of Katherine Anne Porter, one of my professors once remarked), stories with male protagonists, stories with female protagonists, stories with genderless narrators (who represented, in my mind, a portrait of the artist as a young man); I thought I was simply demonstrating my versatility. But no; for these agents, my diverse stories simply indicated that perhaps I was unsure of myself. They thought my writing was "very promising" but that I needed to work harder to develop a consistent voice.

Not knowing how I fit into the world really did affect my capacity to relate to people. I already knew that when one sends writing into the world it has to be grounded in a sense of self that others can relate to, or else the reader won't be able to connect with it and relate it to her or his own experience. At the time, though, I really wasn't sure what it would take to become myself. I thought I already knew who I was, and my difficulty was only that the rest of the world didn't know how to deal with me, a condition to which I was quite accustomed. I believed that being different was a blessing for an artist, not a curse.

I drove back to the East Bay that day feeling frustrated and alienated but still determined not to give up on my goal of being a successful writer. From the dock at Jack London Square, I could look out the mouth of the estuary across the bay to San Francisco, and I felt the distance between me and the world beyond me just as concretely as if I were looking at the city through a television screen with the sound on mute.

I went to my first San Francisco Gay Freedom Day Parade in June of 1978, and it was one of the most moving experiences I had ever had, to be in the midst of thousands of people and feel perfectly safe. San Francisco is like a small town sometimes, in the best of ways and in the worst of ways. At its worst, it can be like a middle school, cliquish and self-absorbed, sniping at the people who are different or in this week's "outcast" group and pushing them into their own areas so they don't contaminate the rest of us. At its best, San Francisco can be like a graceful diplomat, welcoming everyone, speaking out for social justice, evoking the qualities that make us all better human beings. Drums and trumpets, dykes on bikes, cheers and whistles, shouts of joy, pounding bass guitars catching the pulse in my chest, naked men and bare-breasted women, leather and chains gleaming in the sunlight, flags waving, colors flying, sequins and satin sashes, and all the smiling faces and waving hands, hundreds of thousands of people who were not afraid to say who they were and not what someone else expected them to be. San Francisco was alive with defiance of the norm, and I was proud to be on the sidelines, feeling the city breathe.

On November 27, 1978, Harvey Milk and Mayor George Moscone were assassinated in City Hall by former Supervisor

Dan White. In my office on California Street, one of my cowork-
ers heard the gunshots in the distance over the telephone as she
spoke to someone in some civic office. I looked up when she
pulled the receiver away from her ear and stared at it. Then she
put it back to her ear and shouted, "What happened? What's happening?" She heard screaming, and then the person she was
speaking with said, "I'll have to get back to you," and hung up.
She put the receiver down and said, "Something horrible is happening. Someone just got shot at City Hall." We turned a radio
on and got the numbing, depressing, frightening news.

San Francisco mourned and waited for justice. But on May 21,
1979, White was given a meager seven-year sentence, and the gay
community reacted with outrage and violence at City Hall. Police
retaliated on Castro Street, and more than one hundred sixty
people were injured. With characteristic resiliency, the gay community celebrated Harvey Milk's birthday with a party on Castro
Street the very next night. White served five years in prison before committing suicide shortly after his release. But the community was galvanized by these events, and would never again be
marginalized, not in San Francisco. These events politicized and
encouraged thousands of gay and lesbian people across the country and around the world, and they moved me forward, too, toward a keener sense of what it meant to be responsible for one's
beliefs, especially when one's beliefs were at odds with the mainstream but clearly were in line with the principles of democracy.

Nearly a decade elapsed before I was able to acknowledge my
transsexualism and begin to transition from female to male in
1988. Ten years of gay and lesbian friendships, visits to bars and
restaurants and bookstores, on Castro Street and all around the
city, that were known queer enclaves. Ten years of career-building
and of family formation, ten years of writing and thinking about
who I was and what I had to say. Becoming a man changed my relationship to San Francisco yet again, because as I became comfortable with myself at last, San Francisco gave me the opportu-

nity to influence public policy. My father used to tell me, "You can't fight City Hall." I think he just didn't want me to get hurt emotionally or spiritually, and he thought if one just goes along with the program, one finds less resistance, thus staying under the radar and shaping your independence by avoiding trouble. But there were some things I had to fight against, like the prejudice that existed (and still exists, though to a lesser extent) against transsexual and gender-variant people, and San Francisco opened up its City Hall to me and to other transgender and transsexual activists in the early 1990s.

I never imagined that the ideas that I expressed in the Report on Discrimination Against Transgendered People that I wrote for the San Francisco Human Rights Commission in 1994 would have such far-reaching effect, nor that my opinion on transgender issues would be sought by journalists, psychologists, policymakers, and other professionals around the world. For this, I owe a debt of gratitude to San Francisco, to its diverse people, to its proud queer community, to its courageous politicians, to its public servants who continuously plug away under conditions that are often less than ideal, to the spirit of individual freedom and independence that San Francisco has historically represented, and to its oft-acknowledged inspirational beauty. When I walk into San Francisco's Paris-inspired marble and golden City Hall, I feel the civic pride that has gone into creating the sense of civility that it represents, and I feel I have a stake in that building, like I am a part of the foundation that supports the city and all its institutions, public and underground. I feel that I belong, and that I have found my place in the world. Castro Street, a once-sleepy neighborhood of Victorian houses and a few blocks of storefronts, got up in the night and slid downtown while no one was looking, and in the morning everyone said, "Look! Rainbow flags are everywhere," and life goes on, same as always.

I make my living now managing other writers in a software-development environment, but I am a writer first and foremost. I think as a writer thinks about how to change the world through words, how to express ideas and emotions that will come alive in other people. I have found my voice and my footing in the search for self and for community. My nonfiction work keeps me extremely busy, and the need for exposition and policy work on behalf of the LGBT community is still very great. But one day I hope to return to fiction writing, to creating characters, and to listening to the natural world again, leaving politics and institutions behind, or at least just over my shoulder.

Since I have come into my own in my own male body, since I have found the balance between my gender and my physicality, because of what transgender and transsexual people have been able to accomplish politically and socially in San Francisco, I feel much more connected there. I'm still proud to be a native of Oakland, but I feel that I've become an inextricable part of San Francisco history, perhaps more indelibly than I may ever manage to become in the East Bay. I still look at San Francisco from across the Bay and hear my long-deceased parents' voices marveling at how beautiful the city is, and I have to smile and say to myself, "Yes, it is. Imperfect, real, and beautiful."

god's radar screen

stephen beachy

IN THE SUMMER OF 2004 I was visiting most days with Vera, my partner Jonathan's aunt, in her room at a hospice. We'd hung some of Vera's artwork on the wall, a watercolor she'd made of a peacock, a collage of outer-space imagery. Vera had lung cancer and she was going to die. She'd smoked Mores, or something very much like them, for fifty years. The hospice was in the Castro, the ghosts of gay men who'd died of AIDS lingering in the atmosphere. Vera had always seemed to us, to me and Jonathan, like a drag queen in a woman's body. She had a drag queen's extreme sense of style, wearing her blond wigs decades before Lil' Kim, her gold tooth with a star in the center, the hot pants she'd worn well into her seventies, and the clothes she'd designed for herself, full of color, always color. "I like colors," Vera used to say, which was a euphemism for the things the lives of those around her maybe didn't include.

Several years earlier, she'd been in a car with her sister, Jonathan's grandmother, Hattie, coming from Oakland to San Francisco to visit Jonathan and his mother, but was stuck in traffic because of the Folsom Street Fair, San Francisco's annual S&M Disneyland. Hattie was driving, Hattie was always driving. Hattie was the ant to Vera's grasshopper, a pathologically practical woman, but she'd been the one who'd saved Vera's country property by making the payments after Vera had sold an acre to buy a pair of shoes. South of Market, Vera saw all those people partying, and she wanted to see what was going on. They were quarreling anyway, she and Hattie, as they were often quarreling. When the old Volvo stopped at a red light, Vera jumped out, and Hattie could only watch as Vera disappeared into the crowd. Although I wasn't there, it is one of the images I will always carry of Vera, well into her seventies, her blond wig disappearing into a crowd of God knows what, masters paddling their slaves, queens with inflamed nipples, doms walking hooded creatures on leashes, and all the other "colorful people" South of Market.

Throughout her many trials and tribulations, euphemisms were one way that Vera had avoided becoming, like me, a jaded bitch. Back in the fifties she worked in North Beach as a "shake dancer," entertaining old white men alongside Maya Angelou, wearing spangles and pasties and various costumes she'd designed herself. Maya Angelou got to keep her clothes on, but Vera had no rhythm, or she had her own rhythm, a rhythm from Pluto. "Shake dancer" was precisely accurate about one aspect of Vera's job, but also a euphemism for "whatever else" she did. Those were the good days. She was a country girl who'd grown up sharecropping on a Mississippi plantation; she'd married a soldier with a plate in his skull, and there are stories of beatings, guns held to her head. She "had to get out of there"—Mississippi—and moved to Chicago, then California, where her stage name became "Amber" —which was also the color of her skin. She made her living as an exotic, and "whatever else" she did paid her enough money to buy a house in the Avenues and another property up north, outside of Sebastopol.

In the sixties, it all fell apart. There she was, sitting up in her dark house in the Avenues with more guns and another crazy boyfriend, waiting for Jonathan's father to bring them money for cigarettes, the Mores, or something very much like them, that she'd smoke for fifty years. The electricity had been lost, and the bank was taking back the house. Like Gloria Swanson in *Sunset Boulevard*—very much like Gloria Swanson in *Sunset Boulevard*—she was a faded star, but she hadn't invested in any oil wells. There was nothing pumping, pumping, pumping in the background to provide her with a continual income, so that was when she began to lose touch with reality, reality fell out from underneath her. She lost the San Francisco house, and sold an acre of her "country property" to buy herself a pair of shoes. She heard voices, and she scrawled thousands and thousands of sentences in the notebooks she kept as a record of her insane spiritual journey, sentences about God's radar screen around the world and the deep dark sunless prison of insanity, the bottomless pit where the Devil is at, which has no form and which is void of everything that lives. "Your Ass Ain't No Magnetic Mountain," she also wrote, addressing, I believe, either God or the Devil directly, "Your Ass is a Maggot Mountain to Get the Fuck Out of Babylon is Strength to the Knees."

In the seventies she got it together again, took art and secretarial classes at a local community college, created the paintings and collages that we'd used to brighten up her room in the hospice. Vera didn't think of me as a jaded bitch, bless her heart, but as a fellow artist and Aquarius; we shared the same birthday. In her room one afternoon, she wondered what I thought about reincarnation, and she told me how she would like to come back as a sort of perfected image of herself. I didn't tell Vera that there in the Castro, surrounded by the ghosts of gay men dead of AIDS, my own ghost never felt very far away. I didn't tell Vera that to me

oblivion often seemed preferable to most notions of reincarnation. The thought of going through another human childhood.
Sometimes as I wandered through the foggy summer days outside…of that hospice room I'd come across families on vacation,
or just families. Mobile prison cells crisscrossing America. Thousands of years turn into millions of years; the vast wasteland of
time. I did tell Vera that I'd rather wait a spell before I came back,
to spend as much time in "that other place" as possible before returning to this world. Vera agreed.

I didn't tell Vera that a shallow and willful belief that death
entailed a luxurious bath that would wash away all of my tired
memories and all of my hard-gained knowledge was one way to
deal with being a jaded bitch. I didn't tell Vera, I'm not sure why,
about a Gnostic sect known as the Carpocratians. They believed
you needed to experience everything, every pleasure, every pain,
in order to avoid reincarnating back into the prison of a human
body. They believed that becoming a jaded bitch was a path toward spiritual enlightenment, a vision I found appealing, for obvious reasons. The only ideas I wanted to share with Vera, as she
was dying, were comforting ideas. I didn't say that there's nothing but flux, most likely, a constant eruption of new forms and a
constant dissolution of old ones, or that a flux like that may as
well be death.

Several months earlier, during the time that Vera could still
get around but we all knew that she was doomed, we'd taken a
drive in the country with her old friend May. Vera was always
wanting to take a drive in the country. "A drive in the country"
was her euphemism for visiting the property she used to own, the
property she'd recently sold in its entirety, and which she had
once sold an acre of to buy a pair of shoes. "Old friend," we'd
suspected, was also a euphemism for a more complex relationship
with May. During the beginning of my relationship with
Jonathan, before Vera began to refer to me as Stephen, or sometimes Stephens, with a mysterious s tagged onto the end, she had

always tactfully referred to me as Jonathan's "roommate." These days there is an enormous vocabulary to describe my relationship with Jonathan, but there still may not be one to describe Vera's with May. Nobody seemed to know exactly how old May was, maybe close to ninety, a tiny dynamo of a woman who sat in the backseat telling us stories of the glory days she'd shared with Vera in North Beach. While Vera was shake-dancing, May had worked as a dominatrix, Miss Zidella. If you wanna get whipped, she'd say, you'd come to Miss Zidella. And she told us of how she'd protected Vera, innocent, beautiful Vera, the most beautiful woman May had ever seen, a country girl having her moment of stardom in San Francisco. At one point, when May declared how much she'd loved her Vera, Vera spoke up. "Let's not get carried away now, May," Vera said, which was, for Vera, as direct as it got, the equivalent of saying, "Please shut up." May exhausted me, too. At ninety, or however old, she had more energy than I did. She rushed around the East Bay collecting cast-off clothes from rich people which she'd sell for a tidy profit. She'd find someone to drive her to the casino in San Pablo, and she'd stay up night after night, losing it all.

After visiting the old property, we stopped at a restaurant and had an afternoon that Vera and May considered the height of graceful living: overlooking the ocean, drinking champagne and eating shrimps—another mysterious *s* on the end. It seemed like the ideal of graceful living from a different era, the fifties in fact, Vera and May's glory days. When we were done, and I was help-ing Vera out to the car, May stayed inside with Jonathan and came clean: although Vera had never wanted her own family to know, May's family had known she was a dyke for fifty years, she and Vera hadn't only been best friends, and all those no-good men in both of their lives, well, who knew, May never explained their role exactly. A few years back, the last one, Charles, had made the mis-take of bad-mouthing Vera to May, on the phone. "Who do you think you are?" May said to Charles. "Who do you think you are to talk about Vera that way? Don't you know I have things in my bag," May told Charles, "and I will cut you?"

Charles was gone for good now, and so were all the others, but May was still around, and Vera was dying. Like the men in Vera's life, I will never know exactly what the things were in May's bag and what they'd been doing there. That summer I would have my own things for Vera, in a bag—the cheap wine that she was fond of, which she had been drinking daily to help her through the past few decades, and which I would buy chilled in gallon jugs at the Cala Foods around the corner from the hospice. I hadn't spent so much time in the Castro in years. The neighborhood had seemed haunted and melancholy when I first arrived in San Francisco in 1991, but the dot-com years had erased or buried the melancholy of that time. "Life goes on" was the message of the new restaurants, spiffy Victorian exteriors, ambitious haircuts of tech-savvy newcomers, and puzzled or thrilled expressions of tourists from whatever vast deserts of the world that weren't so gay-friendly. "Life goes on" was supposed to be some kind of consolation amid a constant eruption of new forms and a constant dissolution of old ones. The summer that I was going back and forth between the Cala Foods and the hospice with my chilled gallon jugs, Ronald Reagan died, finally, the man who'd presided over so many of those AIDS deaths with whatever crushing combination of disinterest and senility, and the atmosphere was now full of testimonials about the "great communicator." The fog would just be beginning its late-afternoon tumble over Twin Peaks, spectral wisps at turns occluding or revealing the late-afternoon sun. The cheap gallon jugs of sweet, chilled wine I carried, in a neighborhood full of stores selling more prestigious post dot-com-brands, added to the feeling that I, along with Vera, was one of those older forms—not inhabiting the neighborhood so much as haunting it.

One day in the hospice, Vera woke up disoriented. While I was out of the room, she told Jonathan that she felt as if she'd been "blown away to another world." "You should tell Stephen about that," Jonathan said. "He feels that way sometimes." When I returned, she described her feeling. I said that it reminded me of a feeling of dissolution that comes sometimes in dreams. During an afternoon nap, maybe, you might feel some part of yourself flying toward the far north and the rest of yourself dispersing into a haze of summer sky. You feel as essentially yourself as you ever have, but so far away from every fact, person, or thought of normal waking life that it's as if you've entered that future where they've already passed away. There is nothing else that's real. By which I meant that it's all real, it's all a fever dream. And what is left behind is not, has never been, and never will be the point of anything at all. "Yes," said Vera. "I felt like that, just exactly like that." I didn't say to Vera that it felt most times as if those dreams were a practice for death itself.

As entertainment, during her last days, Vera mostly liked to "get into the courts," watching *Judge Judy* on the overhead TV. We were sometimes also subjected to commentary on the death of Reagan, who was presented as having been universally beloved. Vera hated him for having defunded the sort of programs that enabled her to take art and secretarial classes at local community colleges, and to emerge into a different life, after her insane spiritual journey had taken its toll. Reagan will always be associated with primates and our evolutionary past, because he costarred with a chimp in one of his first big movies, *Bedtime for Bonzo*. He played a scientist, located on the nurture side of the nature/nurture debate, who was trying to prove the importance of environment by raising a chimp. In his last big movie—the presidency—he played an "optimist" convincingly enough that at his death, former Missouri Senator John Danforth could say, in all apparent seriousness, "The great American theologian Reinhold Niebuhr wrote *Children of Light and the Children of Darkness*. If ever we have known a child of light, it was Ronald Reagan. He was aglow with it. He had no dark side, no scary, hidden agenda.

What you saw was what you got. And what you saw was that sure sign of inner light, the twinkle in the eye."

Carl Jung thought Americans were especially gifted at viewing themselves as harmless. He thought the process of digesting so many "primitive peoples" had forced us to be blind about our darker instincts, and therefore to believe, as a nation, in the purity of our motives. "Limited" was the euphemism Vera sometimes used to describe those who were less interested in the cosmos than she was, its darkness and its light, its entire spectrum of colors. Despite the astrology, Reagan was more apocalyptic evangelical than optimistic mystic, but on the passing of this cynical old Hollywood whore, his performance of "optimism" was taken at face value. Reagan was just another actor for the death-machine, really, a role-player hiding that particular American darkness under a vapid exterior. Reagan seemed, in fact, animatronic, equal parts organic matter and machine. The life force moves into silicon, but is it still a life force? What would Philip K. Dick have to say? In one of his novels, he described a man whose organs had withered away and been replaced by plastic and stainless steel, a man whose voice issued from a tape. Everything had been replaced, and the man was no longer real or alive—just a structure designed to deceive others.

Philip K. Dick had undergone his own insane spiritual journey, further developing his X-ray vision into the bizarre complexity of consciousness and the organic forms it might take. After the life she'd lived, how Vera managed to maintain a gentle and genteel exterior was some feat; smoking and drinking herself to death may have been a positive move on Vera's part, a necessary step on the road to recovery. Still, nobody would ever say about Vera that she lacked a dark side. One story has her stepping on her brother-in-law's oxygen tube, when he was slowly dying from his own cigarette-caused lung disease. But Vera was a mystic, and a real optimist. "I'm thinking about getting up out of this place," Vera would say during her last weeks. But everyone dies, these days.

The loss of Vera was a real loss for the planet. Her blond wigs may live on, but the particular combination of ethereality and arrhythmic charm is lost forever. She was a true freak, a lovely, wonderful freak, and a brilliant evolutionary possibility; there wasn't another person like her, and there may never be again. She left gracefully, fully herself until almost the end, although on her last day she was never really there. On her last day we brought May over from Oakland, and left her alone for a moment to look one more time at the woman she'd loved for fifty years, and to cry, and then we drove May to San Pablo. We dropped her off at the casino, leaving her to gamble through the night, imagining perhaps that when Vera passed, later that evening, her ghost would mingle with the machinery of the slots and continue to animate this world's deceiving structures, and maybe bring May some necessary luck.

621-8108

thea hillman

I'M WRITING TO TELL YOU I miss you terribly. Sometimes I think of coming back. Sometimes I think nothing amazing will ever happen to me again. But I thought that once before, and I was wrong that time, too.

I had just graduated from college. And I was resigned to the fact that nothing interesting was ever going to happen to me again. And then I chose you, San Francisco. More specifically, Dolores Street, between the Castro and the Mission.

I remember walking by 75 Dolores and waiting a month to hear whether the person in front of me on the waiting list was going to take from me the best studio in San Francisco. I marched by the building during what must have been the second annual Dyke March. And I prayed for that apartment. The next day, the landlord offered it to me.

You were a wish come true. An eight-year adventure. Sometimes I wonder if everything that happened could have happened anywhere else. And then, just as quickly as I wonder, I know the answer: of course not.

The decision had been between New York City and San Francisco. It had been agonizing: I had my pros-and-cons list, financial considerations, family proximity, but in the end, it was the pagan sex party at 848 Divisadero that made the decision for me. At the time, I was still living in Santa Cruz, where I'd gone to college. I was nervous going to the party, and volunteered to help set up. 848 was an art space, a two-floor storefront with a dance floor and conceptual art on the walls. For the next few hours, I met tons of people who would become my friends, lovers, and community in the years to come. A curvy woman with short hair and a soft voice helped me lug mattresses up the stairs from the basement. A tall, skinny boy about my age asked me to help him hang tapestries. Muscled dancer-looking boys built a low stage and risers. Two gray-haired boys with skirts and blue eyes set out gloves, latex, lube, sharps containers, condoms, paper towels, and small garbage pails. We all joked and sweated and together created a space that would make people feel like taking off their clothes. I was amazed by the diversity of the party, the strangeness of the people, and the radical acceptance of every kind of weirdness. I felt very, very normal for the first time. And like I'd found a place I could be myself, and be accepted.

After immersing myself in that world, I found another one, a world that couldn't have seemed farther away, where punk-rock dykes were gathering South of Market at the CoCo Club in another kind of mating ritual, one which included gathering in dive bars, drinking copious amounts of alcohol, and reading incredibly intimate poetry straight out of their journals. Sister Spit made this scene fabulous, and then made it famous. The sex in this world was hidden between the crooked penscrawls, under stairwells, and in back alleys. I liked the alcohol and the girls, especially the ones with white tank tops and chains holding their empty wallets to their sagging pants, but I typed my poems out, and sometimes memorized them, and this kind of polish made me somehow unclear and hard to recognize.

Three blocks away, another scene entirely embraced my crafted lines and careful words. The open mic at Poetry Above Paradise welcomed every kind of urban dweller, as long as we kept under the time limit. It was there that I learned to listen to poetry, really listen, to look past someone else's idea of crazy, look past someone else's idea of normal, and witness the magic that comes out of someone's mouth when the band downstairs is quiet and the poets packing the room stop gossiping because that someone just said the most beautiful, perfect line, and then did it again, and again, and devastatingly again.

Just a few blocks from there and five short blocks from my house were Muff Dive and Red and Junk, and a few years later, one block away, was Rebel Girl. This is where I went after the suffocation of holiday dinners with the family, escaping the closet of not coming out because it just didn't come up in conversation. I would run to Blondie's, dance my ass off, and remember myself. There was a particularly weird wedding, of my closest childhood friend. One of her friends, whom I'd met at the bridal shower, was this wild blonde girl who drive a Miata with no glass in the windows and who applied mascara while driving sixty miles per hour. She must have known I was queer and decided to live out her bicuriosity by flirting with me on the dance floor at this wedding, in front of everyone I'd known since I was a kid. The reception was at this fancy place downtown with an iridescent ceiling that looked like the inside of a shell. I kept joking that it was fabaloney. As soon as I left the reception, I headed to Red. The girl followed me there and came on to me, trying to make out with me, totally wasted. After a few dances, I convinced her she was too drunk to drive and I hailed her a cab. As I walked home, I passed her naturally air-conditioned Miata and pictured the guy who'd probably sleep in it that night. As I turned onto Dolores, I spotted two abalone shells, lying on the sidewalk, still dripping with kelp and seawater.

My favorite club was Litterbox. I found many dirty girls there. One time I went looking and left after twenty minutes with a girl I'd never seen before. She took me home on her motorcycle, to her room equipped with a Saint Anthony's cross. I told her no hickies the night before Passover. She didn't listen, of course, or it happened too fast, or it felt too good. She spanked me hard and I didn't sleep over and we never talked again, although I saw her around for years.

Later, Mecca opened a block from my house and forever stole any legal parking spaces. I was only in there one time. I went in with friends, I can barely remember who, except I think it was with one guy that I bonded with while at a circuit party in Potrero on Pride Day. There were two people amidst the sea of dancing boys that didn't fit in: me—the girl—and him, the boy in overalls who wasn't super-fit and muscley. He was Mormon and had just moved from Utah. At Mecca he introduced me to a dot-com girl who'd just cashed in her stock options. She didn't look gay; she looked nervous. She was only in the United States for a short time because she was going to travel the world now that she didn't have to work anymore. I found myself with her in the backseat of one of those new-at-the-time Beetles, with this girl who didn't seem gay at all. Her name started with a K, which always seems straight to me, except she let me fuck her in the backseat and made little noises as these two boys I barely remember drove us downtown to her car, even though I lived a block away.

•

WHEN I THINK ABOUT YOU, what I miss the most is walking down Valencia, or walking up Market from Dolores to Castro and seeing five people I know, who know me and are glad to see me.

And the thing is, today, not one of the parties, poetry readings, or clubs still exists as they were back then, except Mecca, which should never have happened in the first place, but which was a harbinger of things to come.

Sometimes I think when I left you I lost my edge, that nod, dark T-shirt, recognition, worn pants, tall boots, instant urban understanding.

Now I live in the place of my childhood, Oakland, which has a different kind of edge: unknown or at least unrecognized from far away, and most of us here are unknown to each other even from across the street; race and class between us like bulletproof glass.

Oakland needs me, though, more than you do, for she is on the edge, her queerness unfolding, fresh and wet, something to shape and be shaped by.

a moonlit serenade

paul reidinger

AT THE PARK ONE MORNING, long ago, a man and his dogs met a boy and his dog. The morning: bright but cool, a reminder that San Francisco was and is a marine city, a ship of rock moored at the edge of the foggy, chilly Pacific. The park: of the urban, postage-stamp variety, a narrow sward of lawn flanked on one side by a basketball court and an oft-flooded tennis court while gently descending on the other to a small dell with a sandbox and jungle gym for toddlers. The man: That would be me, and the dogs, dogs were not allowed in the sand, as my own dogs well knew, and although they were young and rambunctious in the summer of 1992, they honored the prohibition, usually.

The boy's dog was older, a genial mixed-breed female, gray and brown like a German shepherd, whose gait had been stiffened by arthritis in the hips: a gift of age. She confined her exertions to the chasing of a grubby old tennis ball that skittered across the empty basketball court. The skitterer of the ball was the boy. He was plainly a teenager, clad in a T-shirt and shorts despite the sea breeze, and with the beginnings of a mustache on his upper lip and bristlings of hair on his muscular legs. He was beautiful in that delicate, first-rose-of-spring way, with skin smooth and white as milk, although a certain surliness, an air of the thug, made me wary.

That summer I was thirty-three, *l'age du Christ*, and a newcomer to a neighborhood I had briefly lived in nearly a decade earlier, just out of college and on the eve of plague and earthquake, a pair of catastrophes that by the early 1990s would leave the city dazed and supine. In the white warmth of those first afternoons of my return, our neighborhood could be as still and quiet as a country town, only occasionally intruded on by the rasp of a passing bus or the faraway wail of an ambulance hurrying some unfortunate to San Francisco General Hospital.

The neighborhood, Noe Valley, had been, in my postcollegiate years, a kind of suburb of the Castro: a haven of quiet rusticity and, yes, funkiness—of greasy diners serving meat loaf, and knickknack shops and musty used-book stores, of faded Jaguars with peeling paint and handsome Victorians with original millwork and peeling paint, of crew-cut lesbians in granny glasses and leather jackets bestriding the sidewalks—separated by one steep little hill from the more festive neighborhood to the north. In the sepia-tinted days of yesteryear, a cable-car line had traversed that hill, carrying its human traffic between the valleys. It must have been like a funicular railway, I supposed, in some vertiginous little Swiss or Italian alpine town.

The cable cars were long gone by 1992, replaced by prosaic trolleys, and an influx of the married-with-children upper-middle classes was already becoming apparent, as one long-neglected Victorian after another acquired fresh paint and skylights, but the neighborhood's air of quaint intimacy persisted, from the Main Street USA main street on the floor of the valley to, a few blocks up the hill, the sloping little park. The park, I was discovering, really served as a village green, a place where people met and exchanged news, where their quotidian routines intersected and they became neighbors and friends. People whose ordinary lives were entwined made up a community rather than just a collection of people who lived next door to one another, and dogs were powerful agents of entwinement. Dog people immediately gravitated to other dog people, and as I was the keeper of two teddy-bearish canines, a matched set of chows, black and red, who resembled Christmas toys come to boisterous life and were irresistible to small children, I often found myself acknowledging others' coos of delight and inquiries as to whether it was safe for this or that toddler to pet them.

Indeed it was, I said and hoped, while holding my breath and crossing my fingers. For dogs do not always approve of small children and their erratic movements, of little boys in particular, and the male dog in my charge, though intelligent and friendly in a rather theatrical way, had a streak of high-spiritedness that could be unpredictable, along with a set of spectacularly large, porcelain-white teeth.

The bristly-legged boy was no cooer, as teenage boys tend not to be. Matters of manliness are of desperate importance to them, and the manly man does not coo. Still, I knew the boy was aware of me, just as I was aware of him: I felt his awareness. He barked a pair of shapeless syllables at his dog, and I took these sounds to be the animal's name and, at the same time, an oblique signal to me. I could not make the syllables out and asked the boy for clarification: one dog person casually querying another on a matter of joint interest. This was all exactly as he intended. Without looking at me, he barked out the same incoherent two-part cry. I questioningly repeated it, and at last, having gained the upper hand and feigning irritation at my denseness—or perhaps not feigning irritation, perhaps being genuinely irritated yet pleased nonetheless to have established control of the situation—he spoke the dog's name so I could understand. I repeated it, as if learning a difficult phrase in a foreign language, and we were both, suddenly, relieved.

This is the story of a man and a boy in a park, yet it is not one of those stories, even as morning quickly became evening, and soon enough—by autumn? By the following spring at the latest— the boy and I were talking long into the night, not every night but often, once or twice a week, with the clammy wind rustling in the tops of the Monterey pines that stood sentinel at the edges of the park and the occasional brightly lit, empty Muni bus sailing by, like one of those legendary ghost ships plying the lonely seas, the Mary Celeste perhaps. At first I took these after-hours rendezvous to be coincidental, the boy giving his dog her evening trot at the same time I was doing the same with the chows, but at some point it occurred to me that, under cloak of spontaneity, he was turning up in hopes of seeing me, just as I was hoping he would turn up so I could see him.

There was an expansiveness to the night, a romance to conversations under the glitter of stars. I had not had such conversations for years—not since my own youth, not since I was a freshman in college and was staying up every night until three in the morning, talking and listening, because there was so much to say and to hear—and the boy's questions, his wishing to know life's secrets, his turning to me for wisdom, made me feel young and old. I was once again a youth talking to another youth about God and meaning and desire, about all those largest questions of life, so easily flooded out or muddied by the rising tide of the mundane, and I was a man, too, expected to know something about these high matters—to have answers, not merely questions, to have lived, not merely anticipated.

There is no answer, of course, to desire, since desire is not a question but a spirit, a presence, a heat that warms the night air between two people and draws them closer. I knew something of desire, the agonies and ecstasies it could bring, its thrilling and often perverse derangement, its oblique but intense contacts with feeling, with love, its wavelike pattern of crescendo, ebb, recurrence, unending, like the swell of a limitless sea. Desire was always heat, not always light—and even when the flames of desire did cast light, it was light that could distort and mislead as easily as illuminate.

I knew, too, what men were like, what they tasted and felt and sounded like, what they acted like, what they could and could not say and what they were apt to do, for better and for worse—often for worse—when words failed them. I suspected he knew that I knew these things, for I did not talk about women nor pretend to special knowledge of or passion for them, but he did not ask me directly. Instead, we danced in the moonlight, we pirouetted, we thrust and parried, we talked.

Homophobia is not merely name-calling or egg-throwing or worse, although those coarse manifestations are real enough and do lie near its dark heart. Homophobia can be cleaned up and made sophisticated and, in its more elevated, more liberal forms—and what was San Francisco if not a liberal city, city of the liberals?—becomes even more insidious and more damaging. It is not automatically true, for instance, that when two men are attracted to each other and the attraction is in part erotic, the attraction is really altogether and only erotic, that the other elements of mutual interest, of intellectual, emotional, psychic, political, and spiritual connection, are a complex sham, nothing more than camouflage to mask the shameful flare of eros.

The stereotype—gay man as predator and recruiter of the young—I knew too well, and I was determined to resist it. Yet an intimacy had flowered between the boy and me, and I was equally determined to protect that. I did not need to be told that, as an openly homosexual man who could sometimes be seen at the neighborhood park, talking long into the night with a handsome teenager, I was at measurable risk of being seen as a sexual danger, a contagion of deviance, by other adults, by parents and neighbors, most of them well-educated and well-off liberals proud of their politics and their ease with nonhetero people in casual social settings, yet full of anxiety that their own children, if not vigilantly monitored and guided, might somehow stray from the righteous path of heterosexuality.

So I, too, was anxious: In their eyes, I supposed, my only real interest could be in seducing the boy by using my adult wiles to make him trust me, lull his instinct for self-protection. All roads, no matter how seemingly high, must lead to a lubricious Rome of man-boy love, and in this scenario (to slightly mix my metaphors), I would be the pied piper casting my sordid spell as the boy followed me along the highway into darkness. Or maybe I just generated this unease out of nothing more than a recognition that yes, I was sexually attracted to the boy, and perhaps I felt guilty about that, as if there was something wrong about it, as if a feeling could be wrong—any more than a feeling could be right—as if the standard of propriety and morality turned on what I wanted to do or thought about doing rather than what I actually did or didn't do.

What if the boy was attracted to me, too? Attraction is so often mutual; we tend to be attracted to those who find us attractive. Of course, the law was an issue, though a narrowing one as he approached his eighteenth birthday. A more subtle matter was the possibility that the boy, a varsity letterman at his high school, was drawn to me not because he was homosexual—for I was quite certain he wasn't; he liked to regale me with his sometimes staggering tales of hetero high jinks—but because he was curious about me. I was a different sort of man from the usual types who people a teenage boy's life; I wasn't heterosexual or married, I wasn't a father or a teacher or a coach, I was a writer who kept odd hours and used big words, an overeducated skeptic in button-downs and khakis who spoke his mind, a latter-day Puritan who embraced both a Puritan tradition of intelligent dissent and the local (and pagan) grant of sexual license, a believer that love of country—

indeed, love of any sort—was not undermined but enriched by doubt and the asking of questions.

He liked me perhaps for these reasons and perhaps for others, and because he was an adolescent male for whom the world in its entirety carried an erotic charge, like the haze of humidity that softens summer nights in the green lands east of the Mississippi where I'd grown up—the old Union, realm of the Puritans and the Yankees—his liking me might easily include a frisson of desire. I found this idea plausible; it would account for the thickening of suggestion, flirtation, and innuendo between us, and it simplified the moral calculus for me. I owed a lesser obligation, as I saw it, to a young man who would make his intimate adult life with women; he would not need the knowledge and guidance I could offer, and—contrary to so much gay mythology, in which seducing straight men is something like finding the Holy Grail, and slightly to my own surprise—his putative future as a heterosexual damped my erotic inclination toward him. I had learned my lesson about straight men the hard way in college, and while I might be interested, I couldn't be tempted, not really, at least not unless I fell in love with him, but how could that happen anyway? I was not worried about that, did not even consider it as a possibility, reposed as I was behind a Maginot Line of age and sexual and cultural difference, of rationalizations and certainties.

And if he was homosexual, but of course he wasn't, what could possibly give me that idea? Just because he accused me of thinking he was, then attacked me for having these imputed thoughts? Just because the subject seemed to be brought up in almost every conversation we had, with a quickening intensity and a growing attention to graphic detail as time passed and he grew older and nearer to manhood?

I did wonder, yes, sometimes, toward the end of his senior year of high school. I wondered if he was wondering, and I thought: *Of course he is wondering; how could he not wonder?* It is natural to wonder, to question, to be unsure, to examine the self, these are healthy activities for a youth about to set forth on his quest of the world. And who better to wonder about the urgent subject of sexuality with than a man—like me—in no position to challenge the young man's hetero bona fides? If I took the bait, if I allowed myself to be lured into open speculation about his sexuality, I could be dismissed as an aging lech with a gross fantasy. He would have defended his honor, his heteroness would have been proved beyond question, I would have been put in my place, and the serenade could begin again, with some other suggestive comment he would mumble, his moonlit face turned away from mine, knowing he would get away with it because he knew how I felt about him and it didn't matter how he felt about me, but it did.

•

MORNINGS NOW, the park is filled with sunshine and with nannies who chat in Spanish while their tiny charges sport in the sandbox. The dogs are still there, running across the still-spotty grass, though the cast of characters has changed all but completely, as in some television show that has been on the air too long. The boy's dog died years ago from a dreadful illness, and my beloved, the black male chow with the fabulous teeth and the thick coat luxurious as a mink stole, died soon afterward from another dreadful illness. The boy himself set off to a college far away, not to be seen again as a boy. Sorrows accumulate, losses mount, the world takes no notice. At night, when it is clear, the moonlight still filters through the Monterey pines, and sometimes I still see a figure approaching over the black lawn. My heart starts, but it is never him; pairs and clumps of people still converse in the shadows, against the concrete wall on the far side of the tennis court, but they are never us. It is colder than I remember, and darker somehow, and I jam my hands into my coat pockets and walk home.

thaw

carla trujillo

FRIDAY, SIX O'CLOCK, the sun spiraled downward as I drove across the bridge toward the City. The warm October day had finally started to cool. I eased my car into fourth and looked across the bay. Even though I'd grown up in the area, I never tired of its beauty. The gray mist settling on the water caught the last rays of the sun as they hit the cobalt bay. I smiled and cranked up the stereo. The islands, sailboats, and stream of cars emerging from the City energized me like a tonic. It was 1985, and I'd recently returned to the Bay Area for a new job. Five years in graduate school in a land of too much white—a wind-screaming, snow-filled town in the Midwest—left me hungry to escape. That town had also stifled my spirit, since the only color around was me—give or take a few other tokenized souls. Each day I lived there I'd feel a small part of myself disappear, as if watching shards of my body slip away like a melting iceberg. I had no idea where the parts went, but to save my soul, I rushed through my program, hoping something might be left when I finally returned home.

As a kid I'd lived in the North Bay, and since my job was now at UC Berkeley, I moved to Oakland to be closer to work. If you count my undergraduate years, I'd been away from the Bay Area too long, losing most of my connections from high school. Cherishing the new friends I'd made, friends actually of my housemate, Diana, I plunged into their good times, laughter, and fun. These women lived in the East Bay and worked in the City, so staving off the rush-hour madness, they invited me to join them for drinks at the Baybrick, the sizzling dyke bar on the south side of Market.

San Francisco had plenty of men's bars but not many for women. None of the bars at the time attracted the cute girls like the Baybrick. *Where the hell did they come from?* I wondered as I slipped through a bevy at the door. The Friday mood was festive with scrambled kisses, laughs, and hugs. My eyes flicked around the room, settling happily on the women of color. *Thank you, Baby Jesus!* I almost shouted out with joy. It took all my willpower to keep from staring at the beauty around me. There posed only one small problem: Not a single woman knew who the hell I was. So the best I could do was muster a shy smile and a nod as I made my way to the back of the club. Finally spotting my housemate at a table with her friends, I dove into their warmth, settling down at last by their side.

The Baybrick's managers knew how to throw a good time. Great drinks, killer snacks, and the muscular energy of music amped up the atmosphere, drawing women in like honey. As the night air thickened, the place seemed to quiver, the thrill of the weekend resonating like a hunger. The dance floor in the back, filling fast with all the overflow, had a stage against a wall, with chairs and tables arranged around it. The evening's predance performance featured comedy by Marga Gómez and Monica Palacios—two Latina lesbians well known throughout the city, yet never seen by my new-to-town eyes. The show was the secondary reason my friends had joined one another at the club and their excitement was palpable as they smiled in anticipation. As showtime approached, we moved to the dance floor, settled in, sat back, and waited.

Finally, accompanied by the flash of a cornball corrido, the two comedians sashayed onto the stage. Their show—garnered from the sepia-colored fringes of old movies and TV shows—offered a Latina twist to some of life's most vexing questions:

1. Was Doris Day a secret Latina? Did you ever wonder why she sang "Que Sera, Sera?"
2. And how about Honey West? Was she really from Laredo, using moles and blond wigs to cover up her Latinadad?
3. And could it be the doll, Barbie was originally known as Barrbi? That sexy *muñeca* from East L.A.?

Only Marga and Monica, clad in ditsy, sex-charged gold lamé, knew the answers. And those answers, juxtaposed with their own mix of race, class, and hilarity, left everyone in the audience falling off their chairs in laughter. And the four of us most certainly did laugh. In fact, the decibel strength of our laughter caught the attention of Marga and Monica, who moved us even closer as their personal audience warmers.

But alas, the show had to end. And the two women, lovers at the time, left the stage tossing back the most original material I'd ever seen, their routines so memorable, they could carve out laugh lines across the toughest lesbian eyes.

Now the chairs and tables melted, the dance floor heating, almost buckling with the beat. The deejay etched out funk-filled rhythms as my friends and I danced in all that heat. I don't know how long or how many numbers I worked my body through, but at the stroke of two, I finally had to call it one sweet night.

Regretfully, I left the Baybrick, the fog-filled air doling out a cooling kiss. As I got in my car, I was surprised to find those lost parts of my body. My legs, my arms, my torso stretched out long and past their former shadows. And suddenly I knew that I'd come back, come home, to me.

beach blanket babylon and me

jim van buskirk

I FELT AWKWARD seeing so many handsome men. They all seemed so sure of themselves, so comfortable in their gay identities. I was trying to make my way through the crush when suddenly the front door flew open and in burst a Santa Claus, a Christmas tree, a poodle playing the piano, and "Carmen Miranda." With her bugged-out eyes, her over-the-top Brazilian accent and outrageous headdress, Carmen Miranda and her campy troupe performed "Brazil" and other old songs. The crowd loved it, and so did I. Was this what being gay in San Francisco was? I silently sang a chorus of "If they could see me now." I was Gwen Verdon playing Sweet Charity.

I wasn't in Kansas anymore. How had little Jimmy Van Buskirk from Buena Park ended up in the big city?

I had dropped out of classes at the University of Washington, given notice on my room in the apartment shared with two guys from the bookstore where we worked, and loaded my Toyota with all the belongings I could fit. I hadn't given much thought to where I was heading. I just needed to move away from my family, friends, and go somewhere new, become someone new. I drove to San Francisco and got a hotel room. Within a week I moved to the southern suburbs of Belmont to a job and a free apartment. Every weekend I drove up the peninsula into the city and wandered around, looking at male couples.

I told myself I liked the cappuccino and the foreign films. I had no idea that I was one of a large wave of men immigrating to what was becoming the "gay mecca."

It was 1972 when I finally moved to San Francisco with a boyfriend, who soon returned to his former partner, leaving me adrift in the city, as it was self-satisfyingly referred to. I had never lived in a city, only suburbs: of Los Angeles, Seattle, San Francisco. I knew no one. I was excited and scared to be on my own. I couldn't quite believe I had achieved my dream of living in San Francisco.

I delighted in my furnished one-bedroom apartment at the Lucerne, 766 Sutter Street. I worked two blocks away at Scott Martin Books, 527 Sutter Street.

I had been hired by Scott Martin to develop a new paperback-book section in the small bookshop catering to the carriage trade. Our customers included the libraries of the local private clubs (Pacific-Union, Metropolitan, Olympic) as well as many of their high-class members. Their names—a who's who of San Francisco society—with private phone numbers and addresses, appeared in the Social Register, the slim black volume kept at each telephone. I was the shop's token "real person."

One afternoon a large, not particularly attractive woman browsed the tables. She had scarcely closed the door behind her when the bitchy store manager sniffed: "Hard to believe that Audrey Hepburn came out of that." How had he recognized Audrey Hepburn's mother? Celebrity sighting seemed a natural trait to gay men, at least the witty ones. I listened attentively to his gossip about the cocktail parties, the dinner parties, and the goings-on of the tony customers.

The small staff at Scott Martin Books, mostly gay men, frequently socialized with the staff of Williams-Sonoma, the gourmet cookware shop directly across the street. Scott and the owner, Chuck Williams, were old friends. Daniel, who ran our shipping and receiving department, lived with Terry, who worked at Williams-Sonoma. Shortly after I started working, Daniel and Terry invited me to a party.

That Saturday night, I nervously entered the apartment full of good-looking men. In the middle of the room was a film projector through which spooled a sixteen-millimeter print of *Gentlemen Prefer Blondes*. I had never seen a Hollywood movie projected in someone's private home.

Previously, most weekends I had explored my new town: up Nob Hill, through North Beach, across Aquatic Park, along Polk, and back to Sutter. To alleviate my loneliness, many nights I wandered through the Emporium department store on Market Street, usually ending up at Club Rendezvous, at 567 Sutter. It was my Sutter Street triangle: home, work, bar. I wasn't yet twenty-one, but perhaps some combination of my youth, my height and my looks motivated the doorman to wave me in without asking for ID. Night after night, I ascended the steep staircase to the dark bar on the third floor, where a background of Barry White, Roberta Flack, and Al Green sang about love.

I would order a beer and assume a posture that I simultaneously hoped and feared indicated my availability. I would wait for someone to initiate the insipid bar chat that sometimes segued to sex. I wasn't looking for sex as much as love, and, the Waylon Jennings song title to the contrary, I had no idea that I was looking for love in all the wrong places. I got involved with a variety of men whose skills at establishing a relationship were as rudimentary as my own.

Now, at this party with Carmen Miranda and her friends, I was even more impressed with the unexpected entertainment that had happened so spontaneously. After the madcap performance, the poodle came up and introduced himself to me as Bob Bendorff. I felt special as we chatted briefly. I must have mentioned where I worked, because a few days later he appeared at the bookstore. I was both excited and embarrassed to see him there. I hustled him out of the shop by agreeing to go out with him. As we began dating, he proudly paraded me, his new boyfriend, around town, introducing me to his friends.

One morning he dragged me to a small apartment on Union Street. *What now?* I wondered uncomfortably, as he rang the doorbell. His friend, a woman still in her bathrobe, was obviously humoring Bob when she invited us in. That morning Nancy Bleiweiss looked more like a Jewish hausfrau than a Brazilian bombshell, and it took me a while to recognize her as Carmen Miranda. Then I met Nancy's sister Roberta, who everyone called "Bug" and who had a crush on Steve Silver. She had been the singing Santa Claus, while Steve, the leader of the group, was the Christmas tree. For a while they called themselves Tommy Hail Group after the name on an old suitcase they had found. Then they became Rent-a-Freak. I felt I was meeting major celebrities, thrilled at being granted entrée to the backstage theater world.

Daniel and Terry invited me to a holiday party at Williams-Sonoma, where Chuck Williams always made sure there was plenty of food and alcohol. Everyone seemed to drink a lot, and so I followed suit. When I got home, somewhat tipsy, I felt like I was still camping it up, just as I had been at the party. I called an old friend for confirmation.

"Do I sound gay?" I demanded.

"Not at all," she assured me.

I didn't believe her. I was leaving to visit my family the next morning, and I was afraid my transformation would be obvious to everyone. Apparently, I managed to hide my newfound sexual orientation. I was happy to return "home" to San Francisco.

Bob Bendorff supported himself by playing piano in gay bars. For a while he accompanied a young, zaftig performer named Sharon McKnight at the House of Harmony on Polk Street. In those days "Polkstrasse," between about O'Farrell and Washington Streets, was the heart of the gay neighborhood.

Sometimes I would walk the few blocks from my apartment at Sutter and Taylor to the bar to hear the buxom brunette sing "Hard Hearted Hannah, the Vamp of Savannah" and "My Funny Valentine." I didn't know these old songs, not even from my parents' LPs on the blond hi-fi. I immediately responded to their witty lyrics and sophisticated melodies.

Other times, because the Lucerne had no street buzzer, Bob would call me at two A.M. from a pay phone on the street. I would groggily pad down the stairs from the second floor to let him in, then listen to him recount the events of the evening as I slowly fell back to sleep.

Bob was eager to introduce me to more of his friends: Angela, the lovely Irish lass who sang at the Sea Witch in Ghirardelli Square; Judy, the vivacious actress who worked in improv; Jim, the handsome singer; Mary Cleere, the beautiful redhead with the silky voice; Greg, finishing his degree in directing at San Francisco State; Randy, also studying at State, who later became a jeweler. I was impressed to be on the periphery of show business. When Steve Silver and his troupe opened a show in a back room at the Savoy-Tivoli restaurant and bar in North Beach, of course I was at opening night. I wouldn't have missed the irreverent fun of the newly named "Beach Blanket Babylon" for anything.

Now, Nancy was Glinda the Good Witch from *Wizard of Oz*, surrounded by multiple singing and dancing Christmas trees, M&M's and a Mr. Peanut. They sang a mix of standards like

"Stardust," "Twilight Time," and Cole Porter's "Night and Day," juxtaposed with more contemporary compositions like "Hello Dolly" and the Carpenters' "Close to You." Mary Cleere was the ultimate cosmopolitan as she performed "Put the Blame on Mame," wearing an exact replica of the sexy gown from Gilda. Even though I had never seen the movie, I knew from the crowd's hooting, as she slowly tugged off her long glove, that she accurately captured Rita Hayworth's persona. The evening ended with a rousing rendition of "San Francisco," simultaneously invoking Judy Garland, Jeannette MacDonald, and the others who had sung about "comin' home again, and wanderin' no more." At that moment I felt I, too, was coming home.

A few Sunday mornings later, on June 2, 1974, Judy called and woke me up. "Have you seen the *Chronicle* magazine section today?"

"No. Why?" I was still asleep.

"Run down and get one."

I immediately turned to the four-page spread on *Beach Blanket Babylon*, not noticing that it was written by Armistead Maupin. There, on the last page, amid photos of the cast, was a picture of me laughing with Nancy on opening night. I had arrived.

Mary and Bob put on some cabaret shows at the Eureka Theater, in the basement of a church at the corner of Market and Noe. Mary Cleere was sensational, especially singing Sondheim's "And I Shall Marry the Miller's Son." Then she starred in a production of *Dames at Sea*. When I recognized her one New Year's Eve at the intersection of Columbus and Broadway and Grant, I considered it a good omen to have seen a star in San Francisco's version of Times Square.

Shy and insecure, I was overwhelmed by Bob. He was bright, sensitive, and a talented musician. He was also childish, manipulative, and an alcoholic. But none of that mattered: he liked me. Bob got invited to parties, and insisted I accompany him. We moved in together and threw festive dinner parties. I thought I should be having fun, but I wasn't. As his drinking worsened, his jealousy increased and he became abusive. We fought frequently. I threatened to leave him. At one point I ended up with a broken hand, later a black eye. Always he coaxed me back, promising it would never happen again. I wanted to believe him. I didn't recognize my role as the typical "battered wife" until long after we broke up.

I noticed another pattern: I seemed to have a propensity for piano players. I slept with Mike, accompanist for Charles Pierce, the "male actress" famous for his impersonations of Jeanette MacDonald and Bette Davis. Then I had a brief affair with Barry, a pianist who played at the Sea Witch, among other local spots. This was all new for me. I was trying to find my way in the world as a gay man. I didn't understand that this was new for a lot of other people, too. They all appeared much more adept with this newly found freedom, sexual and otherwise. I stayed on the periphery, uncomfortable and awkward.

Occasionally on the 38 Geary bus I ran into Mary Cleere. Fresh from therapy appointments, her face was tear-stained and she looked nothing like her stage persona. I couldn't imagine what this beautiful, talented star needed a therapist for. Even admitting to having one seemed chic.

Beach Blanket Babylon moved to Club Olympus on Columbus Avenue before finally landing in Club Fugazi, the old Italian social club on Green Street. Now there was an entire orchestra of poodles. The headdresses had evolved from replicas of Carmen Miranda's pineapples, bananas, and feathers to spectacular constructions featuring hot-fudge sundaes, Christmas trees, even, in the finale, the San Francisco skyline. Now the star was Snow White singing "Some Day My Prince Will Come," a longing I could relate to. My pal Jim Reiter was in the show, dressed as a cowboy and popping out of the pocket of an oversize pair of jeans to sing "Me and My Shadow."

I didn't see *Beach Blanket Babylon* all that often. I was busy dancing at Buzzby's on Polkstrasse and the End-Up, south of Market. After the bars closed, we would often stop at Pam Pam West, on the corner of Geary and Mason. In a corner booth of the twenty-four-hour coffee shop would be Steve, Nancy, and Roberta, sipping sodas and carrying on like teenagers at the malt shop. Brainstorming new ideas for the show, no doubt.

When I did see *Beach Blanket Babylon* over the years, the hats got even larger and more numerous, and the skits and musical numbers became more outrageous. Rather than spoofing classic movies, the show began parodying current celebrities, ultimately becoming self-referential. The tourists and locals still loved it, but I had moved on.

Bob had introduced me to Bobby Short and Barbara Cook's interpretations of the *American Popular Songbook* and the Broadway shows of Stephen Sondheim, and I continued my exposure to cabaret and theater. Bob left *Beach Blanket* to pursue other activities. Steve and Nancy and Roberta had a nasty falling out over ownership of the show. What had started out as kids having fun ended up in court, and in the papers.

By then I was back in college, getting a master's degree in library sciences at UC Berkeley. There I met Doug, a French major. We moved to Paris after we both graduated. Returning from our year abroad, Doug and I moved into an apartment in North Beach—one block away, it turned out, from Club Fugazi. When the tenth anniversary rolled around in 1984, I invited Jim and Mary Cleere, who were both living in New York at the time, to stay with us. As an assistant buyer in Macy's handbag department, Doug was especially thrilled to meet Mary Cleere, whom he recognized as the star of an industrial called "In the Bag." Then I met Rob.

On May 24, 1994, Jim invited me to the San Francisco Opera House for the twentieth anniversary of Steve Silver's *Beach Blanket Babylon*. As I sat in the very last row of the balcony, watching one hundred people celebrate the city's longest-running theatrical revue, I marveled at the extravaganza spreading across the stage. As everyone around me laughed at the singing and dancing and the huge hats, I found myself reminiscing, unprepared for the long parade of characters dancing in my head.

From high in the balcony, I admired guest stars Frankie Avalon and Annette Funicello, figures from my youth. I remembered them from Walt Disney's *Mickey Mouse Club* and the "Beach Party" from which *Beach Blanket Babylon* had adapted its name. I remembered the fresh, fun frolic that Beach Blanket had been, and winced at the excessive exercise it had become. Tears filled my eyes as I realized how it paralleled who I had been and who I had become. The show inadvertently celebrated my own coming-of-age as a gay man in San Francisco.

Afterward, in the crowded lobby of the opera house, I noticed a familiar face, a man a little older than myself. As I walked over to greet the good-looking man, I tried to remember his name. I knew we had once worked together.

"Hello, Jim. It's Daniel," he said with a smile. Of course—the shipping and receiving clerk at Scott Martin Books who had inadvertently changed the course of my life. We chatted briefly, then drifted apart. As I stood talking to Jim, I noticed Armistead Maupin across the room.

Just that morning I had made a photocopy of the first installment of *Tales of the City*, Armistead's serial novel from the May 24, 1976, *San Francisco Chronicle* for an exhibit I was preparing at the San Francisco Public Library. I had brazenly called my exhibit "Tales of the City: Lesbians and Gay Men Since Stonewall," and had written to Armistead requesting permission to use the title. I was too shy to walk over to meet him.

Little did I know that I would soon be chatting on the phone with Armistead, asking him to write a foreword for the book I was writing with Susan Stryker. When I made the cold call, Armistead was charming and gregarious, eventually penning the perfect preamble to *Gay by the Bay: A History of Queer Culture in the San*

Francisco Bay Area. Published in April 1996 to coincide with the opening of the James C. Hormel Gay & Lesbian Center at the San Francisco Public Library, it chronicled a history I had been only peripherally part of.

In June of 1995, Steve Silver died. Jim and I attended the memorial service at Grace Cathedral, knowing it would be a production. Apparently, every detail had been planned by Steve. But a strange, surreal quality lay at the foundation of the event. No mention was made of Steve's sexuality or the fact that he had died of AIDS. His surviving wife, Jo Schuman Silver, played the part of his grieving widow, and Charlotte Maillard Swig, San Francisco's Chief of Protocol, eulogized a man I had never met. Jim went on to the gravesite service, but I couldn't take any more of what I perceived as hypocritical obfuscation of the truth.

Sometime later I met playwright, director, and stage manager Allen Sawyer. According to his version of the story, we dated for a year without me knowing it. I wondered why he kept inviting me to lunch and the theater. When Theater on the Square closed in 2003, Allen landed a job managing the box office at *Beach Blanket Babylon*. I marveled at the coincidence.

Of course I accepted when Allen invited me to a dress rehearsal of the thirtieth anniversary celebration. As I sat upstairs at Club Fugazi, watching the parade of parodies and chapeaux, once again I had an odd perspective on the past, once again I sat alone with my memories.

Today, Steve Silver, Bob, and Randy are all gone, lost to AIDS. My friends Jim and Angela have stopped performing. I've lost touch with Judy but occasionally run into Roberta and Greg. Mary Cleere is a well-known cabaret singer in New York. I still manage the James C. Hormel Gay & Lesbian Center at the San Francisco Public Library, one floor away from the Steve Silver Room. I write a regular column about San Francisco for *Cabaret Scenes* magazine and sometimes interview singers for the *Bay Area Reporter*, the local gay weekly. Ever supportive, Armistead Maupin blurbed my new book about sites from movies made in San Francisco, *Celluloid San Francisco*, which includes Club Fugazi because a scene from the *Tales of the City* series was shot there.

Recently, Allen confided that during a brief visit to the Bay Area, Prince Charles and Camilla were scheduled to attend a performance of *Beach Blanket*. I might be allowed to attend the special event, to which all San Francisco society and politicos were hoping to be invited. Allen worked for weeks with Jo Silver and Charlotte Maillard Swig Shultz, negotiating guest lists and planning seating charts. The more he regaled me with the inner machinations of the major event, the less interested I became in attending. I realized I had no interest in British royalty, San Francisco society, or the popular attraction that *Beach Blanket* had become. The popular show with its wacky headdresses would go on without me. The celebrity evening, from all reports, was a success. *Beach Blanket Babylon* is such part of me that I didn't need to be there.

where one size
does not fit all

karin kallmaker

SHE WAS A STUDY IN BLACK, creaking leather as she walked past me, her jacket dotted with stickers and patches. The one easiest to read blazed in neon orange, L.A.B.I.A.: Lesbians Against Boys In Anything.

A pink peace symbol adorned one shoulder. The opposite sleeve read *DYKE*. Across her back, when I looked after her, a rainbow bumper sticker proclaimed: *It's your book, your God, you burn in hell.*

All in all, she was in my sight for about thirty seconds. I've never forgotten the moment.

I was nineteen. And she terrified me.

Everything about her called attention to what she was. The city was still bleeding from the loss of Harvey Milk. All that hope had fizzled, and in 1979 we didn't know it would come back, go away, and come back again.

All I knew, from the scary confines of my bland personal closet, was that we were hated. Even on Castro Street, she was drawing the occasional hostile glance. I wouldn't have been surprised if a passing car had tossed a bottle in her direction. I walked with my gaze lowered. All I knew was that she made a great target and I wanted to be as far away from her as I could get.

I wanted to be as far away from dyke, lesbian, femme, butch, leather, and homophobes as I could get, too.

I didn't even live in San Francisco. I hailed from homogenous Sacramento, and I was only in the Castro as a day trip. It had taken all the courage I could screw to a sticking point to walk my jeans-and-pullover self down the street. I was aware of my handbag, my ordinary shoes. Aware that while I was on the street, it was possible that everyone who looked at me would think I was a lesbian. But it was also true that I would be able to leave, to go back to "normal." The belief that I had an escape route was the only thing that got me moving that day.

The woman in leather never left. It was a very long time before I would appreciate that she didn't want to leave. She carried "normal" with her, redefining it everywhere she went, and so broadly that it included every version of the woman I'd be for the rest of my life.

As I stood on Castro Street in 1979, my feelings were so mixed that they took years to sort out. The leather dyke scared me, but she also gave me a real, live vision of how pride walked. Her butch created room for my femme. Still, I didn't feel queer. I felt like a scared middle-class white girl who'd first heard the word "homosexual" nearly a year after she'd discovered she was one.

As scared as my closeted lesbian was, the woman in me was oddly comforted. Though I was prudishly repelled by the skin displays and obvious leering from men lounging in the open windows of bars, I was also relieved that none of that had anything to do with me. We were mutually irrelevant to one another. Though gender politics were still present, the Castro felt like a place where men and women could co-exist. The battle of the sexes wasn't about sex, at least.

The generic American in me saw little that was familiar. Though there was diversity from one end of the street to the other, I saw no young women who looked like me, and it just wasn't in me to relish being one-of-a-kind—at least, not yet. At nineteen, I saw only clothes I hadn't earned, clothes that I did not want, and, of course, clothes I knew I wanted but wouldn't fit me if I tried. I lusted after that sticker-studded jacket—and, truth be told, the icon who wore it—but I'd have been a mouse in borrowed plumage.

Everything I could take in with my selective vision told me I didn't belong on that street. Yet I couldn't stop smiling. To me this street was the birthplace of my people. I was, in spite of feeling distinctly like a visiting alien, a member of the family in the kind of family that can't disown you. The clothes that fit me were the ones I was wearing, and I was walking on Castro Street.

For the first time in my life, I could wear the correct *Hello My Label Is* badge: lesbian. Over the next few decades I would add, discard, reclaim and work at owning more labels: dyke, femme, mom, writer, and more. The street offered the choices and I learned to dress myself.

•

CASTRO STREET IS CROWDED, potholed, overparked, and scary to drive down. It's just a street with a few landmark buildings and a lot of people rushing around, living life. There are ubiquitous shops and parking meters, homeless, corporate businesses, and mass transit. Petition tables dot the landscape, along with trash, chained bicycles, and unleashed pets. It could be an urban street nearly anywhere, with a penchant for multicolor flags. That is, until a person stops seeing the background and studies instead the people. At the height of the lunch or dinner hours, the variety is dazzling.

Not everyone looks beyond the obvious, however. In the early eighties, Dan Rather visited the Castro to report to the nation about gay politics and power, and represented the district with footage from a sex shop and the proprietor discussing penetration using a nightstick. Those clothes only fit some of us, yet all of us were wearing them, like it or not, during that broadcast.

•

AFTER THE 1989 Loma Prieta earthquake, local news stations found voluble gay men mourning their lost wainscoting and monosyllabic lesbians with tool belts proclaiming a flattened ruin would be rebuilt by next week. Part of me to this day remains amused even as I bemoan that the rest of the country saw only stereotypes. Where was the coverage of bucket brigades and bare-handed digging? Who would see the totality with which the gay residents of San Francisco would devote themselves to their city's recovery? Even in our local newsrooms, the clothing of heroes eluded us.

We could be our own worst enemy, too, with epic family squabbling over exactly who and what we were. A documentary about lesbian couples, their families, and their jobs was dismissed by a prominent "thinking lesbian" of the time as perpetuating the myth of lesbian affluence. The women portrayed, nurses and schoolteachers among them, clearly should not be wearing the same clothes she was. I was as excluded by her intellectual fashion attitude as I was by heterosexual ignorance.

I was tired of other people picking out my clothes.

•

WHEN I MOVED TO THE BAY AREA, finally, shortly before Loma Prieta, the hope was coming back in spite of Harvey, and in spite of AIDS. These were the gay nineties. Buildings had changed, but the leather dykes were still there and there were more of them. How many, I would wonder, owed their comfort on the street to that leather dyke I had seen more than ten years earlier?

The leather community mingled, too, with lesbians carrying little ice chests, bound for home and a turkey-baster moment. There were lesbians who thought motherhood was a sellout, and lots who thought kids were great, as long as someone else had them. On Castro Street, family took on, yet again, new meaning. AIDS activists and Lesbian Avengers would also stretch and forever change the street.

Gay, bi, lesbian, butch, femme, trans, queer—they all took on new meanings for some while others stayed with the definitions that had worked for them. On this street, over time, everyone learns to choose their own clothes. Though there are always those who insist on being the arbiters of fashion, one size does not fit all in the Castro.

Absolutes came and went. Debate raged hotly over defining the "right" way to live, though the subjects were always new. Even on that glorious Valentine's Day 2003, when hundreds of couples scored official marriage licenses, there was debate. We're queer—what does marriage have to do with us? We're queer—they say we can't have it, so we'll take it anyway. We're queer—why should that limit anything we want to experience? We're queer—we've survived without sanction, and we always will.

The marriage licenses were rendered symbolic, but wedding finery looked grand on Castro Street. It fit those who wore it. After all, the street might be the stage where family disputes play out, but it never takes sides.

•

AS FOR DISPUTES outside the family, for the freaked-out fascism that goes away, comes back and stays way too long, the Castro is now my chill pill. No longer terrified, I can go there for solace, for energy, for a refresher course in the reality that matters to me. In one short block I'll experience "We're here, we're queer, and we'll overcome" to a three-snap and heartfelt "Fuck it, let's dance." Surrounded on all sides by what I now call "normal" I can pretend, for a short while, that the rest of the world is a depressing work of fiction. I'm aware now, going on thirty years after that encounter with the leather dyke, that I don't want to leave "normal." But when it's time to go, I carry my own version of "normal" away with me.

•

I LIKE TO TAKE SHY FRIENDS on their first visits to the Castro. We start at the top of the street and wade in. I watch in their faces that journey I started when I was nineteen. I see the surprise, shock, a little fear, the glance down at a shirt or slacks that suddenly don't seem nearly hip enough. We stroll through the hardware store, farther down to look at books, assess the handcrafts, and all the while we people watch. Every race and ethnicity seems present, and my ability to characterize gender and sexual identities is quickly exhausted, and an all-encompassing "Now that's queer" is the only sentiment that fits.

It's easier to spot styles at the edges, but I've learned to look for the center as well. Is that other forty-something flashing traces of riot grrl? That buzz-cut baby butch—that's a rhinestone ankle bracelet mingling with that tattoo, isn't it? What other styles should I think about, and if something doesn't appeal to me, then why not? Every once in a while there's also a mousy young woman with wide eyes frozen on a corner, at whom I can smile as if to say *You're safe here, really.*

After a couple of hours, and maybe a coffee, ice cream or a hot meal, my shy friends' inner nineteen-year-olds are long gone. Some can talk for hours about what they've seen and thought and how it made them feel and reflect on who they are. For others, it can be summed up with a pleased, wide grin in answer to my "Cool, huh?"

On Castro Street, I learned to dress myself with the clothes I choose, to keep the styles that felt right, and to try on new hats once in a while. Now I can remember that leather dyke with delight and pleasure, comfortable at last that not wanting to be her doesn't mean I reject her. Quite the contrary, that sticker-studded jacket is a part of my wardrobe, and I put it on at my keyboard and it influences all that I write. That scared young woman who felt she would never fit the street's definitions finally learned that she is part of what defines it. When once I was terrified that everyone who saw me would assume I was a lesbian, I am now offended when I meet people who don't.

Castro Street's fluidity is its constant. No matter what my clothing of the day might be, from a shy writer offering to sign her first novel to a seeming soccer mom with two kids in tow, Castro Street has never refused me entry. The potholes, the crowds, the scary traffic are still there, but somehow the street is larger than ever.

about the editors

katherine v. forrest is the internationally known author of fifteen works of fiction including the lesbian classics *Curious Wine* (reprint, Alyson Publications) and *Daughters of a Coral Dawn* (reprint, Alyson Publications), the first novel in her Lambda Literary Award-winning lesbian-feminist utopian trilogy. The final two, *Daughters of an Amber Noon* and *Daughters of an Emerald Dusk* are also Alyson Publications. Her eight-volume Kate Delafield mystery series is a three-time winner of the Lambda Literary Award. She has edited numerous anthologies, and her stories, articles, and reviews have appeared in publications worldwide. She was senior editor at Naiad Press for ten years, and continues to edit as well as to teach classes in the craft of fiction.

jim van buskirk's writing has been featured in various books, newspapers, magazines, radio broadcasts, and websites. He coauthored, with Susan Stryker, the Lambda Literary Award-nominated *Gay by the Bay: A History of Queer Culture in the San Francisco Bay Area* (Chronicle Books, 1996), and, with Will Shank, *Celluloid*

San Francisco: The Film Lover's Guide to Bay Area Movie Locations (Chicago Review Press, 2006). He coedited, with Jim Tushinski, the anthology *Identity Envy: Wanting to Be Who We Are Not: Creative Nonfiction by Queer Writers* (Harrington Park Press, 2007). Jim is the program manager of the James C. Hormel Gay and Lesbian Center at the San Francisco Public Library. For more information, visit jimvanbuskirk.com.

about the contributors

A lecturer, writing instructor and one time literary agent, victor j. banis is a legendary pioneer in the field of gay writing, and the critically acclaimed author ("a master story teller"—*Publishers Weekly*) of more than one hundred forty books, fiction and nonfiction. His verse and short pieces have appeared in numerous journals, including *Blithe House Quarterly*, and several anthologies, among them *Cowboys: Gay Erotic Tales* (Cleis, 2006), *Paws and Reflect* (Alyson, 2006), and *Charmed Lives* (Lethe, 2006). A native of Ohio and longtime Californian, he now lives and writes in West Virginia's beautiful Blue Ridge.

stephen beachy is the author of two novels, *The Whistling Song* and *Distortion*, and his most recent book, *Some Phantom/ No Time Flat*, two novellas published by Suspect Thoughts. His fiction has appeared in *BOMB*, *The Chicago Review*, *Blithe House Quarterly*, *Best Gay American Fiction*, and elsewhere, and his essays and criticism have appeared in *New York* magazine, *The New York Times Magazine*, and the *Bay Guardian*. He lives in San Francisco, where he is currently completing a book of essays, *Dreams of Terror and Abuse*.

lucy jane bledsoe's most recent book is *The Ice Cave: A Woman's Adventures from the Mojave to the Antarctic*. She's also the author of two novels, *This Wild Silence* (excerpts of which won a California Arts Council Individual Fellowship in Literature), *Working Parts* (winner of the Stonewall Book Award), and a collection of short fiction, *Sweat*. Her next novel, *Biting the Apple*, will be published in 2007. Bledsoe has also published several children's books. Visit her website at www.lucyjanebledsoe.com.

jim duggins, PhD, began writing for his high-school newspaper, and followed that as a U.S. Navy Journalist in the Korean War. After attending college, he taught in high school, community college, and finally at San Francisco State University. In addition to articles for academic journals, he has done freelance and work-for-hire writing. His most recent work has been articles about what has become known as Mid-Century Modern Architecture in southern California. Now, retired from teaching, he lives in southern California where he is working on his fourth historical novel.

elana dykewomon is a pioneering novelist, poet, editor, teacher, and activist. The author of the classic work *Riverfinger Women* and the Lambda award-winning historical novel, *Beyond the Pale*, she is finishing up her seventh book, *Risk* (a novel). For more information about her books, or her classes and editing services, check out www.dykewomon.org. She lives in Oakland with her beloved, Susan, among friends, stirring up inspiration whenever she can.

charles q. forester has been active in the gay and lesbian community in San Francisco since coming out in 1973. He worked for three mayors of San Francisco and in nonprofit organizations. His last position was executive director of the Friends of the Library. He was national cochair of the Human Rights Campaign and the fundraising campaign for the James C. Hormel Gay & Lesbian Center at the San Francisco Public Library. He also served on the board of KQED. He is now writing poetry, and his interview with Thom Gunn was published in 2005.

jamison green is the author of *Becoming a Visible Man* (Vanderbilt University Press, 2004) and *Eyes* (Olive Press, 1976). He writes an occasional column for PlanetOut.com, contributes articles to academic journals, and serves on five nonprofit corporation boards. He is also an internationally known educator, public speaker, and policy consultant specializing in transgender and transsexual issues.

According to a special report by the Traditional Values Coalition, entitled *Homosexual Urban Myth*, thea hillman is a radical who "conducts erotic readings for homosexual groups" as part of the "homosexual revolution." According to herself, that's pretty much correct, but she would add that she is also the author of the critically acclaimed book *Depending on the Light*. Her second book, *For Lack of a Better Word*, will be released in 2007. For more information and performance schedule, visit theahillman.com.

fenton johnson is the author of two novels, *Crossing the River* (1989) and *Scissors, Paper, Rock* (1993), as well as *Geography of the Heart: A Memoir* (1996) and *Keeping Faith: A Skeptic's Journey among Christian and Buddhist Monks* (2003). Johnson has contributed to *Harper's Magazine*, *The New York Times Magazine*, and many literary quarterlies, and has received numerous literary awards. He is on the faculty of the creative writing program at the University of Arizona, and is completing his latest book, *The Man Who Loved Birds*, a novel. For additional information, visit www.fentonjohnson.com.

karin kallmaker is the Lambda Literary Award-winning author of more than twenty romances and fantasy-science fiction
novels. Her Lambda finalists include *Seeds of Fire* (as Laura
Adams), *Substitute for Love, Just Like That, All the Wrong Places,*
and *Once Upon a Dyke: New Exploits of Fairy Tale Lesbians.* Her
short stories have appeared in anthologies from Alyson, Circlet,
and Haworth. Her writing career began with the venerable Naiad
Press and continues with Bella Books. She and her partner are the
mothers of two and live in the San Francisco Bay Area. She is descended from Lady Godiva, a fact she'll share with anyone who
will listen.

michael nava is a third-generation Californian of Mexican descent. He was born and raised in Sacramento. He was the first
member of his family to go to college, graduating with honors
from the Colorado College and receiving his law degree from
Stanford Law School. Since 1999, he has been a judicial staff at-
torney at the California Supreme Court, where he currently
works for Associate Justice Carlos Moreno. In addition to his legal career, he is a novelist and the author of an acclaimed series of
crime novels featuring a gay Latino criminal defense lawyer
named Henry Rios. He has been the recipient of numerous
awards and honors, including five Lambda Literary Awards, the
Whitehead Award for Lifetime Achievement in Gay and Lesbian
Literature, a fellowship from the California Arts Council, and an
honorary degree as a Doctor of Humane Arts from the Colorado
College. He is a stalwart, if often disappointed, fan of the San
Francisco Giants.

carol queen got a PhD in sexology so she could impart more
realistic detail to her smut. She's an award-winning author (with
a Firecracker Alternative Book Award for her erotic novel *The
Leather Daddy & The Femme*) and editor (with a Lambda Literary

Award for *PoMoSexuals*, coedited with Lawrence Schimel). See www.carolqueen.com for a complete list of her books and anthology appearances. (And e-mail her there if you want to chat about *Rocky Horror* if she ever gets around to that book!) She lives in San Francisco, where she works as staff sexologist at Good Vibrations and directs the Center for Sex & Culture (www.sexandculture.org).

andrew ramer has no pets or children. His next book, *Queering the Text: Biblical, Medieval, and Modern Jewish Stories*, is forthcoming from Suspect Thoughts Press.

kirk read is the author of *How I Learned to Snap*, a memoir about being openly gay in a small Virginia high school. He is an HIV counselor and phlebotomist at St. James Infirmary, a free health-care clinic for sex workers. He is working on two projects: a memoir about sex work called *This Is the Thing*, and a collection of essays and performance works. He cohosts the San Francisco open-mic events Smack Dab and K'vetch. He is spending time lately with a group of hippie gourmet chefs who gather food in the wild and cook meals for large groups of people. Community is not an abstract, idealistic concept to him—it's a strategy of creative living.

paul reidinger is the author of several novels, the most recent of which is *The City Kid* (Southern Tier/Haworth). He is a writer for the *San Francisco Bay Guardian* and lives in San Francisco.

carol seajay resigned from the Old Wives' Tales Bookstore collective in 1983. After a brief stint as a FedEx driver to finance her next venture, she has been devoted full time to the *Feminist Bookstore News*, which she had been publishing on a part-time basis since the first Women In Print Conference in 1976. She published *FBN* until 2000. In 2003, she launched *Books to Watch Out*

For, a collection of three book-review newsletters—one for lesbians, one for gay men, and a more general edition for feminists and feminist-thinking women. Find more details and read sample copies at www.BooksToWatchOutfor.com. She currently lives in England where she is Director of *Mslexia*, a magazine on women and writing, and publishes *BTWOF* from afar, with the able help of managing editor Suzanne Corson. Old Wives' Tales closed in 1995 after a nineteen-year run.

aaron shurin is the author of a dozen books, including the poetry collections *Involuntary Lyrics* (Omnidawn, 2005) and *The Paradise of Forms: Selected Poems* (Talisman House, 1999), as well as the essay collections *Unbound: A Book of AIDS* (Sun & Moon, 1997) and *King of Shadows* (forthcoming). His work has appeared in more than twenty national and international anthologies, and has been supported by fellowships from the National Endowment for the Arts, the California Arts Council, and the San Francisco Arts Commission. Shurin codirects the MFA in Writing Program at the University of San Francisco.

f. allen sawyer was born in San Francisco. He is the author of many plays, including *Gross Indulgences: The Trials of Liberace*, *Whatever Happened to Sister George*, *Hot Pants Homo*, *Senator Swish*, and *Lavender Lockeroom*. He was profiled in Contemporary Gay American Poets and Playwrights from Greenwood Press.

k. m. soehnlein is the author of the novels *You Can Say You Knew Me When* and the Lambda Award-winning *The World of Normal Boys*, both published by Kensington Books. His essay, "The Story I Told Myself" appeared in the anthology *From Boys to Men: Gay Men Write About Growing Up*. He lives with his partner, Kevin Clarke, in San Francisco, and shows no sign of moving anywhere else.

michelle tea lived at 251 14th Street, aka The Blue House, for seven years. Now she lives in a cleaner place in North Beach, though an exterminator did stop by this morning to lay some mouse traps. She has written a bunch of books, including the Lambda Literary Award-winning novel *Valencia*, and most recently *Rose of No Man's Land*. She curates the Radar readings and salons in San Francisco, and the Sister Spit: Next Generation national tours.

mark thompson is a journalist and photographer, and was former senior editor of *The Advocate* for almost twenty years (1957–1994). He is the author of five books and many essays on gay history and culture, including the widely acclaimed trilogy *Gay Spirit*, *Gay Soul*, and *Gay Body*. He has worked as a therapist with gay youth and people living with AIDS, and has belonged to many community organizations, including the board of directors of the ONE Archives, the largest gay and lesbian library in the world. Most recently, Mark has been touring an exhibition of his photographs of noted gay artists and spiritual leaders, "Fellow Travelers: Liberation Portraits." He lives in Los Angeles with his life partner of more than two decades, writer-priest Malcolm Boyd.

carla trujillo is the editor of the anthology *Chicana Lesbians: The Girls Our Mothers Warned Us About* (Third Woman Press, 1991), which won the Lambda Literary Award and the Out/Write Vanguard Award for Best Pioneering Contribution to the field of Gay/Lesbian Lifestyle Literature. Her novel *What Night Brings* (Curbstone Press, 2003), won the Miguel Mármol prize, the Paterson Fiction Prize, the Latino Literary Foundation Latino Book Award, the Bronze Medal from *Foreword Magazine*, Honorable Mention for the Gustavus Meyers Books Award, and was a Lambda Literary Award finalist. She is the editor of *Living*

Chicana Theory (1998), and the author of short stories and articles on identity, sexuality, and higher education. Born in New Mexico, she received a PhD in educational psychology from the University of Wisconsin. She is a director of the Graduate Diversity Program at UC Berkeley, and has lectured in ethnic studies at the UC Berkeley and Mills College and in women's studies at SF State University.

jim tushinski is the author of the novel *Van Allen's Ecstasy* (Harrington Park Press), which was a finalist for the Ferro-Grumley Fiction Award and the Violet Quill Award, and is the director, coproducer, and editor of the feature-length documentary *That Man: Peter Berlin*. His latest book is the creative nonfiction anthology *Identity Envy: Wanting to Be Who We're Not* (Harrington Park Press), which he coedited. A former longtime resident of San Francisco, he now lives in southern California, where he is working on a biography of cult filmmaker Tom Graeff, a new novel, another anthology, and a new documentary project. For more information, visit www.jimtushinski.com.

jess wells is the author of thirteen volumes of work, including *The Mandrake Broom* (Firebrand Books), a historical novel about the fight to save medical knowledge during the witch-burning times. Her novel *AfterShocks* has been reissued internationally, and was re-released as a Triangle Classic by InsightOut Books. She lives in San Francisco with her son, and can be contacted through her website, www.jesswells.com.

helen zia is author of *Asian American Dreams: The Emergence of an American People* (FSG, 2000) and coauthor with Wen Ho Lee of *My Country Versus Me* (Hyperion, 2002). Her essay in *Love, Castro Street* is adapted from a longer piece that first appeared in *AmerAsia Journal: Asian Americans in the Marriage Equality Debate* (UCLA Asian American Studies Center Press, vol. 32, no. 1, 2006).